Negotiating Hospitality

T0293729

How do hosts and guests welcome each other in responsible encounters? This book addresses the question in a longitudinal ethnographic study on tourism development in the coffee-cultivating communities in Nicaragua. The research follows the trail of development practitioners and researchers who travel with a desire to help, teach and study the local hosts. On a broader level, it is a journey exploring how the conditions of hospitality become negotiated between these actors. The theoretical approach bases itself on the ethical subjectivity as responsibility and receptivity towards 'the other'. The ideas put forward in the book suggest that hospitality, responsibility and participation all require a readiness to interrupt one's own ways of doing, knowing and being.

This book provides a conceptual tool to facilitate reflection on alternative ways of doing togetherness and will be of interest to students and researchers of hospitality, tourism, development studies, cultural studies and anthropology.

Emily Höckert is Postdoctoral Fellow in Tourism Studies at the Linnaeus University in Kalmar, Sweden.

Contemporary Geographies of Leisure, Tourism and Mobility
Series Editor: C. Michael Hall, Professor at the Department
of Management
*College of Business and Economics, University of Canterbury, Christchurch,
New Zealand*

The aim of this series is to explore and communicate the intersections and
relationships between leisure, tourism and human mobility within the social
sciences.

It will incorporate both traditional and new perspectives on leisure and
tourism from contemporary geography, e.g. notions of identity, representation
and culture, while also providing for perspectives from cognate areas such as
anthropology, cultural studies, gastronomy and food studies, marketing, policy
studies and political economy, regional and urban planning, and sociology,
within the development of an integrated field of leisure and tourism studies.

Also, increasingly, tourism and leisure are regarded as steps in a continuum
of human mobility. Inclusion of mobility in the series offers the prospect
to examine the relationship between tourism and migration, the sojourner,
educational travel, and second home and retirement travel phenomena.

The series comprises two strands:

Contemporary Geographies of
Leisure, Tourism and Mobility aims
to address the needs of students
and academics, and the titles will be
published in hardback and paperback. Titles include:

Tourism and Citizenship
*Raoul V. Bianchi and Marcus L.
Stephenson*

Co-Creating Tourism Research
Towards Collaborative Ways of
Knowing
*Edited by Carina Ren, Gunnar Thór
Jóhannesson and René van der Duim*

Routledge Studies in Contemporary
Geographies of Leisure, Tourism and
Mobility is a forum for innovative
new research intended for research
students and academics, and the
titles will be available in hardback
only. Titles include:

Memory, Migration and Travel
Edited by Sabine Marschall

Negotiating Hospitality
Ethics of Tourism Development in
the Nicaraguan Highlands
Emily Höckert

For more information about this series, please visit: www.routledge.com/
Contemporary-Geographies-of-Leisure-Tourism-and-Mobility/book-series/
SE0522

Negotiating Hospitality

Ethics of Tourism Development in the
Nicaraguan Highlands

Emily Höckert

LONDON AND NEW YORK

First published 2018 by Routledge

2 Park Square, Milton Park, Abingdon, Oxon OX14 4RN
605 Third Avenue, New York, NY 10017

Routledge is an imprint of the Taylor & Francis Group, an informa business

First issued in paperback 2022

Publisher's Note

The publisher has gone to great lengths to ensure the quality of this reprint
but points out that some imperfections in the original copies may be apparent.

British Library Cataloguing-in-Publication Data
A catalogue record for this book is available from the British Library

Library of Congress Cataloging-in-Publication Data
A catalog record has been requested for this book

ISBN: 978-1-138-55149-7 (hbk)
ISBN: 978-1-03-233912-2 (pbk)
DOI: 10.4324/9781315147604

Typeset in Times New Roman
by Out of House Publishing

Contents

Preface   vii

1   Introduction   1

2   The ethics of hospitality   33

3   Unconditional welcome of tourism to Nicaragua   66

4   Negotiating the conditions for rural hospitality   100

5   Envisioning hospitable encounters   137

6   Conclusion   159

    Bibliography   171
    Index   200

Preface

It was early July in Finland, and most people were escaping from the cities to begin their summer holidays. My daughter was enjoying time at our summer cottage with her grandparents. I had decided to dedicate myself to work for one more week, and continue writing the second last chapter of this book. After a few days of writing in solitude, I jumped on a bicycle and decided to go visit my grandparents. It was a spectacular summer evening and the sun was shining warmly even though it was already seven o'clock. Not warning them about my coming, I took it almost for granted that they would be happy to see me: this must be one of the great things about being a grandchild. They received me with open arms and warm hugs as always, but Grandma was worried – as always – that they did not have anything to offer their surprise guest.

While Grandma was filling the table with wine, cheese and different sorts of cookies and pastries, Grandpa asked me how it was going with my research. I answered that I was really enjoying the opportunity to dwell on the theoretical discussions on hospitality, but that I was also longing to start the holidays. I said that for me it would be great to hear how they understand the concept of hospitality and what hospitality as an idea means to them. Grandma looked at the kitchen table and pointed out how on the west coast of Finland, where we were, the main requirement for hospitality was to serve good food and drink to guests. Grandpa and I agreed that hostesses were often very focused on feeding their guests. However, Grandpa continued by suggesting that, in his opinion, hospitality was not only a duty of the hosts; the guests also had a responsibility to be welcoming towards the hosts. He used our discussion as an example and argued that I was being a hospitable guest as I was interested to hear their ideas about hospitality. For me, that very moment included a glimpse of ethical encounters and hospitality between ourselves: we had been ready to be interrupted, we were sharing our time, and we were open towards each other. On my way back a few hours later on my bike, I was smiling, thinking about the irony of having travelled all the way to Nicaragua to find out something I could have asked my own grandparents about.

At the same time, without engaging in this research on rural tourism development in Nicaragua, I probably would not have become interested in the different ways people welcome each other. What is more, during my three field visits to Nicaragua between 2007 and 2013, I constantly asked new questions about the possibilities and challenges related to tourism encounters. On the broadest level, this research journey could be described as a search for ethics, fairness and responsibility in the context of tourism development. Based on previous discussions in cultural studies of tourism, one of the best settings to identify responsible host-guest relations is in small-scale tourism initiatives based on active local participation (Stronza 2001; Singh, Timothy and Dowling 2003; Tosun 2005; Smith 2009c; Jamal and Dredge 2014; Kontogeorgopoulos, Churyen and Duangsaeng 2014). In these discussions the starting point for tourism development lies squarely in the well-being of those being visited instead of in promoting the tourism industries as such (e.g. Salazar 2012a; Grimwood et al. 2015, 23). In recent decades there have been calls for community participation as an alternative way to develop tourism, yet research in that vein has largely remained a counter-discourse to more business-, resource- and performativity-oriented tourism studies.[1]

It is clear that the notion of community participation is deeply ideological, reflecting the beliefs derived from social and political theories about how societies should be organized and how development should take place (Midgley 2011; Tosun 2000). Moreover, the interest in the potentialities of community participation can be interpreted as a sign of people growing tired of competition, consumption and weakened social relations in contemporary societies. As solidarity and communality are often described as virtues that have been lost in the midst of urbanization and technological development, it is hardly a coincidence that travellers, tourism researchers and development practitioners have sought these values in economically marginalized rural villages around the Global South. In most cases this means experiencing, studying or promoting community participation somewhere far away from one's own physical home.

Continuing the tradition of community case studies in tourism research (e.g. Smith 1978; Tucker 2003; Stronza 2008; Dredge and Hales 2012; Mostafanezhad 2014), my study includes a longitudinal ethnographic study in the coffee-cultivating communities of San Ramón, in the northern highlands of Nicaragua. Nicaragua is a country with a strong history of cooperative movements and resistance against foreign invasions, which makes it an interesting case for studying how local participation is supported by foreign and external actors. The research is driven by curiosity regarding the assumption that the people living in rural communities welcome all kinds of guests unconditionally (see also Szczesiul 2017). Hence, the purpose of the study is not to describe how the members of rural communities 'do' participation among themselves, but to train the focus on the host-guest relations in supposedly responsible, participatory tourism encounters. The research journey begins in the year 2007, when I lived in Nicaragua for the first time, mixing the roles of tourist, development practitioner and master's student in tourism research. I think that conducting a longitudinal study has given me a great opportunity to reflect on my own preconceptions about academic research, international development cooperation and, most of all, the 'other'.[2] My sincerest wish is that by telling the story of my research, this book can help us to reflect on not only how we relate to others, but also how we relate to ourselves.

Doing this research has given me the privilege of meeting, and enjoying the support of, many wonderful people. It is all these encounters which have made it possible and meaningful for me to complete this book. First of all, I am enormously grateful to the people in San Ramón who opened their homes to me, treated me as a friend, took the time to answer my questions and challenged me with theirs, *muchísimas gracias*. I also would like to thank all the development practitioners, government workers, civil society activists, scholars, teachers and students who participated in my study in Nicaragua during the past years – and even those who decided to keep their doors closed. Many thanks are due to Flora O. Acevedo, Óscar Danilo Barrera Pérez, Ernest Cañada, Olga Gómez, Catriona Knapman and Andrea Siclari for sharing their valuable insights on rural tourism development in the country. I owe special thanks to Damaris Diaz for all her help and care in Managua and beyond: there could be a thick book written about her genuine hospitality.

My wholehearted thanks go to the tourism research community at the Multidisciplinary Tourism Institute (MTI) of the University of Lapland for making me feel at home in Rovaniemi. I am indebted to my world-class supervisor and colleague Soile Veijola, who has been a continuous source of inspiration, ambition, encouragement and guidance since the very beginning of this research process. I would also like to thank Johan Edelheim, Outi Rantala, Maria Hakkarainen, José-Carlos García Rosell, Minni Haanpää, Heli Ilola, Monika Lüthje and Outi Kugapi for all the inspiring discussions and top-notch teamwork.

Since the first chapter of this book, it becomes obvious that without one particular writing camp near Pyhätunturi Fell in Finnish Lapland in February 2013, my book would probably have turned out to be something quite different. I am grateful to Soile Veijola and Jennie Germann Molz, among others, for bringing together a wonderful community of people who participated in and contributed to *Camping Together: A Tourist Experiment in Post-Biopolitical Living*. This unique camping and writing experience allowed me to dive into fascinating discussions on hospitality, relational ontologies and good life with Soile, Jennie, Tim Edensor, Alexander Grit, Olli Pyyhtinen and Gavin Urie. Thank you one more time.

I am extremely grateful to three brilliant scholars for their generous and detailed comments on my manuscript and much-needed boosts to this project. Million thanks to Suvi Ronkainen for our discussions on ethnographic research, to Tazim Jamal's for her insightful remarks on Levinas's work and the asymmetry of welcoming and to Kellee Caton for engaging in a rich dialogue with my research and giving lots of fresh inspiration.

I would also like to thank Jussi Pakkasvirta for his support and remarkable knowledge about the Central American context, and for welcoming me to join the POLITOUR research project (Policies and Practices of Tourism Development in Central America), financed by the Academy of Finland in the years 2011–2014. I am also grateful to the University of Lapland and the Finnish Concordia Fund for financing my research. Sincerest thanks are also due to Katono Ouma, Liina-Maija Quist, Ilona Steiler, Elina Oinas, Julia Jänis, Anja Nygren, Jeremy Gould, Florencia Quesada and Katri Onnela at the University of Helsinki.

Now, when thinking and travelling with hospitality, it is essential to underline that the ideas presented in this book have been greatly improved thanks to inspiration, critique, support and encouragement from many students, journal editors, reviewers and seminar, conference and symposium participants. Special, warm thanks in this regard go to Suvi Alt, Dianne Dredge, Ana Maria Munar, Katrín Anna Lund, Jarno Valkonen, Juulia Räikkönen, Simone Abram, Seija Tuulentie, Veera Kinnunen, Zoe Koivu, Bryan Grimwood, Tiina Seppälä, C. Michael Hall and many others. Working with Richard Foley, such a wonderful person and dedicated practitioner, turned the language-editing process into a treat. I would also like to express my gratitude and appreciation to Carlotta Fanton and Emma Travis at Routledge for all their support.

In the latter stages of working on this book, I have had the privilege to enjoy the company and support of my colleagues at the Linnaeus University in Kalmar, where I have become inspired to envision hospitable encounters in the more-than-human worlds. Many thanks to Martin Gren, Marianna Strzelecka, Per Pettersson Löfquist, Christer Foghagen, Hans Wessblad, Stefan Gössling, and my all-time favourite neighbour, Mathias Karlsson.

During this journey I have enjoyed the outstanding hospitality of very many friends and family members in Managua, Helsinki, Rovaniemi, Curitiba, Kalmar, Pori, Perälä and Boston. You all know who you are – thank you! The research project on ethical encounters, participation and hospitality has also meant, paradoxically, closing myself up at home alone and avoiding interruptions from the outside world. I am thankful to all those who have allowed me to do this, and even more to those who have continued to knock on my door and to welcome me back. Thanks to Iida, Jani, Mikko, Harri, Elina, Þóra, Nonni, Maria, Matthias, David, Alejandra, Karin, David, Kaarina, Satu, Emma, Riikka, Anu, Outi, Kaisa-Liisa, Fammu and Mummo. My gratitude also goes to family and friends in Tärnaby who have helped me to find a better balance between writing and relaxing. I started to write all your names here, and was happy to notice that the list would have been far too long.

Finally, I want to say *Kiitos* Elsa, *Tashakor* Ali Reza and *Miau* Iiris. My greatest appreciation and admiration go to Christofer: this journey would not have been possible without your adventurous mind, friendship, patience and perfect dose of sarcasm. *Tack!*

I dedicate this book to loving memory of my Grandpa Ukki.

Notes

1 For more discussions on the business orientedness of tourism studies, see Saarinen (2006), Ayikoru, Tribe and Airey (2009), Tribe (2009), Hall (2010b), Pritchard, Morgan and Ateljevic (2011), Caton (2012).
2 I have chosen to use the lowercase spelling of 'other' in the expression the 'other' unless there is a clear reason to use the capitalized form, for example, a quotation from Levinas. The complexity of this issue is obvious as even Levinas's own texts include contradictory ways of capitalization and non-capitalization (see also Kallio-Tavin 2013, 25).

1   Introduction

During my first visit to Nicaragua in 2007–2008, the questions of participatory development and democratic decision-making were as topical and disputed as they can be. Nearly thirty years had passed since the legendary Sandinista revolution and the supposedly leftist Sandinistas had just returned to power after an era of more right-wing governments. The streets were filled with big pink posters which celebrated the new president, Daniel Ortega, and his ambition of making Nicaragua 'Christian, Socialist and in Solidarity' again through 'civic participation'. At the same time, the winds of change were splitting the nation, and many were having serious doubts whether Nicaragua was actually moving towards more inclusive and equitable forms of progress. People were asking, with disillusionment in their voices, whether the real spirit of Sandinism and the socialist movement had become replaced by centralization of power, personal interests and clientelism (Equipo Nitlapan 2008b, 3–13). While I was doing my internship at the Finnish Embassy in Managua, I was struck by international aid agencies' concerns over how democracy had deteriorated in the country. It seemed like a growing number of bilateral aid organizations had begun feeling that their help was no longer valued and welcomed by the new government in power.

However, one of the few issues that the Nicaraguan government and international donors seemed to agree upon was the importance of directing funds and support to tourism development. Similarly to other countries in Central America, Nicaragua had recently been seeking, and also seeing, exponential growth in international tourism. In fact, growing foreign interest in the volcanoes, pristine beaches and colonial towns in the country was raising tourism to one of the most important sources of foreign income, alongside coffee beans (Barrera 1997; INTUR 2006; Babb 2010). At the same time, nongovernmental organizations (NGOs) in particular were directing their criticism towards the invasion of luxury resorts and residential tourism on the country's Pacific coast; in their view, it was highly uncertain who was actually reaping the benefits from the boom in the tourism sector (see Cañada and Gascón 2007b; Bonilla and Mordt 2008; Matteucci, Lund-Durlacher and Beyer 2008; Hunt 2011; 2016). In response to the emerging demands for fairer forms of tourism development, the Nicaraguan government and international aid agencies began adopting rural tourism as a model for creating more sustainable forms of that development.[1] The fresh policy and project documents emphasized the importance of developing tourism based on micro and small enterprises, local control, participation, ownership, empowerment and wider distribution of benefits (SNV 2007; PEMCE 2008; INTUR 2009). This led to a situation where many of Nicaragua's rural tourism initiatives were founded as social projects, with a considerable influx of funds from international donors.

With my background in tourism and development studies, I was thrilled to read project documents and newspaper articles on rural, community-based tourism. I even received invitations to participate in seminars and conferences arranged to discuss the great potential of this kind of tourism development. I remember thinking that community-based initiatives offered a much-needed alternative to the prevailing venues of tourism inequalities, such as all-inclusive enclave resorts (Carlisle 2010; Córdoba Azcárate 2014), displacement (Mowforth, Munt and Charlton 2008; Hunt 2011), violation of labour rights (Buades 2009; Cole and Eriksson 2010), sex tourism (Lovelock and Lovelock 2013), exploitation of natural resources (Gössling 2003) and commodification of indigenous cultures (Johnston 2006). My interest in the promise of the new kinds of tourism projects encouraged me to research the area further. I was concerned about the ways in which tourism developers were treating tourism almost as one of the 'productive' rural sectors (Shen, Hughey and Simmons 2008, 8; see Jóhannesson 2015), and irritated by the debates that were bogged down arguing whether local communities should participate in tourism development or not (Mitchell and Muckosy 2008). This meant that the impacts of community-based tourism were mainly measured in economic terms, while the demand for sustainability translated to mitigation of possible environmental costs. Thus, believing in the emancipatory possibilities of this kind of tourism, I wanted to focus on the social and cultural impact and to find theoretical support for my assumption that the local context and local communities' views should be better acknowledged in tourism debates. Knowing the short life expectancy of rural tourism projects (Rocha 2008), I was interested to get to know some of the pioneering communities in the field. I had heard about some older tourism initiatives that had recently contributed to the creation of the coffee route, Ruta del Café, in the northern highlands.[2]

1.1   Welcome to the coffee trails of Nicaragua

In August 2008, after a three-hour bus ride from Managua and one change, I arrived in the small farming town of San Ramón. A local tourist guide came to pick me up at the bus stop and bid me welcome to the coffee trails. She was wearing a green t-shirt with the logo of RENITURAL, which stands for *la Red Nicaragüense de Turismo Rural Comunitario* (Nicaraguan Network for Rural Community-based Tourism). During our walk to her home community,

I got to hear the entire story of tourism's arrival, starting from the Sandinista revolution in 1979. The guide told me how in the 1980s, during the Contra war, the international solidarity movement brought the first foreign visitors to the area. At that point, tourism was not yet organized, and visitors were 'attended as friends, not as tourists', as she put it. The first guests brought their own food and stayed with local families for free. They expressed an interest in helping, but also in learning about the collective spirit of the Nicaraguan socialist revolution and the newly founded coffee cooperatives. These types of visits, as well as different forms of unofficial help, nearly ended when the Sandinistas lost the election in 1990.

The guide also spoke about the global coffee crisis in 2000, which had severe impacts on the cooperatives of small coffee producers in the area (Valkila and Nygren 2009; Ganem-Cuenca 2011). In light of the circumstances, the regional and local coffee cooperative unions introduced the idea of beginning an official tourism programme. In addition to providing supplementary income and new contacts with coffee consumers, tourism was expected to contribute to gender equality and to create new job opportunities, especially for young people (UCA San Ramón 2008). Since then, representatives of many bilateral aid organizations and NGOs, as well as students and researchers like me, had become frequent visitors to the area (Cañada, Delgado and Gil 2006, 56–8; Höckert 2009; Cañada 2010; Pérez et al. 2010; Zapata et al. 2011; McRoberts 2012). In Spanish the initiative came to be called Agro-Ecoturismo Comunitario, while English-speaking visitors preferred to call it the Fair Trade Coffee Trail.[3] After the walk, we arrived in a village of about forty houses, an elementary school, two kiosks and a football field. There was also plenty of tourist signage, making the community more, as tourism scholar Bella Dicks (2003) puts it, 'visitable'. The printed and painted boards welcomed visitors to the community, indicated the houses offering tourist accommodation, showed how to get to the waterfall, the old gold mine and the scenic lookouts, helped identify the trees, explained which coffee plants are organic and provided reminders of generous donations from different aid organizations.

Less than a month after this visit, I returned to San Ramón to collect ethnographic data for my master's thesis. I conducted interviews and engaged in participatory observation with a special interest in the idea of empowerment. I was happy to hear that women and young tourist guides, the ones committed to the tourism programme, were participating in different forms of training in order 'to be able to receive guests'. People told me that although they had felt nervous and awkward with the first 'official' tourists, new contacts, positive experiences and better understanding of tourism activities helped them to gain confidence and enjoy the travellers' visits. I also heard that in the early years of tourism, the guests stayed and slept in the same rooms as their host families, whereas now there were already special rooms built for the purpose. In my analysis I described how local communities had experienced the social and cultural impacts of tourism development as positive for the most part.

I drew the conclusion that the essence of this kind of tourism could be seen in its potential to promote people's control over factors that affect their lives – in other words, to support empowerment (Höckert 2009; 2011; for conclusions in similar vein, see Hatton 1999; Scheyvens 1999; 2002; Cole 2006; Matarrita-Cascante, Brennan and Luloff 2010; Strzelecka and Wicks 2015).

However, when I returned to San Ramón in 2012 to work on my doctoral thesis, the atmosphere with regard to tourism activities had changed. The number of visitors had declined drastically after 2008, and the host families had ended up paying back the loans they had taken for tourism development, and the interest on them, with their coffee beans. Many of the local hosts seemed upset with the development aid organizations and cooperative unions, which had advised them to take relatively big loans, called microcredits, in order to improve the accommodation they could offer tourists.[4] While listening to these accounts, I recalled that people had already told me about their concerns over these loans during my previous visit. However, I must have been trivializing these fears, as I was focusing on gathering tractable data and offering coherent results.

Unlike before, I was now travelling with a smaller amount of development optimism and a bigger load of academic scepticism. This switch allowed me to notice the local communities' resistance towards new development interventions and how weary people were of waiting for tourists who were no longer coming. Although the number of tourists had declined, development consultants, students, researchers and volunteer workers were still relatively frequent visitors in these communities. Many of them, or perhaps more rightly us, were coming to help the locals to participate in tourism and community development in the 'right way'. One of the most drastic examples had been a bilateral development aid programme called 'Moderniza', which included a great variety of different kinds of recommendations on how local families should improve their hospitality – and take new loans – in order to bring back paying customers. As a response to these modernization efforts, some of those participating in tourism development had decided that the consultants representing this particular programme were no longer welcome in their homes and home community.

I had previously travelled to San Ramón with a naïve hope of finding tourism development and tourism encounters noticeably different from those in contemporary global tourism settings, that is, different from host-guest relations based upon the inequalities between the wealthy and the impoverished (see Cole and Morgan 2010, xv; Scheyvens 2011; Bianchi 2015). However, I became frustrated and confused. Even community-based tourism, which was supposed to be based on local communities' needs, seemed to reconstruct the unequal, and uncomfortable, balances of power between the West and the rest, or the cores and the peripheries.[5] Despite the principle of local participation, the problems were commonly found in local communities, while the solutions were provided from outside. Hence, it was unclear whose voices were being heard in participatory projects. I had to admit that despite the recent celebration of local ownership and indigenous knowledges (Jamal, Everett and Dann 2003, 154; Higgins-Desbiolles 2006; Schilcher 2007, 184; Telfer 2009, 153; Pritchard, Morgan and Ateljevic 2011, 14; Zapata et al. 2011, 23), even the emancipatory tourism initiatives I witnessed were struggling in changing the role of economically marginalized 'subaltern populations' from objects to subjects in tourism development (see Tosun 2000; Tuulentie and Mettiäinen 2007; Mowforth et al. 2008, 71; Saarinen 2010). And, above all, as I will argue in more detail later, these tourism encounters lacked mutual openness; that is, they lacked hospitality.

Comparative study on rural tourism in Nicaragua by María Jose Zapata, C. Michael Hall, Patricia Lindo and Mieke Vanderschaeghe (2011) points out that the local tourism projects directed to domestic markets tended to reap benefits faster and in a more sustainable manner than those implemented using the top-down strategies of international development agencies, which reflect prevailing neo-liberal values. However, as Zapata et al. have established, these kinds of 'bottom-up' initiatives are less common. This is unfortunate, and not only for ideological reasons. As shown in a growing number of studies around the world, the development of tourism for long-haul markets – without translation to the local resources available – can easily lead to a problematic dependency situation (e.g. Pleumarom 2012; George et al. 2009; Butcher 2012). In general, tourism initiatives often flag significantly after the withdrawal of external support. While the focus of tourism research has traditionally been on the encounters between hosts and tourists, the definitions of success or failure of even supposedly ethical forms of tourism development seem to depend greatly on the power, goals and practices of intermediaries and tourism experts (e.g. Cheong and Miller 2000; Fennell and Przeclawski 2003; Burns 2004; van der Duim et al. 2006; Zorn and Farthing 2007; Navas-Camargo and Zwerg-Villegas 2014; Wearing and Wearing 2014; Strzelecka and Wicks 2015; Hakkarainen 2017).

Bringing together cultural studies of tourism and development studies, the study at hand draws attention to the encounters between tourism experts and local communities in rural tourism settings. In addition to the empirical data I have collected in rural communities of San Ramón, I have gathered material among various tourism experts working and travelling in Nicaragua. I have chosen to use the term 'tourism experts' to describe guests with special insights into tourism, such as development officials, consultants, researchers, volunteers and students. The pages that follow will focus on exploring the following questions. Why might participatory tourism encounters lead to frustration and criticism among local communities, development practitioners and tourism researchers? How do the risks and responsibilities of participating become negotiated in rural tourism initiatives? In which ways can research on local participation re-construct or de-construct otherness? What would it mean to move towards more inclusive forms of participation? Seeking answers to these questions will then help to illuminate the main question: how do self and other, or hosts and guests, welcome each other in tourism development encounters?

While acknowledging that 'guests' and 'experts' do not form a homogeneous group of actors (rural host communities do not either), I consider that the experts share a common devotion to help the host communities to develop tourism. I have experienced that tourism researcher Mary Mostafanezhad's (2014) notion of 'humanitarian gaze' describes many of the foreign guests' wish to care for the 'other' in the economically marginalized areas extremely well. Drawing on John Urry's and Jonas Larsen's discussions of the tourist gaze, Mostafanezhad (2014, 7) proposes that 'like the tourist gaze, the humanitarian gaze is a relational act, not of an individual, but a field of relations that is mediated by discourses of institutions as well as cultural, political, economic, social and historical experiences of the gazer and gazee'.

The study suggests that one of the possible explanations for the frustration experienced in earlier projects lies in pre-set agendas of participation and assumptions about tourism and the 'other'. These socially constructed and organized presumptions, similarly to anthropologist Edward M. Bruner's (2005, 22–5) notion of 'pretour narratives', are most likely to undermine the possibilities of establishing open communication. Although presumptions adapt and change, postcolonial critiques, in particular, have called attention to the difficulty of addressing the issues of dominance and exclusion without actually perpetuating otherness and the binary oppositions between subject and object, developed and undeveloped, tourists and toured (e.g. Tucker 2014, 199). By postcolonial criticism I refer to that criticism in which the researcher positions herself or himself against imperialism, colonialism and Eurocentrism, as well as Western notions of philosophy (Hall and Tucker 2004, 2–3; McEwan 2009, 22–6). Especially Gayatri Spivak (1988), but also other decolonization theorists, such as Walter Mignolo and Arturo Escobar (2010), argue that the privileged position which academic researchers and development consultants, among other actors, occupy is the reason why the others, or the 'locals', cannot be heard. Instead the 'other' is always already interpreted. The consequence is 'epistemic ignorance' or 'epistemic violence': trivialization and invalidation of ways of knowing that fall outside of one's own, the dominant, the West's or the local elite's, languages, epistemic traditions and philosophies (Sharpe and Spivak 2002, 613; Kuokkanen 2007, 66–8). This means, paradoxically, that those who are expected to participate might become silenced in encounters designed to support local participation.

Reading postcolonial philosophy, and especially Emmanuel Levinas's (1969) thinking on phenomenology as openness to the other, has helped me to realize how tourism development includes not only epistemological conflicts, but equally the potential for conflictive ontological encounters. Thus, exploring the foundations of participation and the social requires sensitivity not only towards different ways of *knowing*, but also towards different ways of *being* with the 'other' and 'multiple others' (see Veijola et al. 2014; Grimwood 2015; Jóhannesson, Ren and van der Duim 2015; Alt 2016;

Grimwood and Caton 2017). By drawing on postcolonial and phenomeno-logical discussions on ethical subjectivities the study offers an alternative approach to participation that can help us to understand how we relate to each other in supposedly ethical encounters. Before presenting the theoretical and methodological approaches I have chosen, I take a closer look into pre-vious academic debates on participation in tourism and argue for the value of, in Gunnar Thor Jóhannesson, Carina Ren and René van der Duim's (2015, 243) words, stronger and nuanced engagements with relationality in tourism.

1.2   Hosts and guests in participatory tourism development

Community participation has become an important orientation in the search for sustainable and inclusive forms of tourism in rural and so-called periph-eral areas. Although the underlying assumption of participation is to guar-antee local communities' role as host in the course of tourism development, the initiatives and guidance for community participation commonly come from outside (Palomo Pérez 2003; Butcher 2007; 2012; Kontogeorgopoulos et al. 2014). This means that rural communities are often considered as poten-tial sites for participatory tourism projects by visitors who see tourism to fit well together with rural ambience, the 'agrarian way of life' and hospitality combined with a romantic picture of communality (see Lüthje 2005; George et al. 2009; Lane 2009). Moreover, as tourism and development scholar David J. Telfer (2003, 160) has argued, during the last decades it has been noticed at the global level that unless funds are targeted to assist in community tourism development projects, the potential for community development may be lost amid the pressures of the global economy.

While diving through the literature on participatory tourism development leaves an impression of local participation as a quite novel strategy for sus-tainable development (see Eadington and Smith 1993; Stronza 2001), the conceptualization of participation really derives from a rich, and even contra-dictory, legacy of ideas and practical agendas. For example, development scholars John Cohen and Norman Uphoff (2011, 34) begin telling the history of development and participation from a much earlier date. In their view, the questions about the relationships between participation and social and human development have been around at least since Aristotle, who analysed which arrangements in the Greek city-states most likely contributed to human happiness and *the good life*. In Aristotle's thought, the best state in the final analysis was one with broad participation, without any class dominating the others. Similarly, Matthias Stiefel and Marshall Wolfe (1994, 20) have connected the Western idea of participation to the idea of a *pluralist repre-sentative democracy*, which includes an underlying consensus that allows all major social groups to feel represented within the system.

However, in their review of historical perspectives on participa-tion in development theories, Andrea Cornwall and Karen Brock (2005, 1046) argue that by remaining 'politically ambiguous and definitionally vague participation has historically been used both to enable ordinary people to gain agency and as means of maintaining relations of rule'. As an illustration, Heiko Henkel and Roderick Stirrat (2001, 170) have proposed that the genealogy of participation can be found in the *Reformation*, where the idea of 'participation' became significant on the level of theology and evangelical promises of salvation. Postcolonial critiques in particular have described the unambiguous relationship between the origins of community development and colonial approaches, making participation a less democratic, radical or alternative development strategy than is often presented. Many scholars have traced the past history of the idea of community participation to the first community development projects run by missionaries and colonial officials (Nederveen Pieterse 2001, 75; Cornwall 2006; McEwan 2009, 234; Greig et al. 2007, 23; Leal 2010, 90). It has also been claimed that colonialism itself – and its dual mandate to civilize while exploiting – created the climate in which community development was to take shape (Mayo 1975 in Midgley 2011, 174).

More radical roots of contemporary ideas of participation theory can be found from anthropological critiques of development, particularly those which evolved in the 1960s and 1970s from the Latin American *dependistas* (Grosfoguel 2008, 307–34; Telfer 2009, 154–5), Paolo Freire's liberation pedagogy (1970/2000; Berkhöfer and Berkhöfer 2007) and Antonio Gramsci's neo-Marxism (1971; Stiefel and Wolfe 1994, 15–17). These approaches called attention to how mainstream development efforts tended to perpetuate dependency and to reinforce structures of inequality with the 'Third World' – a view that was informed by much of Freire's work (see Dussel 2013, 311–20). According to Freire it was necessary to analyse the connections between the culture of silence and the culture that has a voice. His *Pedagogy of Oppressed* (1970/2000), when translated into the development context, implies a radical critique of mainstream development thinking.[6]

An examination of the plurality of theoretical and philosophical discussions on participation indicates a lack of consensus about the theoretical backgrounds of contemporary participatory development theories. Interestingly, the later discourses on participation seem to have paid only sporadic attention to the long historical evolution of theories and practices of democracy, cooperation and communitarian and socialist utopias from which the hopes for participation had earlier been derived (Stiefel and Wolfe 1994). This has resolved in not only a rather limited idea of participation, but also discontinuity of learned lessons and theoretical debates. Especially the connections of participation to the more radical roots of social transformation – such as Freire's liberation pedagogy – were to some extent forgotten when the *community participation* approach was discovered by the mainstream in the late 1980s and 1990s; that is, when community participation became considered a core component of what is known as the *alternative development theory* (Chambers 1983; Cooke and Kothari 2001, 5; Greig, Hulme and Turner 2007, 233–6).[7]

The literature on community participation in tourism studies has for the most part followed the aforementioned *alternative development paradigm* (Telfer 2003, 158–61; 2014). The call for community participation emerged as a response to the dominance of the *neoliberal idea of economic development* and the numerous tourism impact studies and residents' attitude surveys which indicated that only few positive impacts were accruing to the host communities (Cohen, E. 1979b; Keogh 1990, 450; Tosun 2000, 616). The academic discussions on participatory tourism planning were launched in 1985 by Peter E. Murphy in his book *Tourism: A Community Approach*. While several scholars had already conducted studies on host communities' roles in tourism development (e.g. Young 1973; Smith 1978; de Kadt 1979; Jenkins 1982; Mathieson and Wall 1982; see also Saarinen, Rogerson and Hall 2017), Murphy's research became adapted as the first broader platform and catalyst for theoretical discussions about a community's sense of ownership and practical involvement in tourism processes (Olsen 1997; Ross and Wall 1999; Page and Dowling 2002; Boyd and Singh 2003; Simpson 2008).

Ever since, Murphy's call for decentralizing tourism development has offered stewardship to researchers and practitioners interested in developing less reactive, more integrative, approaches to tourism planning at community levels (Reid, Mair and George 2004). The underlying assumption of this approach has been to make sure that people are given the opportunity to shape their own destinies, rather than having the role of passive recipients of the fruits of development programmes or the tourism industries in general. A growing body of research on community participation has connected the phenomenon to *respectful use of resources* (e.g. Jamal and Getz 1995), *poverty reduction* (e.g. Cañada and Gascón 2007b), *typologies and models of participation* (e.g. Timothy 2002; Stronza 2008), *empowerment* (e.g. Scheyvens 2002; Cole 2006; Pleumarom 2012), *place attachment* (e.g. Woosnam et al. 2017), *skills* and *capacities* (e.g. Moscardo 2008; Aref 2011), *trust* (Mair 2014; Nunkoo and Gursoy 2016), *tour guides* (Salazar 2010; 2012), *management* and *leadership* (e.g. Kontogeorgopoulos et al. 2014; Prince and Ioannides), *external actors*, *partnerships* and *networks* (e.g. Zorn and Farthing 2007; Zapata Campos 2014) and *governance* (Bramwell 2014). These streams of studies offer a great variation of theoretical and epistemological approaches and methodological underpinnings, making it unclear whether these studies can be gathered under the umbrella of a 'participatory paradigm' (Jennings 2009; Lincoln, Lynham and Guba 2011; Dredge and Hales 2012). Perhaps the only thing that has been agreed in these studies is the difficulty of defining the concepts of community and participation in practice.

Tourism scholars and social activists Ernest Cañada and Jordi Gascón (2007b, 87) have highlighted the importance of not trying to copy rural community-based tourism from outside, arguing that the potential for local involvement varies a great deal from place to place. Unlike the general discourses of sustainable tourism – those with focus on sustaining resources or on sustaining the tourism industry as such – the community-based discourse has called attention to tourism, sustainability and development as social constructions (Saarinen 2006; see also Mair 2014). It has signposted an important shift towards more holistic understandings of *how* tourism activities might contribute to the multiple goals of development and well-being in different contexts (Stronza 2001; Balslev and Gyimóthy 2015; Jamal and Dredge 2015). During the last decade, a growing number of tourism researchers have questioned the settings where the West and the cores have the power to name, represent and theorize the knowledge of tourism and development (e.g. Holmes et al. 2016). Dianne Dredge, Robert Hales and Tazim Jamal's (2013) analysis on community-case study research in tourism suggests that the essence of research on community participation should be seen in the mutual, transformative learning that occurs between researchers and community members. The discussions on participation have received inspiration and support particularly from critical and hopeful tourism scholars who call for recognition of the neglected power of sacred, local and indigenous knowledges, to foster pluralism, social justice and empowerment in tourism worlds (Ateljevic et al. 2005; Higgins-Desbiolles 2006; Pritchard et al. 2011; Caton 2012; Karst 2017). Heightened attention to Aristotle's ethics, solidarity, consciousness-raising, reciprocity and other non-market values in tourism has moved the academic tourism debates closer to the earlier and 'more radical roots' of participatory theories.

Yet, despite the emerge and re-emergence of these 'hopeful' theoretical and ideological approaches, Donna Chambers and Christine Buzinde (2015, 2–3) encourage us to keep asking, 'Whose "hopefulness" is it?' and whether peoples from and in the South are still largely the *objects* of tourism research rather than the *producers* of tourism knowledge. Based on my own research journey, it is easy to agree that solidarity, empathy and the wish to 'give someone a voice' do not automatically translate to more equal encounters between people (see Mostafanezhad 2014; Tucker 2016). On the one hand, compassion becomes continuously materialized in normative studies on how to run, manage and evaluate participatory projects, without explicit debate about the shared values behind the very idea of participation as such. Consequently, tourism students, among others, are encouraged to memorize the ready-made definitions of local participation, sustainability and empowerment instead of reflecting on the political, epistemological and ontological premises that inform the topic (see García-Rosell 2013). On the other hand, compassion felt for the 'other' leads to studies that embrace the idea of multiculturalism to such an extent that it becomes difficult to discuss why the idea of participation is actually seen as a part of the good life and well-being (Fennell 2008; Jamal and Menzel 2009). Are the goals to promote the ideal of 'homo economicus', to live better and larger, to find solutions that could allow us to 'live well' or, even more, to 'live-well-between-ourselves'? Whose goals are these? And as Maria Puig de la Bellacasa (2017) would ask, 'Who is caring for whom?' What are the assumptions that guide our ideas of what is ethical, good, and desirable?

Reflecting on the contemporary liberal values and Eurocentrism in tourism curriculums, research and practices, the most common approach to good life and ethics seems to be an individualistic cosmology in which everything begins from the self (Smith 2009c). Thus, instead of building on the relational modes of participation, both practical and scholarly discussions are paradoxically celebrating the free individual subject as the protagonist of inclusion and social justice. This has led to debates where there are individuals who know how to help those 'badly done by', and individuals who criticize or ridicule those who engage in helping. Examples of scholars who belong to the latter group are, for instance, those who have condemned community participation as a failed pursuit, one which could be more or less abandoned in the scholarly debates and in practice (e.g. Dixey 2008; Butcher 2012; Goodwin, Santilli and Armstrong 2014). These critiques receive support for their arguments from pragmatic studies that define *how* and *why* local communities *fail* in participating in tourism, without further reflection on whose point of view these questions are being examined from (e.g. Tosun 2000; Simpson 2008; Goodwin 2011).[8] There is a paradox at work especially in the positivist and post-positivist, retrospective assessments of what has worked, what has not, which overlook the effects of one's own participation and agency in the research process (Westwood et al. 2005; Dredge and Hales 2012, 430–1). Furthermore, a considerable amount of participatory planning literature indicates quite instrumental concerns about the ways in which lack of local capacities or resistance of the local population might destroy the industry's potential altogether (e.g. Murphy 1985, 153; Potts and Harrill 1988; Fennell and Pzeclawski 2003; Aref 2011; Weaver 2012). Even though these kinds of debates expose structural and operational limitations of participation, they also reveal assumptions that local communities are expected to do participation in a *certain way*, with *right attitudes*. In these discussions the emphasis remains, as Amanda Stronza (2001, 275) has pointed out, on what is external to local communities.

While the debates for and against local participation in tourism have focused on communities' attitudes and skills, possibilities of achieving material progress, or contributing to environmental conservation (Li 2006; Hunt and Stronza 2014), quite limited attention has been drawn to the ethico-political dimensions of the issue, which supersede the straightforward intentions of promoting fair and alternative forms of tourism development. Above all, the extensive focus on the limitations, and on what does *not* happen in participatory initiatives, has eclipsed any interest in what *does* happen in the presentations of project-based analyses of community participation. Discussion on participatory tourism development would hence need more critical examination of its own *worlding* (Spivak 2003) or *worldmaking* power. That is, more attention should be placed on the ways in which different kinds of representations constitute and naturalize our world and our relations with the 'other' (see Hollinshead 2007).[9] This means asking, for instance, what happens when the intentions to operationalize and assess participation lead to eliminating those relationships between self and other which are not predictable, organized and linear (Singh 2012; Dredge and Hales 2012; Jóhannesson and Lund 2017; Tucker 2017). Or what might be the consequences of those studies on participation that present complexity, messiness and interdependency of human relations as major constraints on progress?[10] In my view, these kinds of discourses echo developmentalism, in which peripheral areas are expected to catch up with a certain kind of rational linearity of enlightened, modern-day thinking.

Whereas the relevance of including local communities will be advocated by parties other than the communities themselves, this approach keeps the communities, paradoxically, in a position of guests – guests who might, or might not, be invited to participate in participatory projects and tourism development. Could it be that even after many years of using tourism as a tool for development, empowerment and poverty reduction, the 'other', who in many cases is the 'poor', remain judged for not being capable of speaking for themselves (Viswanath 2008, 46)? As tourism scholars Stephen Wearing and Michael Wearing (2014) and Allison P. Holmes et al. (2016) have argued, even though community participation can be seen as a way to decolonize existing power relations within tourism, tourism studies have overlooked the unequal power relations that exist within participatory tourism discourses. Similarly, Hazel Tucker (2016, 36–9) warns about the uncritical framing of empathy that fails to address the issues of inequality and dynamics of power. The risks of facilitating unjust and illegitimate use of power in the name of participation has been brought up by development scholars Bill Cooke and Uma Kothari (2001), among others, who have raised the question whether the focus on methodological limitations of participation might have been obscuring the more fundamental problems within the development discourse. In their anthology *Participation: The New Tyranny?* Cooke and Kothari asserted that the problems associated with the orthodoxy of participatory development and the application of participatory practices do not lie with management or techniques, but with politics and discourses. Therefore, as these authors suggested, the debates on community participation should focus more on what kinds of subject positions are created in these discourses.

In sum, it seems like the idea of participation in tourism suffers from a schizophrenic condition where the liberal, self-interested, autonomous subject is simultaneously celebrated and criticized. In the first place, the principle of participation emphasizes everyone's right to benefit from tourists' interest in their home community, to decide what is good for them and to resist dependency from other actors. At the same time, the community participation narrative is perceived as an ethical alternative to individualistic 'just do it' society, driven by the market ideology, where everyone is responsible mainly for themselves. According to sociologist Albert O. Hirschman's (2002 [1982]) hypothesis, society tires of the individualistic mind-set in 10–15-year cycles. This means that after some intense search for solidarity and participation we would gladly return to minding our own business as usual. It seems, interestingly, that Hirschman's estimate of a 10–15-year cycle between faith and disappointment in individual action has been, with a few years' margin, embodied in the tourism literature. In addition to changes in the general tone within tourism research (see Taylor 1995; Timothy 2002; Butcher et al. 2012; Kontogeorgopoulos et al. 2014), there are individual tourism researchers who seem to have gradually lost their faith in the principle of community participation in tourism settings (e.g. Murphy 1985; Murphy and Murphy 2004; Scheyvens 1999; 2011).

Then again, some philosophers, such as Giorgio Agamben (1990), suggest that the search for a community and communality is a pertinent part of being human and hence infinitely present in a 'state of becoming'. Similarly, tourism researcher Shalini Singh (2012, 114) argues that community participation and communitarian reciprocity are human processes which are always emergent. The present book joins discussions in tourism studies which approach participation as a fundamental part of relating to others and where 'tourism comes about through relational encounters' (Jóhannesson et al. 2015, 3). It argues that the illusion of participation as a new or alternative approach to tourism and development has taken the focus away from discussions of the social and relational in participatory encounters. I agree with Singh (2012, 114), who takes issue with the existing scepticism and hopelessness in many community participation case studies. She asks whether it might be possible or meaningful to abandon participation per se as an approach, given that interaction, action and engagement are intrinsic to humankind. Instead, in Singh's (ibid., 118) view, the failures of the past should encourage us to redouble the efforts to look for fresh perspectives to establish participation as a part of our humanity.

The review of the previous research on participatory tourism development raises the question whether local communities have actually ended up playing the role of guests even in participatory tourism debates. During my research journey, I have become sceptical about the goal-driven ideas of participation and recognized the need for new, welcoming spaces for more mobile and hybrid subject positions (see Keen and Tucker 2012, 97; Tucker 2014). Thus, similarly to previous ethnographic research conducted by Hazel Tucker (2003; 2010) in Turkey, Amanda Stronza (2001; 2008) in the Peruvian Amazon, Wanda Vrasti (2013) in Guatemala and Gambia, Mary Mostafanezhad (2014) in northern Thailand, and others, my study uses the case of San Ramón in Nicaragua as a way to gain understanding about the contradictions in emancipatory intentions to help the 'other'. The research discussed in this book focuses on exploring 'hospitality' and 'welcome' as terms for describing, disrupting and shaping social imaginings and arrangements between ourselves.[11] Hence, rather than trivializing the principle of participation, this study describes it as the basis of ethical relations. I will now proceed towards unfolding my approach.

1.3 Hospitality as a means and goal of the research

Hospitality has been practised for thousands of years and is rooted in the survival of the human 'species' (Panosso Netto 2009, 57; O'Gorman 2010).

However, over the last couple of decades hospitality has enjoyed a renaissance with the growing international mobility of tourists, travellers, voluntary and involuntary migrants, refugees and asylum seekers on one hand, and with the powerful philosophical writings which explore the experiences of colonialism and postcolonial xenophobia, on the other (Still 2010, 1; see German Molz and Gibson 2007; Bell 2009; Lynch et al. 2011; Baker 2011; 2013; Candea and Da Col 2012; Lynch 2017). While my study is firmly moored in tourism research, it crosses thresholds and draws inspiration in particular from post-colonial philosophies of hospitality (Levinas 1969; Rosello 2001; Kuokkanen 2007). Reason for this rests in my primary interest in the study *of* hospitality as human phenomenon, instead in the study *for* hospitality as an industrial activity that focuses on the provision of food, beverage and accommodation in commercial and non-commercial settings (Lashley 2000; 2017; Eksell 2013; Lynch 2017, 175).

More specifically, the scientific purpose of this research is to deconstruct and envision alternatives to *participatory development* and *participatory encounters* through the notion of *hospitality*.[12] Hence, the study explores how the notion of hospitality might offer an alternative approach to reflect on the ways we *participate*, that is, how we relate to others and to ourselves (see Germann Molz and Gibson 2007; Baker 2013; Veijola et al. 2014; Innerarity 2017). The approach adopted builds on the discussions of French philosophers Emmanuel Levinas and Jacques Derrida on renewing subjectivity and ethics through the notions of hospitality and welcome.[13] The discussions became public after Levinas's death in 1995, in Derrida's (1999) *Adieu to Emmanuel Levinas*. The book consists of two parts: Derrida's moving funeral oration called 'Adieu' and an essay titled 'The Word of Welcome' based on a lecture Derrida gave in a homage to Levinas on the first anniversary of his death at the Richelieu Amphitheatre at the Sorbonne in Paris.[14]

For Derrida (1999, 21), the first of Levinas's (1969) best-known and extant works, *Totality and Infinity*, should be approached as 'an immense treatise of hospitality'.[15] In this work Levinas suggested that the Western intellectual tendency to *totalize* definitions of subjectivity and ontology should be resisted by the ethical recognition of openness, receptivity and *infinity*. The impetus for this stance can be found in Levinas's disappointment with the oppressive dichotomies between self and other, subject and object, which tend to priori-tize the freedom of being over the relation with the other. Levinas developed his ethical thought in a post-war climate, directing his concern towards the egocentric idea of being that did not do justice to our original experience of the other person, that is, to *the phenomenology of the other* (Wild 1969, 12–13). He built his critique especially on the necessity to move *beyond* Martin Heidegger's (1927/1972) ontology of *Being* (*Dasein*) in order to address our responsibility for the other (Levinas 1969, 179; 1998). For Levinas, ethics are not situated in self, but in the intersubjective relation with the other person, in being-for-the-other.[16] He argued that the obligation to do justice to the other and to *welcome* the other 'calls into question the naïve right of my powers, my glorious spontaneity as a living being' (Levinas 1969, 89).

According to Derrida (1999, 8–12) and Drabinski (2011, xii), it is the Levinasian idea of the other prior to self that has changed and keeps changing contemporary European philosophy. What makes his thought unique in the Western spirit of morality and justice is the idea of the relational mode of being which escapes from the isolated subject by desiring and respecting the alterity of the other (Laachir 2007, 180–1).[17] That is, as ethical subjectivity is constituted in this relationship with alterity, Levinasian ethics *begins* from the Other, who is never a mere object. In Levinas's work the relationship with the other is not based on a particular ontology, but on original responsibility for the other, which is essential in us from the beginning. In this sense, ethics for Levinas is not just one area of philosophy, but first philosophy, in which human existence is always situated in the unavoidable light of infinity (Levinas 1969, 299–307; see also Wild 1969, 13; Hand 2009, 36–7). His approach to ethics, which draws from Jewish thought as an intellectual tradition, is embodied in his presentation of the *face* of the other. For Levinas (1969, 79–81), the face is not a physical detail, but refers to the *infinite alterity* of the other, who is free from any idea which one can produce of the other. It is then the face in face-to-face encounters that issues us with an absolute ethical challenge: it challenges us to engage in acts of welcoming and responsibility without categorizing, systematizing or mastering the other.

In *Adieu to Emmanuel Levinas*, Derrida (1999, 3) suggested that Levinas's philosophy as a whole should be approached from the perspective of an unlimited responsibility and hospitality that precede and exceed one's freedom. As Levinas's ideas have been formed against any conception of subjectivity as totalized and dominant over the other, his thinking has been pertinent to postcolonial philosophy (Hiddleston 2009, 6, 16; Drabinski 2011, 22; Dussel 2013). Most of all, his other-oriented mode of speaking and thinking moves the focus from conceptual constructions towards greater readiness to listen and learn from experience (Wild 1969, 16). Reading Levinas, and Derrida's engagement with Levinas's thought, has encouraged me to look for the irreducibility and 'other-orientedness' in *participation*. By taking 'being-for-the-other' as an ontological starting point, the ambition of this research is to redirect the focus to the idea that, in the context of hospitality and participation, the self and the other are expected to *care* for each other's well-being (see Germann Molz and Gibson 2007; Kuokkanen 2007, 130; Smith 2009a; Jokinen and Veijola 2012; Jamal and Camargo 2013; Grimwood and Caton 2017; Hales and Caton 2017).

A valid way to enter into theoretical discussions of hospitality, as Derrida (1999, 19–20; 2005, 6–9, 19) explains it, is the necessary but impossible conjunction of *laws* and *politics*, of hospitality on the one hand, and the *ethics* of hospitality (an ethics *as* hospitality) on the other.[18] While the former is based on conditions and obligations, the latter invites us to think about the possibility of absolutely unconditional, open and infinite welcoming. In Derrida's work, hospitality which relies on conditions and obligations between people *delimits* rather than *opens up* borders and spaces for new possibilities. While saying this, he directed his critique especially towards Immanuel Kant's thought of hospitality based on juridical and political rights of visitation (Derrida 1999, 49–50). Hence, for Derrida (2002, 349–59; see also Baker 2013, 3) the Levinasian idea of ethics as infinite openness to alterity was to be seen as an inspiration and aspiration to fall short of. Instead of presenting *laws or politics of hospitality* and *ethics of hospitality* as opposite to each other, Derrida (1999, 19–21; 2000, 80–1, 135–7) argues that it is *between* these two conceptions of hospitality that responsibilities and conditions of welcoming become negotiated. Drawing on the writings of Levinas and Derrida, the present research considers that it is in these spheres and spaces – in these encounters – where responsibility for the other could become possible.[19]

In line with Levinas's notions of *totality* and *infinity*, and Derrida's concept of *hospitality*, this book argues that participation cannot be based on totalizing conditions and rules that are meant to master or control the other. Instead, as in the case of hospitality, the conditions of participation become constantly negotiated in intersubjective relations between self and the other. In adopting this approach, the study joins the efforts of what Jennie Germann Molz and Sarah Gibson (2007) describe as 'mobilizing hospitality'. These authors have called for dialogue and mobility between different discussions of hospitality in order to explore how the deployment of the concept in one disciplinary context may provide insights in other fields. In particular, the theme of ethics in mobile relations is one of the strongest threads that ties together diverse thoughts on hospitality and welcoming. Importantly, as Heidrun Friese (2004, 74, in Germann Molz and Gibson 2007, 2) has argued, in different kinds of studies and gatherings the question is not only 'thinking *of* hospitality, but thinking *as* hospitality' (see Lugosi 2017b). Germann Molz (2012) highlights the relationality of hospitality by calling it an act of sharing spatial, material and emotional resources. Her inspiring work on *Travel Connections* encourages us to continue to explore the possibilities of doing togetherness at home and on the move and to ask what hospitality encounters can teach us about living in difference.

Moreover, the call for mobilizing hospitality does not imply only mobilizing the conceptualization as such. Instead, somewhat different from conventional studies on tourism and hospitality management, cultural studies of tourism have drawn attention to mobilization of dualistic subject positions between hosts and guests, self and other, female and male, individual and community, humans and non-humans. For instance, the Finnish sociologists, tourism scholars and feminist theorists Soile Veijola and Eeva Jokinen (1994; 2012) have argued that in the global economic systems it is no longer easy to tell the guests from the hosts, private from public or work from home. Through their extensive discussions on contemporary arrangements of gender and hospitality, Veijola and Jokinen (2012, 40) have introduced the notion of post-host-guest society, which suggests that tourists and their host(esse)s become simultaneously subjects and objects of care. Similarly, the Levinasian notions of host and guest, both *hôte* in French, seem to describe settings where the pre-set roles between self and other cease to exist (Derrida 1999, 41–3; Rosello 2001, 18, 118).

In cultural studies of tourism, much attention has also been paid to the ways in which tourism practices might be based on the re-production of 'otherness', a focus that has made the concepts like 'tourist's gaze' (Urry 1990; Larsen 2014) and 'authenticity' (MacCannell 1976; Knudsen, Rickly and Vidon 2016) central. What is common to these discussions in tourism research, to postcolonial criticism and to Levinasian thought is the central role of 'the o/Other'. This research project embraces the different ways the concept has been used to describe and define the self's relation with the other. While in postcolonial thought 'the Other' is generally understood as the one who becomes silenced, in Levinasian writings 'the Other' (*autrui*), when capitalized, carries a positive connotation of 'the personal other', which evokes the idea of philosophical and ontologically given alterity (Cohen 1987, viii; Kallio-Tavin 2013, 25; Drabinski 2011). To put it differently, in postcolonial critique the Other's alterity becomes defined in comparison to self; for Levinas (1969, 180–1), the Other's difference and infinity is not reduced to totality. What is more, Levinas's idea of the 'Third' – the 'other other' – calls for political obligations, which means that the self is not responsible merely for the singular 'other', but for all others, for humanity as such (see Fagan 2009; Drabinski 2014).

Although Levinas's suggestion of ethics as *responsibility-for-the-other* and *being-for-the-other* echoes in the arguments for participation and inclusion, his idea of a responsible subject is very different from the modern idea of self as a free and independent individual; this can be seen in the way he challenges us to confront the very question of social life itself (Crossley 1996, 174; Oksala 2001, 67; Smith 2009a; Höckert 2014; Meijrt-van Wijk 2017). Accordingly, it seems meaningful to make more space for his reflections in the ethical landscapes of tourism (Duffy and Smith 2003; Fennell 2008; Ankor and Wearing 2012; Grimwood and Doubleway 2013). Tourism scholar Mick Smith (2009b, 614; 2009c) in particular has underlined the importance of welcoming and including Levinasian ethics in the contemporary discussions in tourism and hospitality studies. Although Smith has not engaged in the theoretical discussions on hospitality, his critique of contemporary discussions on ethics in tourism is very much in line with the critique which Derrida directed towards Kantian thought on external laws of ethics. In other words, in my view, Derrida's division of two laws of hospitality is in line with Smith's arguments of contemporary discussions of ethical tourism, in which he views ethics mainly as rules, like the law of hospitality, instead of as the basis for being.

In his analysis Smith (2009b, 263) shows how even more sophisticated discussions of ethics become stuck reconstructing a struggle between, on the one hand, external impositions of social solidarity and, on the other, biologically generated self-centred and egoistic desires. This means that any expression of concern for others is implicitly or explicitly associated with the cultural repression of necessary satisfaction of more primal, instinctual and natural needs. This approach to ethics (also to be seen in development discussions) is built on the idea of how responsibility towards the other, caring for the other, having an enlarged sense of community and so forth might actually be something unnatural, something imposed on us from the outside. Therefore, calling for ethical practices in tourism and development would for the most part be a matter of moralizing and guilt-tripping people into fulfilling their social obligations. Doing so would mean expecting people to engage in something that might be very much against their 'naturally' self-interested inclinations (Smith 2009c, 264).

The idea of modern subjectivity is often presented as a tradition of autonomous and self-determined individuals who are using their rational abilities to promote their own, hedonistic interests (Fennell 2006; 2008, 3). It is the assumption that 'we are all individuals' which is seen to underlie liberal and neoclassical understandings of economics and politics (Smith 2009b, 620; Braidotti 2013; Mostafanezhad 2014). In tourism settings, the notion of subject has been primarily connected to an active, individual tourist who enjoys through consumption and whose travels in the best case lead to the tourist's encountering and finding her- or himself (see Rakic and Chambers 2012; Veijola and Falin 2014). In tourism 'the figure of the Self looms large' (Caton 2014a, 185). Richard Ek (2015, 144) argues, thinking with Derrida (2005), that 'the postpolitical tourist has the status of being immune; exempt from commitments and liabilities'. Nevertheless, as Ek continues, although the current commercial society encourages the tourists to behave in a certain way, it does not mean that the tourist is necessarily a one-dimensional, dominant dupe without reflection and contemplation (see also Bruner 2005, 12; Francesch Díaz 2016).

Mick Smith (2009a, 264) has also lamented how this idea of human existence is 'so self-centred that it initially seems difficult to reconcile with any kinds of ethics at all'. Along the same lines, David A. Fennel (2008) asks whether it is in the 'tourism's nature' to emphasize the value of one over the value of others. I agree that accepting individualism as an intrinsic part of human or tourism's nature – instead as a historically and culturally specific, and increasingly problematic discursive formation (Braidotti 2013, 24) – has regrettably restricted the imaginings, openness and fruitfulness of academic debates on ethics in tourism. It is this tradition of autonomous subject that Levinas's notion of hospitality, openness to the other, seeks to interrupt. This does not mean aiming to 'kill the subject', in post-modern style (see Ronkainen 1999), but to break out of one's ego by redefining subjectivity as the 'subject of the welcome' (Derrida 1999).

Kim Meijer-van Wijk's (2017, 45) wonderful introduction to Levinas's philosophy suggests that

Levinas would probably affirm that there is no sense in thinking of morality or ethics – as philosophers do – from an individual perspective, no more than it makes sense to for one to be hospitable alone. Hospitality is the encounter with the Other and so is ethics.

Although the Levinasian vision of infinitely open welcoming between ourselves can be seen as a mere utopia, Derrida (1999, 51–2) proposed it as a way to interrupt and move beyond the individualist tradition of self.[20] Levinasian thinking, as I read and visit it, resonates well with so-called *indigenous cosmologies*, in which subjectivity is based on relational ontologies. Indigenous cosmologies have attracted special attention particularly in a long tradition of anthropological studies which have sought to denaturalize modern ontological assumptions. One such study is Marion Blazer's (2010, 235) longitudinal learning journey with the Yashiro people of the Paraguayan Chako, which tells a story of the less-acknowledged potentials of relational worlds. During the past years, a growing number of scholars have studied the Andean vision of *suma qamaña* (good life, *vivir bien*), which is seen to embrace an alternative way of understanding reciprocity and the other. In other words, it is described as an alternative to the Western, growth-oriented, development thinking that separates people from each other and from nature (Escobar 2010; Karst 2017; see Alt 2016, 233–9). For instance, in her ethnographic research on indigeneity and state formation in Bolivia, development scholar Eija Ranta (2014) describes the crux of the process as being the political activation of indigenous cosmologies in which all beings exist in relation to others and never in the form of an individual or an object. To my knowledge and experience, the paradigm of *vivir bien*, which means 'living well between ourselves' – instead of 'living better' – coincides with Levinas's notions of subject formation, in which 'subjectivity is not for itself, it is initially for another'.[21]

Nevertheless, Levinas's radical idea of ethics as first philosophy has been treated primarily as a Western alternative to the Western essential ontology of being (Hand 2009; Drabinski 2011; Maldonado-Torres 2010, 94–6). Thus, the most obvious place to look for Levinas is the discourse on the ethical turn in continental philosophy. These discussions are normally traced to Husserl's phenomenology, and then followed through Martin Heidegger, Hannah Arendt and Levinas all the way to Luce Irigaray and Derrida. Phenomenological philosophy does not emphasize participation as such, but the discussions cited include an interest in the origin of ethics and values and encourage consideration of the issues of responsibility and response. As the ethics sought are thought to be found in the encounters between subjects, the central themes of this tradition touch the questions of love, wonder, responsibility, generosity, gift and *hospitality* (Heinämaa and Oksala 2001, 11–14). For Levinas (1969, 304–6), infinite responsibility is also manifest in the never-enough character of giving, gesture and charity (Drabinski 2011, 18).

While drawing on Levinasian thinking on intersubjectivity, this research builds on the discussions of relational ontologies that embrace and call for messiness, openness and unfinishedness in social relations analysed by Soile Veijola, Jennie Germann-Molz, Olli Pyyhtinen, Alexander Grit and myself (2014) in *Disruptive Tourism and Its Untidy Guests: Alternative Ontologies for Future Hospitalities*. The book explores tourism and host-guest relations through deliberately untidy concepts such as *camping, parasite, silence, unlearning* and *serendipities*. By arguing, along with Jean-Luc Nancy and Georg Simmel, that existence is always co-existence, we have contrasted alternative ontologies of tourism to the ones that take reality to exist through clear-cut and self-subsistent beings, subjects and categories. To imagine alternative ontologies, we have introduced the concept of 'the untidy guest' to argue that 'when scholars – and indeed tourism itself – confound and interrupt habitual interactions and assumptions, this may lead to new ideas and understandings of the "good life"' (ibid., 4). In the study at hand I continue to elaborate on the importance of untidiness within the discussions of participation and relationality (see also Keen and Tucker 2012; Dredge et al. 2013; Grit and Lynch 2012; Tucker 2014; 2017; Jóhannesson et al. 2015).

In the following section, I offer a short presentation of how the thoughts presented in the preceding section, on welcoming, intersubjectivity and knowing-with, have been operationalized and applied to the epistemological and methodological discussions of the study.

1.4   Towards hospitable methodologies

Conducting fieldwork, collecting data, making knowledge claims or representing the other are never innocent, objective or neutral activities. As Michael Agar phrased it, ethnographer is actually the stranger who comes into a space where others are familiar with each other. In a chapter titled 'Who are you to do this?', Agar (1980, 91) argues that:

> ethnography is really quite an arrogant enterprise. In a short period of time, an ethnographer moves in among a group of strangers to study and describe their beliefs, document their social life, write about their subsistence strategies, and generally explore the territory right down to their recipes for the evening meal.

Travelling has been historically intertwined with ways of knowing and mastering the world. Jamaica Kincaid's (1988) *Small Place*, Judith Adler's (1989) *Origins of Sightseeing*, Mary Louise Pratt's (1992) *Imperial Eyes*, and Edward M. Bruner's (2005) *Culture on Tour*, amongst others, challenge their readers to acknowledge the colonial antecedents of contemporary travel writing and travel journalism, tourism research, anthropology and ethnographic fieldwork (Edensor 1998; Blazer 2010; Salazar 2013; Abram and Norum 2016). This means asking how the purposes and ways of conducting research might and *should* differ from the ways in which Western officials, missionaries, explorers, intellectuals used to collect reports and stories about the 'noble savages', 'primitive populations' and wilderness of the colonies and other 'remote' areas (Tuhiwai Smith 2012).

One of the most problematic dichotomies back then, and perhaps even today, was the way in which local communities 'over there' were seen as sources of raw material for developing theories 'over here'. The implicit assumption that 'the valuable and legitimate' knowledge would be developed and conserved outside the communities studied has been criticized by post-colonial scholars as highly imperialist and problematic for several reasons (Said 1993; Chambers and Buzinde 2015; Grimwood et al. 2015). First, the assumption perceives the other, similarly to non-human others, as an object of knowledge and in this way reconstructs the colonial subject positions. Second, it strengthens – instead of questions – the Western and ethnocentric epistemes where 'other cultures' become translated into the language of the one who knows (Ahmed 2000, 58–9).[22] Third, separating fieldwork from theory, or reality from interpretation, overlooks, as Veijola and Jokinen (1994) have vividly demonstrated, the presence of the researcher's body in the field-work encounters.

The processes of disrupting and decolonizing the production of knowledge, 'rewriting ethnography' and making a reflective turn of ethnographic research have been ongoing since the 1970s. The most-cited and best-known critique of ethnography, *Writing Cultures: The Poetics and Politics of Ethnography* by James Clifford and George E. Marcus (1986), turned attention to the richness of ethnographic fieldwork as a form of interpretive knowledge production on one hand, and to the risks of (re-)constructing rather than describing other-ness, on the other. By bringing reflectivity and ethicality into the centre of ethnographic research, ethnographers were required to address the issues of *perspective* and *bias*, as well as the ethical obligations to the people with whom they work (Murchison 2010, 8). Ever since, ethnography has expanded rapidly beyond anthropology and beyond the settings where the 'West studies the rest'. Scholars from a wide range of disciplines, including tourism research, keep choosing an ethnographic research strategy as the most suitable one for studying, for instance, actions, cultures and social organizations in their everyday contexts. However, the expansion and popularity of ethnography have not reduced the importance of addressing the unequal power relations in research, the risks of simplifying the diversity of lived experiences, or the limitations of using Western epistemological lenses to interpret the tourism and hospitality phenomenon across the globe (Chambers and Buzinde 2015).

In effect, despite the ongoing efforts to decolonize and democratize knowledge production, and despite the rich history of ethnographers experimenting with different research strategies, sites and styles of storytelling and presentation, there are groups of people who are no longer ready to be objects of academic research.[23] In her book *Decolonizing Methodologies*, Linda Tuhiwai Smith (2012, xi; see also Junka-Aikio 2014) draws attention to the dirtiness of the word 'research' in the indigenous worlds and to the ways in which some groups have taken different actions to limit their hospitality towards researchers. Just as development discourses and practices have changed from developing *for* to developing *with* the other, so, too, researchers have been challenged to search for more ethical epistemic standpoints which would be open to the idea of knowing *with* (e.g. Veijola 1997; Tuhiwai Smith 2012; Haraway 2016; Holmes et al. 2016).

Moving from development encounters towards research encounters means, in addition to trying to live up to the epistemological and methodological criteria of academic research, facing the same ethical issues that are relevant in the context of development (de Sardan 2005, 202; Parsons and Harding 2011; Blazer 2010). Just as in participatory development projects, merely encouraging others to participate in academic research does not automatically mean that the ethnographic subject would want to join or would be able to speak. However, the previously presented philosophers of hospitality and ethical subjectivities, such as Levinas, Derrida or Spivak, have not engaged in writing practical advice for conducting fieldwork. Namely, how to enter and visit the homes of others in order to collect information about them and their homes. In fact, according to Sharpe and Spivak (2002), the entire idea and question of method is quite violent as such. *How* then is one to conduct an empirical study that could move from using invasive research practices towards using more hospitable, or at least less violent, methodologies? It looks like envisioning more inclusive, hospitable research approaches should begin from readiness to question the authority of the academic researcher. This can be done by asking the very same questions that should be posed to those in charge of development projects (Jamal and Everett 2007, 61). For instance, Tuhiwai Smith (2012, 10) demands that researchers must have answers to the following kinds of questions. 'Whose research is it and whose interests does it serve? Who has designed the questions and framed its scope? How will the results be disseminated and who will benefit from it?'[24]

While moving from Levinasian reflections towards methodological discussions means exceeding the scope of Levinas's own texts, the phenomenological method is pivotal for imagining what 'Levinasian thinking' on hospitality and welcome might look like (Drabinski 2011).[25] At this point, I should make it clear that this research project is not an anthropological study that aims to describe what Nicaraguan hospitality or cosmologies might be like. Neither is it my purpose to offer recommendations whether or not tourism should be promoted and developed in rural communities. Also different from most of the phenomenological studies in tourism, a trend begun by Erik Cohen's (1979a) *Phenomenology of Tourist Experience*, I am not interested in the *tourists'* experiences as such, but in the encounters that take place in the context of tourism development. This limitation is guided by the heuristic guidelines of hermeneutic phenomenology (Gadamer 1975; van Manen 1990),[26] which encourage looking at the relations between self and other to explore how meaningful experiences come about (Pernecky and Jamal 2010). Encounters are defined here as spaces and liminal spheres between people in which the conditions of participation become negotiated. Hence, this study suggests that focusing on the micro-encounters and negotiations between tourism experts and local communities can make it possible to understand different ways of perceiving tourism development and ethical relations.

The aim of this research is to interpret and describe tourism development encounters from different standpoints: people who are engaged in tourism in their home communities, local tourism coordinators, tourism developers, consultants, students, researchers, volunteers. Throughout the analysis presented in this book, I ask how, on the one hand, people living in rural communities – the 'hosts' – and, on the other, tourism experts – the 'guests' – experience, interpret and give meanings to the meetings, encounters and entanglements that take place among themselves or, put more aptly, between ourselves (Gadamer 1975; van Manen 1990). Instead of approaching hosts and guests as clear-cut subject positions, I am interested here in the ways in which the 'host' and 'guest' roles become disrupted, negotiated and mobilized in tourism development encounters (see Tuulentie 2006; Germann Molz and Gibson 2007; Tucker 2014; Jóhannesson et al. 2015). Focusing on socially mobile, intersubjective encounters allows one to explore how the hosts and guests welcome each other in always asymmetrical relations of hospitality (Levinas 1969, 215–16; 1985, 98–9).

Between 2007 and 2013 I lived in and visited Nicaragua three different times. During my first fieldwork period in 2007–2008 I collected data among rural communities in San Ramón through group and individual interviews and by observing encounters between tourism experts and local hosts (Höckert 2009). As is normal in ethnographic fieldwork settings, the discussions accompanying and alongside the interviews were a central part of the interaction. I helped women in the kitchen, took many photos, answered questions about my home country, rode a horse, helped to build an eco-cottage, played football, walked to school with children who were wearing their well-ironed white and blue uniforms, bought handicrafts, played card games, picked coffee, learned about coffee production, and drank many litres of coffee with lots of milk and sugar. Although I was holding tightly to my identity as a young researcher, the locals most likely received and perceived me like any of the travellers who arrive with many questions about coffee cultivation, gender equality, history and politics (Höckert 2009; see Hall 2010b; Francesch Díaz 2016). For my second visit to Nicaragua, a four-month period in 2011–2012, I had broadened my focus to rural tourism development in the country in general. Following up this interest, I conducted expert interviews (Goulden and Marcussen 2004) in the Nicaraguan tourism ministry INTUR, international aid organizations and NGOs, and had close contact with two universities in Managua. At the same time, I continued to follow how the people in the communities of San Ramón experienced the heightened national and international interest in rural tourism development. For a Finnish researcher the timing of this field visit was simultaneously exciting and difficult as during these months the foreign ministry of Finland announced its plans to leave Nicaragua after 30 years of bilateral development cooperation.[27] However,

I was not ready to say 'goodbye' to Nicaragua quite yet, but returned one more time in May 2013. By this last fieldwork, the focus of my study had moved from the promises of local knowledge in tourism towards questions of relationality and mutual receptivity in tourism development encounters.

The seven-year period was not a continuous, long stretch of fieldwork, but can be described as longitudinal ethnography which continued even when I was not in the 'field'. Tourism scholar Outi Rantala (2011b, 153–5) has depicted a three-layered ethnographic process as moving between physical, written and textual fields. This means that although I was not present in the physical encounters with the informants, participants, interlocutors, I continued to encounter my data and the literature that helped me to engage with this data. As a result, my research journey included many flights and bus rides, walks and talks, academic seminars, various kinds of travel literature and different types of questions. Especially the drastic change in my travel readings indicates the impossibility of separating theory and practice. Instead of making long leaps between empirical and theoretical worlds, the leaps became constant and entangled. This meant changes in the theoretical and operationalized concepts that I was using to make sense of the studied world. While some concepts turned out to be more limiting, such as 'empowerment' or 'local knowledge', others, such as 'hospitality', suddenly opened new doors. Hence, I follow on the footsteps of those researchers who locate the essence of ethnography in the very openness of the travelogue written during and after the journey (Westwood et al. 2005; Ateljevic et al. 2005; Cerwonka and Malkki 2007; Vennesson 2008; Rantala 2011b; Vrasti 2013; Haanpää 2017).

Crucially, fieldwork diaries that I wrote during these visits later functioned as a good reminder of the challenges of slowing down the research processes and keeping one's mind open. The notes included a whole range of feelings spanning from worry about the ongoing coffee crisis (Olam 2013; Terazono 2013), worry about my own research process, frustration and anger towards tourism experts or local tourism coordinators (see Chapters 3–5), to variations of happiness and annoyance towards the curious children who entered my tourist hut to play and use my laptop. My fieldwork diaries also echo the changed atmosphere in Nicaragua-Finland relations, and allowed me to analyse how the changed tone in the words of welcome had been shaking and shaping my own subjectivity as a researcher. Reading and re-reading these field notes helped me to understand why Quetzil Castañeda (2006) has distinguished the processes of 'being in fieldwork' and 'gathering data'. What Castañeda underlines is the holistic nature of ethnographic fieldwork; that is, how focusing only on the concrete actions of gathering data causes a researcher to neglect her or his experiences and reflections when, for instance, she or he does not succeed in getting the desired or expected data. In other words, *being* in fieldwork embraces the pre-assumptions, confusions, disappointments and 'failures' as part of the data and part of the journey (Caton 2013, 347; Vrasti 2013; Wilson and Hollinshead 2015).

In addition to hundreds of pages of field notes, I gathered tourism policies and strategies, state documents, statistics, newspaper articles and conducted all together fifty-five semi-structured interviews. Perhaps I should mention that thirty-eight of these interviews took place in the area of San Ramón, while seventeen of them were expert interviews conducted in air-conditioned cafés and offices in Managua and Matagalpa. I conducted nearly all the interviews in Spanish, which I had learned while living in Spain and Nicaragua. The analysis was enrichened with material from Nicaraguan artists and authors, such as Sergío Ramirez and Gioconda Belli. However, in hermeneutic phenomenological analysis, the number of informants, or the total amount of data, are rarely seen as relevant (Gadamer 1975; van Manen 1990). Instead, as Johan Edelheim (2015) addresses in his rich and critical examination of tourist attractions, the 'validity' of phenomenological analysis depends on the *vivid* description that allows the readers to recognize the described experiences as something that they have had or could have had. This is what Max van Manen (1990, 27) has called the 'phenomenological nod'. In addition to the phenomenological nod, Edelheim highlights one's devotion to 'aha' and 'eureka' experiences (see also van Manen 1990, 26; Jamal and Hollinshead 2001). In my study I have sought to remain loyal to my own 'moments of insight' by laying special emphasis on the data that helped me to experience the 'aha'.

One of the most sweeping 'aha-moments' took place during my second stay in Nicaragua, in 2012, when I realized how weary the people in San Ramón had become of outside-led development projects. Before coming to Nicaragua for this second time, I had studied about the different possibilities of conducting participatory action research (McIntyre 2008; Grimwood et al. 2012) and ethnographic action research (see Hakkarainen and Garcia-Rosell 2018) with – not on – the subjects of the study, and had become particularly interested in the potential of a methodology called Photovoice (see Hergenrather, Rhodes and Bardhoshi 2010). However, after meeting the people and sensing their feelings of fatigue with projects in general, with constant flow of 'new' ideas and methodologies from outside, I had to abandon my plans of inviting the local hosts to produce, collect and analyse data. Ironically, the local tourism coordinators brought up the need for a study that could help them to advertise the local tourism products and bring in more customers. This was nothing that I was there for, nor was I even capable of doing a marketing research after studying mainly cultural studies of tourism and development. In this situation, I was sure that asking the locals to take part in a community-participation project that I had planned, that would fit in with my previous education and that would help me to gain data and material for my dissertation would have been contradictory to the very idea of participatory action research.[28]

Valuing highly the Levinasian idea of relationality and Spivak's call for acknowledging one's privileges and positionality in one's relation with the 'other', my study has steadily moved towards ethnographic approaches that promote openness, locate ethics in the centre of methodological considerations and demand accountability for one's own biases (Jordan and Yeomans 1995; Hytten and Madison 2012). These approaches are in favour of slower research processes (see Jóhannesson et al.2015) that allow radical reflexivity (Bruner 2005) about the ways in which the potential informants welcome researchers. Moreover, these methodological discussions have urged me to question my own openness towards informants, research participants and the data I have collected, transcribed and analysed in the course of the present research. The first and the last bus trip to the communities of San Ramón were clearly very different: while the first time I was convinced of the need to analyse the social and cultural impacts of tourism development, the last time I was mainly wondering why I had actually been so sure about it. Likewise, I reflected on why I had overlooked the consequences of these kinds of research visits from my earlier analysis (Höckert 2009). In this sense, my recently gained insights about the Levinasian (1969, 82–4) notion of *welcome* had brutally interrupted my own spontaneous freedom to visit and study the 'other'. It had made me realize my own position as a cosmopolitan traveller and researcher who had previously taken for granted the welcome *of* the other – that the other welcomes me. In this situation, I found the hermeneutic circle a liberating and forgiving approach to analysis as it encourages continuous questioning of presumptions and imaginings that we travel with (see Pernecky and Jamal 2010; Edelheim 2015).

Despite the unfinishedness and openness of hermeneutic phenomenological analysis, the focal phenomenon must be temporarily frozen if it is to be described. That is, inviting the reader to participate in the discussions about the phenomenon at hand requires representing the experiences of the phenomenon in some kind of context, painting a picture while the target keeps moving (Büscher, Urry and Witchger 2011). This means, simultaneously, that the representation of the phenomenon of tourism encounters turns into an intersubjective encounter between the representation (this text) and the reader (you). In this sense, just like the encounters in tourism settings, the representations of these encounters must also be viewed in terms of the intersubjective system of linguistic communication (Gadamer 1975 in Crossley 1996, 24). Knowing this, I recognize and fear my power and responsibility when welcoming the reader to encounter my representations of the tourism development encounters. Therefore, I must add that the purpose of telling the stories from Nicaragua, and San Ramón in particular, is not to welcome guests directly to Nicaragua or San Ramón, but to welcome the reader to imagine different forms of relations that can take place between self and other. I also want to be clear that when writing the travelogue of my research journey, I have wished to leave it to the reader to decide what kinds of encounters could be desirable. I also avoid making recommendations whether travellers should or should not engage in future encounters with the communities represented in this study. That is, my position in this research process is not to mediate the words of welcome on the others' behalf.

And yet, my study inevitably joins the stream of emancipatory intentions to 'empower the marginalized voices in tourism' by speaking *for* and speaking *about* the other. Notably, this kind of intention to represent others is not only a complicated and contentious task, but also a political one (Blazer 2010). So while not all representation of the 'subaltern other' are by any means desirable, the question remains whether scholars can actually speak for, and about, the other without preserving otherness (Duffy and Smith 2003, 105–12; Tucker 2010, 941; Chambers and Buzinde 2015). Reporting research results, writing travelogue or telling narratives of the other inevitably includes risks of re-constructing and strengthening the imaginaries about the other. This is not a challenge to be taken lightly; in fact, Spivak (1988, 25) laments how even two of the most famous scholars of subjectivity, Michel Foucault and Gilles Deleuze, have claimed to represent the other as transparent mediums. By doing this, Spivak warns of the ethical dangers associated with representing the previously marginalized from the standpoint of a relatively empowered intellectual in the Western academy. She is in favour of a deconstructive reading of the positivist and essentialist paradigms of 'representation' that support the claims of many benevolent left-wing intellectuals to speak *for* or *about* the marginalized other (see also Morton 2007, 107; Vrasti 2013, 125).

These discussions are continued in the following chapter. My ambition is to explore how, by adapting Levinas's mindset, hospitality could be used to de-establish speaking *for* and speaking *about* the other and to envision the ethical force of *saying*. This ethical saying does not aim to define the other as an object of knowledge, but is merely a desire for infinity, openness and receptivity (Levinas 1998). I suggest that shifting the unit of analysis from individuals, communities, ethnic groups or nations to *encounters* could allow us to take small but pivotal steps from the *said* towards the *saying*. By this 'shift' I also refer to a more careful acknowledgement and articulation of what research, as well as the representations of research, is expected to explain about the social worlds studied. For me, this is a contribution from hermeneutic phenomenology which can help to decolonize methodologies; that is, to make *the methodologies more hospitable* by training the focus on the imaginings and experiences of the phenomenon at hand while keeping the door open to the unexpected (see Derrida 1999, 21–6).

1.5 Structure of the book

Ethical epistemologies, a notion introduced by Soile Veijola,[29] call for responsible relationships between researchers. In this sense, producing knowledge can be seen as an act of opening spaces and welcoming self and others to think differently (Heinämaa 1996, 171). It is also an invitation to imaginations to go visiting yet unknown places[30] and letting our minds to engage with slow travel. In my study, hospitality not only offers the theoretical and methodological frameworks, but also shapes the styles and structure of the book. The division of the work into chapters follows the approach on hospitable writing, which – here – means welcoming the reader to visit the chapters chronologically or in any order she or he wants.[31]

The next chapter, following this introduction, elaborates the theoretical framework of the study – the notions of hospitality and welcome as the foundation of ethical relations. My argument here is that while contemporary searches for ethical encounters within tourism have primarily been driven by self-oriented and ethnocentric ideas of participation and responsibility, the call for hospitality can be seen as an interruption of this individualistic tradition of self. Offering first an overview of Levinas's work, the chapter moves towards exploring Levinas's and Derrida's ideas of *welcoming* as orientation towards the other. Their description of ethical subjectivity as a continuum of hosting and guesting (see also Rosello 2001) calls attention to the interplay between saying welcome *to* the other and receiving the welcome *of* the other (other's welcome). The chapter weaves together Levinas's and Derrida's discussions on unconditional hospitality and Spivak's postcolonial critique of emancipatory approaches that silence other ways of knowing and being in the world. In the course of the chapter, I suggest that the call for openness towards otherness and alterity voiced by postcolonial philosophers can help us to rethink host-guest relations in communal coffee tables.

Chapter 3 takes Levinas's and Derrida's discussions of unconditional and conditional hospitality into the Nicaraguan context. I begin by describing how the pervasive images of foreign interventions, natural catastrophes and poverty in Nicaragua have recently been enriched with touristic imaginaries (Salazar 2010) of exotic nature, volcanoes, pristine beaches and warm Nicaraguan hospitality. Describing the historical, political and social context in which contemporary tourism development encounters take place, my ambition here is to explore how the historical context might be shaping the ongoing negotiations of local participation in tourism. The chapter discusses how, and by whom, tourism development has been welcomed, firstly to Nicaragua, secondly to the rural areas of the country, and thirdly to the farming communities of San Ramón. While rural tourism strategies and development officials seem to celebrate warm Nicaraguan hospitality, the early years of tourism development in San Ramón show that communities sought to calculate and negotiate the risks and responsibilities of welcoming tourism. This section proposes that tourism development is not only based on and shaped by the narratives of a welcoming nation, but it also affects new host-guest relations beyond tourism settings (see Hunt 2016).

The fourth chapter approaches tourism development encounters from the point of view of the local hosts in San Ramón. The focus here is on the local hosts' experiences of the encounters where the conditions, risks and responsibilities of tourism development have been negotiated, asking how material conditions in particular might continue to shape these negotiations between self and other. Although the local hosts in San Ramón appreciated the help that they received from tourism experts during the early phases of tourism development, the hosts found the continuous demand for material improvements to be exhausting. The chapter presents examples of international tourism development projects in which the guests define and evaluate the material requirements needed for successful tourism enterprises. After a decade of tourism development and volunteer programmes, the local hosts' experience was that they had been nearly silenced in their own homes by their guests. As a result, both sides of the Levinasian idea of *ethics of hospitality* were missing: the tourism experts did not welcome the locals within the discourse, and in response the local hosts ended up limiting their hospitality towards the tourism experts.

In the fifth chapter, the last part of the analysis changes the perspective from dwelling on unwelcoming encounters towards imagining alternative and more welcoming ways of doing togetherness. The purpose of the chapter is, first, to envision what open and hospitable spaces between hosts and guests could be like and, second, to discuss how these kinds of spaces might be created and promoted in future encounters. The data used for the analysis primarily consist of local hosts' descriptions of positive face-to-face encounters that have taken place in San Ramón. In light of the analysis, and reflecting my own experiences of open encounters, the chapter focuses on the questions of sharing one's space, experiences and, above all, one's time with the other. Drawing on Levinas's (1969) and Derrida's (1999) discussions of hospitality as 'interrupting self', the chapter suggests that the main prerequisite for ethical encounters might be a readiness to question one's freedom as a spontaneous and individual subject. In sum, the chapter asks how creating more open and ethical spaces between self and other requires a readiness to unlearn one's preconceptions and privileges and to learn anew the significance of the word 'welcome'.

The concluding chapter summarizes how the privileged guests' expectations of open hospitality on the part of the local hosts can be seen as a sign of a colonized imagination and heightened levels of individualism. By taking the discussions to another level of abstraction, I suggest that such premises might undermine the development of ethically sound encounters and representations within tourism. That is, these premises base the debates and practices of participation on self-centred, solipsist and anthropocentric ontologies that might be more likely to maintain than to disrupt the dualistic distinctions between self and multiple others. Instead of being surprised that the Levinasian utopia of unconditional welcoming does not seem to reflect the lived experiences in tourism development encounters, this approach to responsibility and receptivity can be considered to be the fundamental structure of subjectivity and to be a valuable goal to aspire to – and yet, inevitably, fall short of – when doing togetherness among ourselves. In this light, moving towards more inclusive, responsible and hospitable spaces of participation requires a readiness to interrupt self and to embrace the idea of other-orientedness in social relations.

Notes

1 UNWTO's representative María Nelly Rivas, interview in the Nicaraguan newspaper *La Prensa*, 12 December 2007.
2 At that time, the Nicaraguan tourism institute INTUR and the Luxembourg Agency for Development Cooperation Lux-Development were financing a five-year (2007–2011) programme known as *Ruta del Café* with the main objective of supporting local economic development.
3 For Fair Trade in Tourism, see, for instance, Karla Boluk's (2011) research.
4 For critical perspectives on the subject of micro-credits, see Hossain, Rees and Knight-Millar (2014), Hietalahti and Nygren (2014), Geleta (2015).
5 For similar reflection on the West-Rest binaries in a supposedly responsible context, see Kellee Caton's (2008) work on studying abroad via non-profit educational organizations.
6 In the early 1970s, these radical roots of participation theory existed simultaneously with other forms of dissatisfaction towards mainstream development models, which then turned into a search for more people-oriented approaches (Brohman 1996b in Telfer 2014, 54). Cornwall (2006, 63–5) and Berkhöfer and Berkhöfer (2007, 84) point out that in the 1970s the concerns for project efficiency, political empowerment and mutual learning were all voiced at the same time, which meant that there were co-existing divergent understandings of participation. For instance, in 1974, the UN Charter of 'Economic Rights and Obligations of States' instituted economic, political and cultural pluralism at the highest political level; this was the pluralism that stressed the interpretation of participation as a mutual learning experience among 'equals'. James Midgley (2011, 174), among others, explains the ways in which the more recent idea of *community participation* then evolved, at least partly, in response to criticism of the colonial nature of *community development* as a tool for modernization.
7 Recent years have seen an increasing amount of post-development literature, which questions and rejects the dominance of Eurocentric worldviews on development and calls for inclusion of multiple worldviews (Telfer 2009; Escobar 2012). While some scholars have suggested local participation as a way to question the Western dominance in development, some have argued that participatory approaches are for the most part used to continue that dominance.
8 In his extensive critique of the participatory 'orthodox' in tourism studies, Jim Butcher (2012) laments that even the comprehensive critical studies tend to focus on *operationalizing* the concept of community participation rather than on the concept itself.
9 By the concept of worldmaking I refer here to what Hollishead (2007, 167) describes as collaborative processes that essentialize, naturalize and normalize peoples, places and practices. The notion of worldmaking calls here for critical reflection on the ways in which production of knowledge is involved in constituting the world (see also Tucker 2009; 2014; Dredge and Hales 2012, 428; Grimwood and Doubleday 2013). In their research on community case studies, Dredge and Hales (2012) and Dredge et al. (2013) discuss the possibilities of 'unleashing tourism's worldmaking capacity'.
10 Singh (2012, 114) suggests that Murphy and Pauleen (2007) and Reid et al. (2004) are among those few who acknowledge the potential of non-linearity in participatory tourism; see also Law (2004) in Dredge and Hales (2012, 420); messy

epistemologies are discussed also by Caton (2014b) and unfinished and untidy ontologies by Veijola et al. (2014).

11 The fruitfulness of these conceptualizations is explored by the editors of *Hospitality and Society*, Lynch et al. (2011).

12 I follow here Critchley's (1999) approach to 'The Ethics of Deconstruction' which builds on Derrida's and Levinas's thinking. Critchley (1999, 1) argues that 'the textual practice of deconstructive reading can and, moreover, *should* be understood as an ethical demand'. I also agree with Kuokkanen (2007, xiv), who writes 'Deconstruction has proven helpful in its insistence that we pay attention to the exclusions and silences in narratives. It also impels us to recognize how we all participate in what we criticize'.

13 I have also used Raffoul's (1998) translation and interpretation of Derrida's original version from French to English as a source of inspiration.

14 *Adieu to Emmanuel Levinas* is Derrida's third major engagement with Levinas's philosophy after 'Violence and Metaphysics' in *Writing and Difference* (1967/1978) and *At this very moment in this work here I am* (1980). See also Raffoul 1998, 211.

15 *Totality and Infinity* was published in French in 1961 and translated from French to English in 1969.

16 For a comprehensive analysis of Levinas's relation to Heidegger, and Levinas's idea of responsibility, see Raffoul (2010; 2014) and Drabinski and Nelson (2014). For Levinas's argument about the necessity of moving beyond Heidegger's (1927/1972) idea of Being, see also Levinas's *Otherwise than Being, or Beyond Essence* (1974) where he continues to develop his thinking on ethical metaphysics. While Levinas was one of the first philosophers to build on Heidegger's influential thought in *Being and Time* (1927/1972), he has also been faulted for misinterpreting and limited reading of Heidegger's work. For wonderful analysis and exploration of Heidegger's work in connection to the biopolitics of development, see Suvi Alt's (2016) book *Beyond the Biopolitics of Development, Being, Politics and Worlds*.

17 For the significance of Levinas's thought, see Peperzak (1995).

18 In *Adieu to Emmanuel Levinas* Derrida (1999, 19–20) writes about the relationship between an *ethics of hospitality* and *politics and a law* (indefinite, singular) of hospitality. However, in his later work (2000, 75), Derrida uses the notion of *the law of hospitality* (definite, singular) in order to describe unconditional, Levinasian *ethics of hospitality*. Hence, I have chosen to use the singular form – *the* law of hospitality – when I refer to the ethics of hospitality where the other is received beyond the capacity of the self, and the plural form – the laws of hospitality – when I refer to the politics and regulations of hospitality (see also Germann Molz and Gibson 2007, 4–5; Still 2010, 8; Baker 2010, 89–93; 2013, 1).

19 For instance, scholars in the political sciences, such as Mireille Rosello (2001), Sarah Gibson (2003), Rauna Kuokkanen (2007), Judith Still (2010), Gideon Baker (2010; 2013) and Daniel Innerarity (2017), have previously analysed ethics and responsibility using a somewhat similar approach.

20 For Levinas's idea of interrupting self, see Levinas (1969, 39, 82–4).

21 In the second chapter of this book I will focus in some detail on Rauna Kuokkanen's (2007) research on indigenous knowledges in academia, a line of inquiry in which she draws on Levinas's writings on subjectivity and hospitality.

22 Ahmed (2000, 58–9) argues that ethnography can still, in the 21st century, be seen as an explanatory and accumulative discourse which translates a strange culture into the language of the one who knows.

23 Researchers' eagerness to study indigenous cultures is described in jokes like: "How many people live in a Sámi family in Lapland? Mom, dad, 1.5 children and a researcher."

24 These questions are asked by indigenous methodologies in particular, which approach cultural protocols, values and behaviours as an integral part of methodology (Jennings 2009, 683–4; Tuhiwai Smith 2012). In terms of methodological openness, we should also be ready to consider *who* can be the knower and *what* 'truth' test beliefs must pass to be legitimated as knowledge (Humberstone 2004, 123).

25 Levinas's commentator Drabinski (2011, 20, 24, 29) argues that Levinas's relationship to discussions of the phenomenological methodology is so manifold and complicated that it is a matter for an independent study and debate.

26 While Gadamer (1975) operationalizes phenomenological philosophy, he simultaneously warns about providing rules for analysis which could prematurely foreclose possible ways of understanding. Instead, he calls for creative engagement of the method. In essence, this approach encourages becoming open to – and surprised by – different experiences, understandings and meanings that people give to the phenomenon under scrutiny.

27 In February 2012, it was somewhat peculiar to conduct interviews in the Nicaraguan tourism ministry INTUR, when the interviewees had the morning newspaper on their desk speculating on the state of Nicaragua-Finland relations and on broken promises. It is clear that my encounters with the Nicaraguan tourism officials were shaped by the situation in which Finland and other Nordic countries openly announced their disappointment with the Sandinista government then in power.

28 My experiences and decisions correspond to Caton's (2014a) argument that the tension between constructivism and critical theory is pedagogical and care-oriented. That is, in Caton's (2013, 129) view the choice between different methodological and epistemological approaches has more to do with 'the existence of different moral imaginaries about how people (in this case researchers are participants) can best do right by each other than with researcher's basic beliefs about the nature of reality or the point of the research endeavor'.

29 Soile Veijola has introduced the concept of 'Ethical epistemologies of tourism'.

30 See Hannah Arendt (1982) and Vinciane Despret (2005) in Donna Haraway's (2016) book *Staying with the Trouble*.

31 The idea of hospitable writing is also borrowed from Soile Veijola's teaching and writing.

2 The ethics of hospitality

This research journey follows hospitality as an overarching idea that can be used as an alternative way to approach the idea of participation – the idea of being, doing, making, knowing, planning with multiple others. By calling for openness between ourselves, the framework challenges the possibility of treating hospitality or participation as projects of spontaneous and self-sufficient actors. Development scholar Maria Eriksson Baaz (2005) has analysed the idea of participation by drawing on Spivak's call for self-reflectivity in encounters with the 'subaltern'. Her analysis exposes the ways in which the principles and responsibilities of participation and partnership have continued to be attached to the paternalistic idea of helping (see also Seppälä 2013; Junka-Aikio 2014).[1] What this chapter sets out to examine is how the critique on development encounters might correspond with the critique that Levinas and Derrida direct towards Western thought on subjectivity and hospitality. Firstly, these authors on ethical subjectivities lament the ways in which Western philosophy and the Western culture of hospitality have focused on defining conditions and limits (Levinas 1969, 20–6; Derrida 1999, 3–5). Secondly, in Derrida's view, this idea of hospitality has concerned itself with the issue of *invitation* in lieu of *visitation*. Derrida's thoughts have been rephrased by Karima Laachir (2007, 178; see also Innerarity 2017) as follows: 'you invite someone to your country, to your house and you set the rules for that invitation'. According to Derrida (1999, 15–16), the focus on this type of hospitality reasserts the mastery of the host. Hence, I will suggest here that – similarly to self- and ego-centred approaches on hospitality – local participation in tourism might also be told through stories where 'the self' decides to invite the 'other' to participate. By doing this, the active, caring and supposedly responsible self continues to control and set the rules of participation – to reassert the mastery of the host (Germann Molz and Gibson 2007, 5; Kuokkanen 2007, 138).

Before moving in detail into Levinas's and Derrida's discussions on hospitality, the first section offers an overview of various domains and understandings of hospitality in tourism research in particular. I begin from the historical meanings of the concept and then present Kant's (1996 [1795]) well-known idea of cosmopolitan hospitality. From there I move the focus to the development of the tourism and hospitality industries and the ways in which the dominance of managerial studies in the field of hospitality has somewhat reduced the connections between hospitality and ethics to concerns of how to make the hospitality business more responsible.

The second section presents Derrida's idea of the 'double law of hospitality', which draws a distinction between the idea of *laws and conditions of hospitality* and the idea of *ethics as hospitality*. I explore and explain here how Derrida's work can help to understand the possible limitations of contemporary ideas of ethics and hospitality, which are based for the most part on the laws and conditions embraced by Kant. Furthermore, Derrida's interpretation of Levinas's thinking on ethics can offer an alternative way of understanding ethics in relations to the other. In the third section, I delve more deeply into the Levinasian notion of ethics. His conception of ethical subjectivity as receptivity can be seen as a radical alternative to the Western idea of the individual, isolated subject, which makes it meaningful to examine the influence of Levinas's ideas on later criticism of the colonial legacy. The fourth section discusses the issue of privilege in postcolonial relations. Drawing especially on Spivak's ideas regarding privilege and epistemic violence, I argue that those with a relatively privileged position tend to take it for granted that they are welcome to visit, care for, help and study others (see Mostafanezhad 2014; Chambers and Buzinde 2015). This leads to a situation where even emancipatory intentions to help, or 'give a voice' to, the other, maintain overbearing subject positions between self and the other. The chapter suggests how Levinas's and Derrida's notions of hospitality and welcoming can help one to become aware of one's privileged position in relation to the other, and then – as Spivak (1990, 20) puts it – to learn to unlearn one's privilege as loss. The fifth and last section summarizes the idea of hospitable encounters presented in the chapter. It proposes that the idea of hospitality calls for making space for the other in the encounters between self and other. With reference to the idea of a *home*, the chapter describes how hospitality – in different levels of abstraction – can help to understand how we welcome each other in supposedly responsible encounters.

2.1   Realms of hospitality

In engaging with Levinas's and Derrida's writings on hospitality in the course of my research, I have observed that in practice the issue of hospitality is commonly treated as a question of aesthetics, rather than a question of ethics. For instance, when taking long walks around the suburbs of Stockholm (my previous home town), I noticed that many families had stylish 'Welcome' signs hanging on their front doors. Instead of expecting that the families would welcome any passers-by into their homes, I consider that these signs appeared more as decorative details. I believe that the welcome signs are most likely hung on the doors to create a cosy atmosphere without further consideration of the people who are actually welcomed and allowed to enter these homes.

In fact, I assume that some people might even have quite limited tolerance of surprise guests who interrupt the families' planned routines or time set aside for relaxation. Moreover, when a guest arrives without notice, a host is left without a chance to prepare her or his hospitality by cleaning the house, fixing something to eat or at least dressing properly for visitors.

In the conventional formulation of hospitality, the guest is the traveller who receives hospitality in the home of the host. However, the home can mean different spaces, different forms of homes where a space is made for the guest to arrive (Gotman, 2001, 2; Bell 2009, 22). While there is no clear definition, or unanimous theoretical framework of hospitality, hospitality is generally used as a description of self's relation to the other (Lynch et al. 2011, 5; Lynch 2017). In contrast to contemporary connotations of the concept, the historical meaning of hospitality directed thoughts towards encounters between strangers (Lashley 2000, 6; O'Gorman 2007). As Germann Molz and Gibson (2007, 1) phrase it, hospitality is a phenomenon that, even where it fails, evokes an ancient and persistent question: how should we welcome the stranger, the sojourner, the traveller, the other?

The question of hospitality is a phenomenon as old as human history and the accounts of hospitality often hark back to the antecedents of encounters in the glorious days of the Greeks, Romans or the Enlightenment. In these accounts hospitality entails a sacred obligation not only to accommodate the guest, but to protect the stranger who arrives at the door (Still 2006; O'Gorman 2007; 2010; Baker 2013, 2). In medieval times, hospitality was understood not only as accommodating foreigners and travellers for free, but also as showing compassion for the other in monasteries, guesthouses and hospitals. Later on, hospitality acquired new meanings, among these the mutual obligation to protect, receive, accommodate and feed each other – and to receive others, especially the poor, without compensation (Gotman 2001, 13). Sociologist Helmuth Berking (1999, 82) has presented hospitality as one of the most significant social inventions in the history of humankind. He uses the concept of the 'guest situation' to describe a means of tempering the potentially life-threatening arrival of a stranger into a ritual that upholds and celebrates the local way of life. This ritualistic welcome, Berking (1999, 92) continues, gave the host the power to define the guest situation. Hence, hospitality changed the threat connected with the arrival of a stranger to its opposite, to an opportunity. Instead of seeing receiving a stranger as a threat, hospitality gave the receiving community an opportunity to present the best sides of their homes to the honoured guest (Veijola et al. 2013, 19).

Tracing the trajectory of 'hospitality', Kevin O'Gorman (2010) and Paul Lynch et al. (2011) describe the ways in which different scholars have found a wide range of connotations for the term through Middle English, Old Norse, Greek and Latin. These include *sacrifice, army, power, obligation, reciprocity* and *protection*. Especially interesting from the etymological perspective is how *guest* and *host* share the same root meaning of 'stranger', 'enemy' (Benveniste 1973). Consequently, *hôte, hospis* and *hostis* can be combined in different ways in order to refer to hospitality and hostility: to a guest, a host, a hostile party and a friend. Thus, although the concept of *hospitalitas* might have originally referred to charity and receptivity, it also refers to a possible hostility amongst hosts and guests (Wadron 2006 in Germann Molz and Gibson, 2007, 4; Welten 2017).

Kant's (1996 [1795]) *Perpetual Peace* argued that on a geographically restricted planet our natural destiny and necessity is to come into contact with other people and to live in each other's company. He approached this 'natural law' of living together on earth as a 'cosmopolitan right' to move from one place to another and encounter each other. Thus, Kant's universal idea of hospitality guarantees the right to mobility around the globe and to be received without hostility. In his view, it is only through the principle of cosmopolitan hospitality that humanity can gradually come closer to establishing world citizenship and thus *perpetual peace* (Kant 1996 [1795]; Laachir 2007, 179). At the same time, Kant maintained that the traveller should not use this mobility as a means of abuse, exploitation or oppression. Later he criticized the commercial states of Europe for advancing their economic wealth through inhospitable actions and exploitation of colonialized regions. However, although Kant pointed out the Western tendency to abuse the hospitality of 'virgin territories', his idea of cosmopolitanism neglects the question of how peace may be decided differently between those who have wealth and influence and those who do not. The idea of cosmopolitan hospitality is in fact based on the power of wealth, which is exclusive to certain powerful states and subjects (see Rosello 2001; Derrida and Rottenberg 2002; Baker 2013).

It is obvious that Kant's ideas on cosmopolitanism and 'being the citizen in the world', written more than two hundred years ago, have framed the contemporary debates of international encounters and hospitality between people and nations (Laachir 2007, 179; Germann Molz and Gibson 2007, 4; Lynch 2017, 174). Ever since the 1800s, hospitality has been increasingly shaped by laws, customs and commercialization, and thus come to mean more than simply private relations between people (O'Gorman 2010). What is more, it seems like the ideal and romantic image of the tourism industry – and even more of the 'ideal tourist' who is free to roam for whatever she or he desires (Ek 2015, 145) – can be drawn to Kant's notions of cosmopolitan mobility and hospitality. In fact, cosmopolitanism can be traced back to the founding father of the Cynic movement in Ancient Creek, Diogenes of Sinope (c. 412 BC). Asked where he came from, Diogenes supposedly answered: 'I am a citizen of the world' (kosmopolitês). Ulf Hannerz (1996) connected the notion of cosmopolitans to the small elite of the world's population who are financially well-off, socially and geographically mobile and culturally literate. He argued that cosmopolitanism is above all an orientation: 'a willingness to engage with the Other' (ibid., 103). As a result, the cosmopolitan vision is contradicted by the celebration of openness toward divergent cultural experiences and a competence to master the signs of cultural difference and authenticity (Dicks 2003, 57–9).

While the image of the 'citizens of the world' originally described anthropologists, explorers and missionaries, the group of 'select elite' has since become substantially larger. In fact, the number of tourists – citizens of the world – and their interests are expected to continue to expand, despite the knowledge of tourism's negative contribution to environmental change (see Hall et al. 2015; Hales and Caton 2017). Or, as Jokinen and Veijola (1997, 38) describe it, during the past decades, the explorers have become sex-tourists, the *flâneurs* have become paparazzi, and today's au-pairs are like the nomads of the past. Ever since the rapid growth of mass tourism in the 1970s, the tourism sector has turned its attention towards managing hospitality in hotels and restaurants and other hedonistic enclaves (see Vainikka 2013; Ek 2015, 145). Especially the postpolitical tourist (Ek 2015) with limited interest in engaging with others and otherness – the type of tourist whom Stanley C. Plog (1991) categorized as *psychocentric* – is assumed to feel pleased about the opportunity to dwell in secure, commercialized and managed forms of 'hospitality culture'.

Before the label *hospitality* was widely adopted in the academic journals, curricula and strategies of tourism, the business sector was known as *Hotel and Catering* (Veijola et al. 2013, 18). However, this has changed, especially in the English-speaking world, where hospitality – as an imported and commercialized idea – forms the core of and metaphor for *tourism* (Lynch et al. 2011, 6). Or perhaps more precisely, hospitality can be seen as the *brand* of tourism, a label for selling products and services.[2] Today, the tourism industries are based on commercial hospitality, commercial accommodation, transportation, restaurant services and different kinds of programmes and experiences, and even on commercial friendships, as described in the context of homestay forms of tourism (Hultman and Andersson Cederholm 2012). It is uncertain whether hospitality loses its value when commercialized, or whether commercialized hospitality could or should embrace the idea of reciprocal forms of caring. While studying or managing hospitality includes learning the rules of performing in the settings of commercial hospitality, there are those who claim that in fact mass tourism is not about hospitality at all (e.g. Aramberri 2001 in Germann Molz and Gibson 2007, 7).

Development of mass tourism seems to have established fixed roles between those who receive visitors in their homes (read: hotels) and those who visit the homes of the others. However, there are many who claim that the question of hosting and guesting is far from an uncomplicated one, particularly considering the unequal power relations where the other serves the self (Bell 2009; Cañada 2015). The issue of tourism as work has recently been discussed in a growing strand of literature. The question of tourism work in postcolonial settings has been explored in particular detail in Gmelch's (2012) book *Behind the Smile*, which takes the viewpoint of tourism workers in the Caribbean Islands. Soile Veijola (2009, 109–10), in her article 'Gender as Work in the Tourism Industry', proposes that the discussions of tourism as work offer a new horizon of thought and a new meeting place for critical and industry-driven approaches in Tourism Studies. Furthermore, Tara Duncan, David G. Scott and Tom Baum (2015) have also broadened the conventional, one-dimensional focus on skills in hospitality work, by drawing attention to mobilities and immobilities of tourism and hospitality employees.

It appears to be the fine line between commercial hospitality, on the one hand, and the idea of reciprocal and altruistic hospitality, on the other, that continues to fascinate not only tourists, but also tourism researchers and developers (Tucker 2003; Lynch et al. 2007; Lugosi 2008; 2017a; Poulston 2015; Lynch 2017). Tourists' travel stories are often coloured by descriptions of hospitable locals who help and served their guests so well, or of rude hosts who do not take care of paying customers. What is more, many of us are keen to find authentic, non-touristic places where we can arrive and be received as non-tourists. Tourism scholars have been commonly interested and highly sceptical about the narratives and experiences of the authentic, pointing out that by entering supposedly 'non-touristic places', tourists tend to transform those places into touristic ones (see MacCannell, 1976; Urry 1990, 7–11; Dicks 2003, 30–2; Lüthje 2005; Edensor 2009).

Hospitality studies scholar Conrad Lashley (2000, 5–16; 2017, 2–4) has proposed a model which visualizes and conceptualizes hospitality in terms of three domains: the social and cultural domain, the private and domestic domain, and the commercial domain. While Lashley admits that the domains presented are interwoven, each informing the other, the main purpose of this Venn diagram is to show that studying hospitality as commercial activity is only one of the domains. In practice, tourism literature seems to happily mix different forms of hospitality, which makes it questionable whether it is possible or meaningful to treat these dimensions separately. The 'mix' becomes evident, for instance, in the sector of commercial homes discussed in the work of Johan Hultman and Erika Andersson Cederholm (2012) and Paul Lynch et al. (2007; 2009). Another great example is Szilvia Gyimóthy's (2017) *Dinner Sharing: Casual Hospitality in the Collaborative Economy*, where she draws on Zygmunt Bauman's notion of 'cloakroom communities' and Georg Simmel's 'sociability' to problematize the illusion of the social in the business model of dinner sharing in people's private homes. Such settings bring together the expectations and promises of different domains of hospitality and keep enriching and messing around with our understandings of hospitality (Bell 2009, 22).

It is clear, as Lynch et al. (2011, 4) have also argued, that hospitality is approached in very different ways, for instance, in the social sciences and in managerial studies. At present, a considerable segment of the tourism literature has adopted the managerial approach where hospitality is perceived as something that can be managed, learned, worked with and above all charged for (Veijola et al. 2014; Lynch 2017). For instance, in the recent *Handbook of Hospitality Studies*, edited by Lashley (2017), the concluding words are followed by a 'hospitality questionnaire', which surveys personality traits relevant for the service industry. Gazing through the survey makes one wonder what is actually meant by Hospitality Studies. Is it a home hosted by scholars within Hospitality Management? A home where other social scientists can visit, inform and improve management practices within the service industry (Höckert 2017)? Another illustration can be found in John Tribe's edited volume *Philosophical Issues in Tourism*, published in 2009. In this anthology, tourism scholar Alessandro Panosso Netto (2009, 57) defines the principle of hospitality as 'a social-cultural phenomenon that includes the food, drink and accommodation offered to the guest'. While acknowledging that hospitality is related to an act that has been practised for thousands of years, he divides hospitality into three areas: domestic, commercial and public. Nevertheless, the ontological and transcendental dimensions of hospitality, which I was hoping to find in the *philosophical* discussions in tourism, are utterly lacking in Panosso Netto's chapter.

The managerial and instrumental approach to hospitality makes a pessimistic prognosis about the search for ethics or, shall we say, corporate social responsibility, in the hospitality industries. This mind-set strengthens an idea whereby the interest in receiving strangers, and treating them with respect, is understood in utilitarian terms, that is, in terms of the outcome and results of doing so. Until recently the wider discussions of ethical dimensions in the hospitality-tourism nexus, and the roles, values and spirituality behind hospitality, have taken place more in the margins of tourism discussions (e.g. Inayatullah 1995; Berno 1999; Fennell 2008; Bell 2009; Smith 2009a; Caton 2012). It is clear that the notion of hospitality between hosts and guests can lead tourism researchers and scholars from other fields of studies in multiple different directions. Lynch et al. (2011, 3) have lamented that while hospitality industries have hijacked the concept per se, tourism studies have become more inhospitable towards the interdisciplinary study of hospitality. One example of this has been the overall reluctance among tourism researchers to tackle the issues of exclusion, silence and inequality in, paradoxically, an industry based on welcoming, caring and hospitality (see Cañada 2015). For instance, Darlene McNaughton's (2006) research titled 'the host as uninvited guest' highlights the need to keep asking how the roles of hosts and guests become negotiated and shaped along tourism development. In saying this, I see that it is time to examine the influence of Derrida's 'double law of hospitality' on the contemporary discussions of ethics in a mobile world.

2.2 Double law of hospitality

The recent theoretical mobilization of hospitality towards ethics of social relations has primarily drawn on Derrida's writings on hospitality (Germann Molz and Gibson 2007, 4; Still 2010; Baker 2013; Lashley 2017). In his work, Derrida focuses on the limitations of Kant's definition of the 'law of universal hospitality', which guarantees the rights and responsibilities associated with global mobility. While acknowledging the importance of the Kantian right to travel and to be received in other lands, especially in the context of migration, asylum and citizenship, Derrida (1999, 86–91) criticizes Kant's way of defining hospitality in terms of juridical and political conditions. For Derrida, hospitality in Kant's *Perpetual Peace* means being responsible before the law, and being subject to the law. Derrida (2000, 27–9) uses the example of interrogating the stranger at the moment of arrival by asking for the newcomer's name. By way of contrast, he asks whether hospitality could be *given* to the other before the other has been identified by family name or legal status (Derrida 1999, 87).

As brought up briefly in the introduction (1.3.), Derrida (1999, 19–20, 48–51), drawing especially on Levinas's discussions on ethics, points out that Kant's formulation of hospitality excludes unconditional and absolute hospitality, that is, the *ethics of hospitality*. According to Derrida, it is not possible that particular laws or politics would be *deduced* from ethical discourse on hospitality. However, Derrida (1999, 20–1) does not describe the *laws of hospitality* and *ethics of hospitality* as opposites. Instead, in his view, it is between these two conceptions of hospitality that responsibilities must be taken. Derrida (2002, 2–14) refers to this situation as the 'double law of hospitality' – negotiating and calculating the risks of welcoming while not closing the door to the unexpected.[3] Hence, what Levinas brings into the discussion of hospitality is the idea of ethics as opening the door to the Other, to exteriority, to the idea of infinity that can come to us through that door (Derrida 1999, 26).

While tourism scholars have recently engaged more with Derrida's discussions of hospitality (see Lashley 2017), Derrida (1999, 21–6; Raffoul 1998, 212) tried to make it clear that it is in fact Levinas whose thought as a whole should be approached from the perspective of hospitality. Although Levinas does not use the concept with any frequency, Derrida perceives that it is Levinas's *Totality and Infinity* in particular that invites us to think what is called hospitality. In addition to conveying Levinasian thinking on ethical subjectivity, the two essays in *Adieu to Emmanuel Levinas* – *Adieu* and *The Word of Welcome* – underpin Derrida's own conceptual work and moral claims of cosmopolitanism and the deconstruction of borders (Derrida 1967/ 1978; Drabinski 2011, 188). Derrida continued these discussions later in *Of Hospitality* (2000),[4] *On Cosmopolitanism and Forgiveness* (2001),[5] *Negotiations* (Derrida and Rottenberg 2002) and in *The Principle of Hospitality* (2005), where he develops further and underlines the idea that all cultural and social bonds include a 'principle of hospitality'. Derrida (2001, 16–17) described hospitality as a condition of humanity:

Hospitality is culture itself and not simply one ethic amongst others. Insofar as it has to do with the *ethos*, that is, the residence, one's home, the familiar place of dwelling, inasmuch as it is a manner of being there, the manner in which we relate to ourselves and to other, to others as our own or as far as foreigners, *ethics is hospitality*; ethics is so thoroughly coextensive with the experience of hospitality.

It is clear that Levinas's thinking on totality and infinity has helped and guided Derrida to formulate his critique of Kant's definition of laws and conditions of hospitality (totality) and to point out the absence of unconditionally open welcoming (infinity). Although Levinas has not always been acknowledged in the contemporary discussions of ethics, a growing number of scholars have drawn attention to the ways in which his view of ethics has been transforming the phenomenological tradition and contributed significantly to the ethical turn of continental philosophy (Derrida 1999, 8–12; Critchley 1999; Hiddleston 2009; Drabinski 2011; Meijrt-van Wijk). Maurice Blanchot (1993, 51–2)[6] described the importance of Levinas's thought by saying,

> we are called upon to become responsible for what philosophy essentially is, by welcoming, in all the radiance and infinite exigency proper to it, the idea of the Other, that is to say, the relation with *autrui*. It is as though there were here a new departure in philosophy and a leap that it, and we ourselves, were urged to accomplish.

Levinas built his thought on the modern phenomenological movement with special attention to various forms of human experiences (Wild 1969, 11). As Levinas's commentators point out, development of his work would have been impossible without his knowledge of phenomenological thinkers, such as Edmund Husserl, Martin Heidegger, Jean-Paul Sartre, and Maurice Merleau-Ponty (Derrida 1999, 10–11; Hand 2009, 12–13). However, Levinas found these thinkers' theories to be one-sidedly egocentric and reductive, meaning that they did not do justice to the 'other' (Wild 1969, 13). According to Derrida (1999, 11), Levinas slowly bent 'the axis, trajectory, and even the order of phenomenology or ontology'. Levinas (1969, 51; 109–17) directed his critique particularly towards Heidegger's (1927/1972)[7] intentions to renew 'the question of *Being*' (*Dasein*) in a way that was caught up in the idea of individual solitude. What Levinas (1969, 89) found problematic in Heidegger's thinking is the way it places the freedom of the self before justice towards the other and hence fails to fully address the question of responsibility. Therefore, Levinas's philosophy builds, in particular, on his dissatisfaction with Heidegger's vision of sociality which is at best, in Levinas's view, a *being-with* (*Mitandersein*) rather than an interpersonal face-to-face relationship (Hand 2009, 33; Hiddleston 2009, 17).

Levinas's philosophical vision was influenced by his own early experiences of growing up in a Jewish family in Lithuania during the First World War. His post-war philosophy was undoubtedly shaped by his deep disappointment with humanity during the horrors of the Second World War and by his desire to understand why one human is capable of doing such things to another. Levinas was shocked by Heidegger's association with Nazism, which also explains the intensity of the critique that Levinas directed towards Heidegger's philosophy.[8] Levinas's commentators have later pointed out that his presentation of ethics signalled a hopeful and much-needed idea of a different mode of being in the post-war climate (Hand 2009, 34; Hiddleston 2009, 17–23; Drabinski 2011; Meijer-van Wijk 2017).

Levinas published his first two shorter volumes, *Time and the Other* and *Existence of Existence*, in 1947. Of these, *Time and the Other* in particular has been viewed not only as a critique of Heidegger's thought of being, but also as a clear and strategically important text on the nature of being, solitude, materiality, encounters with the Other and the Other's significance (Wild 1969, 11). The work presents time not as the achievement of an isolated or lone subject, but as the very relationship of the subject with the Other. After these volumes, Levinas continued to develop his explicit critique of the Western philosophical tradition, which he saw as being based on an ontology that tended to generate totalizing concepts of being (Hand 2009, 36; Ladyga 2012, 226). This then became pivotal argument in Levinasian ethics, which he discussed in detail in *Totality and Infinity*.

Totality and Infinity is a work of ethical metaphysics where only a desire for goodness can do justice to the radical otherness of the other person (Cohen 1998, xii). Here Levinas pairs *totality* and *infinity* with another, to advance his critique of totalizing and restrictive definitions of *subjectivity*, *reality* and *metaphysics*. He writes that '[T]he idea of totality and the idea of infinity differ precisely in that the first is purely theoretical, while the second is moral' (Levinas 1969, 83). By saying this, Levinas expresses his disappointment in Western philosophy, which in his view has treated ethics as a theoretical consideration and as a project of a spontaneous, free subject. In his words, '[T]he idea of the perfect is not an idea but desire; it is the welcoming of the Other, the commencement of moral consciousness, which calls into question my freedom' (Levinas 1969, 84). This means that for Levinas ethics and morality occur as questioning the ego, the knowing subject, self-consciousness – or what Levinas calls (following Plato) as the Same (le même) (ibid. 43; Derrida 1999, 17–18; Critchley 1999, 4).

In *Totality and Infinity* Levinas presents the *face* of the other as a moment of infinity that goes beyond any idea or description that one can produce of the other. Levinas's idea of face cannot be reduced to a fact or an obstacle. Instead, the *face* embodies all Levinas's (1969, 151, 194–201; Derrida 1999, 21) aims; the face of the Other is infinitely foreign and manifests the Other's inviolability and holiness. For Levinas the face calls upon and obliges self to take on a responsibility that transcends, or goes beyond, knowledge. It issues us with an absolute ethical challenge; it challenges all our philosophical attempts to systematize or thematize and therefore reduce the other. In Levinas's (1969, 305) words, the notion of the face signifies 'exteriority that does not call for power or possession'; it signifies the existence of fundamental pluralism, meaning that the other exists before the self (Hand 2009, 43). Although it does not feel right to summarize Levinas's thought, it can be said that his idea of ethics is radical in that it always begins from the Other, who is never a mere object to be subsumed to a category (Wild 1969, 12–13).

In his other major work, *Otherwise than Being or Beyond Essence* (1974), Levinas moved from the questions of *ethical alterity* towards the idea of *ethical subjectivity*. This means that Levinas's focus changed from the radical and overwhelming alterity of the Other to the effect of that alterity on subjectivity (Cohen 1987, 11; Hand 2009; 5). In *Otherwise than Being*, he elaborated the idea of ethical metaphysics by turning back to the moral sensibility of the subject that is awakened by the other (1998, xii). He introduces another set of terminology in order to describe the role of language in establishing ethical relations that are *beyond being*. One of the key messages and clearly articulated lessons here is the actual ethical force of *saying*. Levinas (1998, 5–7, 153–62) frames his conception of the other person's radical and irreducible alterity within the domain of language, that is, the *saying* and *said*. In connection with *the saying* and *said*, Levinas presents the view that his task is not to construct ethics but merely to seek its meanings.

In *Otherwise than Being*, Levinas opens up the question of ethical subject anew by claiming that subjectivity and responsibility are not for the self, but *initially for the other*. This thinking on responsibility strictly follows the ousting of the subject from its masterful position vis-à-vis the other, for whom the subject is now responsible. It means that for Levinas it is the ethical relationship *between* self and other – and other others – which constitutes the social fabric. In *The Origins of Responsibility*, Levinas's commentator Francois Raffoul (2010, 163–4) writes that for Levinas responsibility is not the responsibility of the free subject, but responsibility that arises out of the demands that the other makes of me. Hence, when the self becomes the respondent who is first and foremost responsible for the other, responsibility is no longer limited to the measure of what 'I' foresee and want to do. Regarding ethical and political obligations, Levinas (1998) writes, 'as a responsibility for the other, it is also responsibility for the third party, the justice that compares, assembles and conceives, the synchrony of being and peace, take form'.

In the foreword of *Otherwise than Being, or Beyond Essence*, Richard A. Cohen (1998) suggested that the title and the content of the book alert us to the priority that Levinas gives to his critique and contestation of Heidegger's idea of *Being*. Levinas (1998, 17) accuses Heidegger of trying 'to conceive subjectivity in the function of Being …' and uses a rather provocative rhetoric about the need to move 'beyond Being' and beyond ontology (Drabinski and Nelson 2014, 6). In Cohen's (1998, xiii) words, the title could also be interpreted as 'Otherwise than Heideggerian *Being*; beyond Heideggerian essence' – beyond Heidegger's ontology of 'totality'. As Raffoul (2010, 167) describes it,

> For Levinas, the access to ethics (which for him should be raised to first philosophy) and to responsibility takes place in the rupture with ontology, that is, in a rupture with Heidegger. Far from being included within the

horizon of being, ethics is situated in the relationship to the other person, in the "intersubjective".

In light of Levinas's interpretation, Heidegger's idea of being is an ontology that begins from and is directed towards self, while Levinas's ethics is metaphysical and strictly oriented towards the other. Levinas aims to distinguish his ethical philosophy – which relies on alterity and otherness – from the search for responsibility that leans on the conception of personal, individual good (Woods 1997, 53; see also Lynch 2017). However, it is important to point out that not many Heidegger scholars have been convinced or challenged by Levinas's criticism. Those researchers who have taken a thorough look at the relationship between the two philosophers have also called attention to Levinas's somewhat simplifying and weak reading of Heidegger's *Being and Time*. While diving into these discussions would make a too long side-track to my own research story, the anthology *Between Levinas and Heidegger* edited my John E. Drabinski and Eric S. Nilson (2014) offers a great exploration of the topic.

Critique of Levinas does not end here. While writing so beautifully about the radical difference which trivializes our learned categories of difference, Levinas peculiarly fails to reckon with alterity in the transnational context. Drabinski (2011, xii–xiii), among other commentators on Levinas's work, argues that while Levinas focuses extensively on the European context, he also explicitly articulates the differences of 'other Others' with cultural prejudices and chauvinism (see also Spivak 1993, 166–7; Critchley 2015). By 'other Other' Drabinski refers not only to non-Europeans and Palestinians, but also to women, who sometimes appear to Levinas as so radical and alien that they do not register as obligating. Discussions within posthumanism have also addressed and lamented Levinas's reluctance to extend his moral considerations to nonhuman animals (Atterton 2011; Zylinska 2014). Consequently, the meaning of the Other in Levinas excludes, at least to some extent, the 'other Others' and the more-than-human-world from the sphere of responsibility (Ahmed 2000, 142–7; Ladyga 2012). Although Levinas (1985, 65–72) addressed some of this critique in his later work, his writings exhibit inconsistencies that cannot be taken lightly.

But despite – and partly because of – these contradictions, Levinas's ethical philosophy has recently gained unprecedented popularity among commentators in theology, philosophy, political analysis and feminism who wish to carry his thinking further (Atterton and Calarcos 2010). While Levinas aims to describe something that cannot really be described in words in philosophy, reading Levinas requires almost a certain degree of forgiveness of occasional contradictions. In fact, the infinity of his thought makes him a human – the self and the other – who cannot be systematized and placed in a neat package. Derrida (1999, 3) also writes that the work of Levinas 'is so large that one can no longer glimpse its edges'. In the present study, I have, with great regret, chosen to leave out Levinas's writings on God, holiness of the holy, death, sensibility, Eros and uprightness, among other thought-provoking themes. However, not even the idea of ethics as hospitality can be thoroughly explored within one research project. According to Derrida (1999) and Raffoul (1998, 212) the idea of hospitality as 'subject of welcome' can be considered one of the overarching questions in Levinas's thinking. Especially in times of increasing global mobilities and entanglements, Levinas's idea of hospitality and responsibility can be seen more relevant than ever.[9]

I think here with Levinas's idea of welcoming and hospitality, and with Derrida's interpretation and development of this thought, and use their writings as guidance in gaining understanding about the formations of subjectivities in tourism development encounters. Levinas's thought helps to point out the ethical limitations of contemporary participatory development initiatives based on dichotomies between self and the other. By imagining more welcoming, ethical encounters in tourism settings, I put forward the possibility of moving *beyond* the self-centred, individualistic, solitary idea of participation. Accordingly, instead of applying the notion of hospitality as it has been widely used in the tourism industries, my theoretical framework aims to contribute to the recent explorations of hospitality and reciprocity in the contexts of micro and macro mobilities (see also Kuokkanen 2007, 130; Lynch 2017). This engagement also means questioning and resisting the assumption that our social relations would be permeated by the logic of the market (Vrasti 2013). Veijola et al. (2014, 2–7) have previously asserted that

> the focus of tourism research has been laid extensively on the conditionality, limits and laws of hospitality while trying to close the door on the incalculable. The unexamined ontologies of many lines of tourism studies leave little room for thinking and doing togetherness between and among hosts and guests differently.

Consequently, I suggest that Levinas's and Derrida's discussions on ethics and hospitality *do* provide a theoretical framework for approaching participation among hosts and guests, and well-being among ourselves in general, apart from codes or laws of ethics. As Levinas (1969, 83) makes clear, the idea of infinity – which is moral – should not be reduced to totality – which is theoretical. This means that from the perspective of totality, ethics are seen as something external and imposed; and, if one subscribes to the idea of infinity, ethics can be found in each of us.

I will now continue to examine Levinas's idea of *welcome* as constitutive to ethical subjectivity and then move on to discuss the ways in which his ethical thought has been welcomed into recent discussions in postcolonial philosophy.

2.3 Subject as welcome

Although all intentions to describe infinity are assumed to fall short, searching for answers to the question 'What does welcome mean?' can help in trying to capture the conception of ethics in Levinas's work. The word *welcome* operates everywhere in his writings to speak about the first gesture in the direction of the Other. In his analysis of Levinas, Derrida (1999, 5, 51, 54) interprets the idea of welcome as consciousness and *attention* towards the other, as saying *yes* to the other. In his view, saying *yes* to the other means to speak the language of goodness, friendship and hospitality. Indeed, for Levinas (1990, 49–50) the first word or response that makes all the other words and responses possible – including *no* – is the 'unconditional *yes*', a *yes* that is 'older than that of naïve spontaneity'. However, in the idea of infinity there is no *first yes*; rather, the *yes* to the other is already a response. Hence, the ethical and responsible response to the other is surely a *yes*, but a *yes* preceded by the *yes of* the other.

The profound and immutable ambiguity of hospitality is reflected in the French word *hôte*, meaning both 'host' and 'guest'. As indigenous politics scholar Rauna Kuokkanen (2007, 138) highlights in her research on the logics of hospitality and gift at the university, the etymology of *hôte* demonstrates the inseparability of 'host and guest' or 'self and other'. This inseparability means that there is never only one who could claim a mastery or sovereignty over the role of the host. Or when there is, as Kuokkanen (2007, 138) argues, 'this host is an arrogant imperial hôte and does not deserve either the right to hospitality, or the right to say welcome'. In Levinasian philosophy the idea of hosting and guesting turns into a game where both self and other are hosting (hôte) and being a guest (hôte). This means that the *hôte* can be the one welcoming (host) or the one being welcomed (guest) (Derrida 1999, 23–5, 41–3). In this sense, hospitality and welcoming cannot be seen as the 'duty' of a host, but as a mutual virtue in ethical encounters. The way Levinas defines host or/ and guest results in there being no subject 'as a pre-given substantial identity that would constitute the basis for a capacity to welcome' (Raffoul 2010, 214). This means that the subject is not a self-identity or an ego or consciousness. Instead the subject in Levinas's thought is the very openness to the other – it is the subject that welcomes and receives the other 'beyond its own infinite capacities of welcoming' (ibid.; see also Levinas 1969, 84). One way to understand the idea of the 'continuum between hosting and guesting', as postcolonial philosopher Mireille Rosello (2001, 18) calls it, is to draw special attention to the prepositions between *welcome* and *the other*. Michel Serres with Bruno Latour (1995, 101–5), also French philosophers, have pointed to the different ways in which the *prepositions* can be understood as *pre*-positions that indicate 'relations that precede any fixed positions'.[10] The two prepositions central in this context are *of* and *to*: welcome *of* the other and welcome *to* the other. In *Adieu to Emmanuel Levinas* Derrida (1999, 23) aims to clarify the importance of these two prepositions in the following way,

> the welcoming *of* the other (objective genitive) will already be a response: the *yes to* the other will already be responding to the welcoming *of* the other (subjective genitive), to the *yes of* the other.

Both 'welcome *to* the other' and 'welcome *of* the other' (others' welcome) call attention to self's responsibility to welcome the other and to *the other*'s responsibility to welcome the *self* (ibid., 22–5). Raffoul (2010, 216) explains that acknowledging and understanding the welcome *of* the other as a subjective genitive (the other's hospitality) means that the subject as host (hôte) immediately turns into a subject as guest (hôte). However, although these prepositions are fundamentally intertwined, they are not conditional on each other. That is to say that while I am responsible to say the unconditional word of welcome *to* the other, my welcome cannot be conditional or dependent on the welcome *of* the other. If my response *to* the other depended on the response I receive from the other, this would make my welcome conditional. Hence, Levinas's (1969, 216; 1985, 98) idea of multiplicity in being and in infinitely open welcoming requires acceptance that the 'space' where welcoming is situated is always asymmetrical. It requires consciousness and attention towards different kinds of hosts who express their welcome in multiple ways (Kuokkanen 2007, 139). In *Totality and Infinity*, Levinas (1969, 215) writes, 'The other who obligates me in his transcendence is thus the stranger, the widow, and the orphan to whom I am obligated'. Hence, in Levinas's (1969, 299; 1985, 98–9) thought the ethical subject – the subject of welcome – is the *host* who welcomes unconditionally the stranger, the neighbour, the Other. Derrida (2003 translated and quoted by Hill 2010, 246[11]) reflects on Levinas's idea of Welcome,

> We set off from thinking about welcome as the primary attitude of the self before the other, from thinking about welcome to thinking about the hostage. I am in a certain way a hostage of the other, and that hostage situation where I am already the other's guest in my own home, that hostage situation defines my own responsibility.

For Levinas (1998, 114) the responsibility for the Other 'is not an accident that happens to a subject, but precedes essence in it ...'. In fact, it is not the idea of responsibility for the other as such that makes Levinasian thinking radical or alternative in comparison with other Western philosophers such as Søren Kierkegaard (see Fennell 2008) and Heidegger (see Raffoul 2014; Lynch 2017). Rather, it is his redefinition of ethics and responsibility in a thoroughly intersubjective and interpersonal way. For me the central contribution of Levinas's idea of welcoming is the attention towards the welcome *of* the other (the other's hospitality) – and the fundamental responsibility of responding to the other by unconditionally welcoming the other. Without highlighting the importance of this continuum of welcoming – of saying yes – the Levinasian idea of transcendence as a relational human 'affair' faces a great risk of falling to pieces. More specifically, it faces the danger of falling back into the realm of individual and spontaneous subjects; that is, subjects that might stand next to each other, even next to those who are marginalized or disempowered, without the kind of 'reversals of subjectivity' that Derrida and Levinas talk about.[12] It would mean being stuck with the ontological figure of a postpolitical tourist, a figure that 'shows itself beside', free from engagements and responsibilities (see Ek 2015).

For Levinas, it is the very welcome which interrupts the self and the tradition of the autonomous, egological subject. Thus, Derrida (1999, 51) asks '[I]s not hospitality an interruption of the self?'. According to Derrida, one will understand in fact nothing about hospitality if one does not understand the idea of interrupting self. This thought is alternative and opposite to the idea of freely saying 'as for myself, I, *ipse, egomet ipse*', which Derrida (1999, 23), like Levinas (1969, 92–3), calls the most powerful tradition of ethics and philosophy. Hence it is not a surprise that in the dominant tourism discourses, the entire sector is characterized by, and also dependent upon, modernity's promotion of self-gratification and consumerism (Smith 2009b, 620; Urry and Larsen 2011, 6–7). Tourists' mobility – unlike global flows of immigrants, refugees, asylum seekers, and also tourism workers, those who Bauman (1998, 240) called the 'vagabonds' with no other choice than remaining adrift – is based on the idea of the free and voluntary movement of individuals who are capable of exercising their choices as active consumers.[13] Wanda Vrasti (2013) has argued that even the recent search for more ethical forms of travelling, such as volunteer tourism in the Global South, is based on the same individualistic logic. In these kinds of settings, merely visiting the other seems to be performed and perceived as a responsible and ethical act as such. Hence, it becomes too simplistic to assume that, for instance, NGOs were engaged with altruistic forms of travelling as opposed to hedonistic forms of mass tourism (see Butcher 2012).

All things considered, tourism should not be treated as an exceptional playground for spontaneous individuals as this self-centredness has permeated our social lives nearly to an extent that it has become difficult to even recognize it (Agamben 1990; Alt 2016; Haraway 2016). Even the entire idea of human development has been celebrated on a grand scale as freedom. Looking back at the history of this development, the idea of 'global responsibility' has largely been based on the image of active individuals from the industrialized countries helping the poor masses in the developing countries to participate in development and to become more like they are.[14] In this conceptualizing of development, the right and freedom to become an individual and spontaneous subject can be seen as the 'primary ends and principal means of development' (Sen 1999, xii). Both sides – those promoting development and those being developed – are drawn to celebrate the empowerment and freedom of the individual subject (see Chandler 2013, 67–9). Today's understanding and indicators of human development have been influenced by the work of the Nobel Prize-winning economist Amartya Sen. His prominent book from 1999, *Development as Freedom*, argues that 'without ignoring the importance of economic growth, we must look well beyond it', meaning that attention should be shifted to individuals' capacities for and capabilities of making choices that affect their lives. As a critique by international relations scholar

David Chandler (2013, 69–78) highlights, in Sen's idea freedom and development become defined in relation to the interior life of the individual subject.[15]

At its simplest, this could mean that 'the freer you are, the more developed
you are'. In this scenario the hope is that the 'other' will achieve progress in
the form of material and human rights, yet in a way that keeps the privileges
of 'the self' untouched. Taking seriously Levinas's idea of ethical subjectivity as hospitality – where the obligation to welcome and to do justice to the
other questions one's freedom – would lead to an approach radically different
from the tradition of autonomous subject. In Levinas's (1969, 87; see also
Hiddleston 2009) thought, the ethical relation is not simply a conscious decision made by a rational, ethical subject to be responsible to the other; instead,
for him 'morality begins when freedom, instead of being justified by itself, feels
itself to be arbitrary and violent'. This means that the decision and responsibility would no longer entail the development of 'egological immanence',
but these would always revert to the other (Derrida 1999, 53). Decision and
responsibility would always be *of the other*, as Derrida (1999, 23) phrases it.[16]

While Levinas wrote his works during anti-colonial struggles and the
rise of postcolonial critique, he was mainly concerned about a small part of
Europe. Although Levinas's work is firmly rooted in the drama of European
history, his orientation to the other without any prerogative of conquest has
made his work pertinent for postcolonial philosophy (Ahmed 2000, 142;
Hiddleston 2009, 16). In *Levinas and the Postcolonial* John E. Drabinski
(2011, 2)[17] suggests that it is the Levinasian ethical dimension that 'lies in the
heart of so much theory (of postcolonial philosophy) as an underthematized
cornerstone'. In addition to Drabinski, the philosophers Jane Hiddleston
(2009) and Zuzanna Ladyga (2012) have explored the ways in which postcolonial thinkers such as Gayatri Spivak, Franz Fanon and Homi Bhabha
have been *implicitly* carrying Levinas's ideas to the boundary zone between
ethics and politics. Just as Levinas was developing his notion of difference,
theorists from the historical and cultural places of Levinas's 'other Other'
theorized radical difference. Although the tone and resonance of the postcolonial debates were and are different, they ask very Levinasian questions,
such as 'What does it mean to be on the margins of the knowable and the
known?' (Drabinski 2011, xiii). By describing the 'other' as the weak, the poor
and the marginal, Levinas's logic seems to have underpinned the work of
subaltern scholars who became interested in mapping the links between the
domain of ethics and the domain of politics of oppression (e.g. Spivak 1988).
However, while postcolonial writers underline the ways in which historicity
and materialist sensibility mediate the encounters between self and the subaltern other, Levinas's call for responsibility means responsibility beyond the
historical, political and social context.

Interestingly, Levinas's most loyal commentator, Derrida, did not seem
to be disturbed by Levinas's legacy as a thinker who was European through
and through. Instead, it was Levinas's work in particular that helped Derrida
to lay emphasis on how colonialism operates within the very language of

philosophy (Critchley 1999; Hiddleston 2009, 104).[18] Levinasian ethics came to strengthen Derrida's entire deconstruction of Western metaphysics and ethnocentrism, which then had a significant and wide-ranging impact on postcolonial ethics (Hiddleston 2009, 103). Spivak, in particular, has constantly borrowed from both strands of postcolonialism – Marxism and post-structuralism on the one hand, and Levinasian ethics on the other. Notably, it was Derrida's critical engagement with Levinas's ideas that provided Spivak with tools for her work 'deconstructing the colonial legacy of the anthropological paradigm and to formulate the conditions of possibility for an ethical dialogue with the subaltern' (Morton 2007, 61). Hence, Spivak has been considered one of the few intellectuals putting into practice the suggestions made by the post-Enlightenment ethical movement associated with Levinas and also Derrida (Hiddleston 2009; Ladyga 2012, 221–30).

It is clear that Levinas has left it to his commentators to explore whether his work actually has relevance on the ethical across borders, that is, to continue to explore what it would mean to infuse postcolonial explorations of difference with Levinas's notions of the ethical. According to Drabinski (2011), this line of inquiry has not yet really begun in Levinasian scholarship; the scholarly debates have remained mainly in the European context. A rare exception is Enrique Dussel, who has opened up Levinas's work towards the 'other Other' in his *Liberation Theology* using Levinas as 'inspiration' in his writings on intersubjective ethics and the philosophy of liberation in Latin America. However, the story goes that when Dussel asked Levinas why his work only addresses the horrors in the Holocaust, and not the millions murdered in conquest, slavery and under colonialism, Levinas answered 'that is for you to think about'. Hence, as Drabinski (2011, 3–4) highlights, Levinas turns the task of theorizing the disasters that define the historical experience of Latin America into a problem for the Americas.

Yet, a growing number of Levinas commentators have questioned the meaningfulness of trying to keep ethics somehow *local*. This movement unquestionably continues the work started by Derrida. Drabinski (2011) in particular calls for approaching Levinas's thinking in embodied, politicized space – on the boundaries of the ethical and political – in order to maintain the relevance of Levinas's work to contemporary theorizing about the ethical in global encounters. This means exploring the fruitfulness of Levinas's scholarship in questions of subalternity, migration and exclusion in transnational and transcultural contexts. The task is not only a matter of keeping Levinas alive as a thinker. The rhetoric of subalternity needs the Levinasian nuance of the ethical in order to retain its political and other purchase (Drabinski 2011, 11), that is, to open up new kinds of ethical spaces for those in the 'margin'. This ethical space is the liminal sphere between ourselves (Levinas 1969, 109) – a space and a place which often remains closed in postcolonial writings (Parry 2004, 23; Hiddleston 2009, 162).

In this research project I approach hospitality as an 'alternative' ontology (although Levinas would call it transcendence and metaphysics) that allows disruption of the boundaries between subjects and categories. I place a special focus precisely on the ways in which attention to the 'welcome *of* the other' and to one's responsibility to say 'welcome *to* the other' could open up spaces for more ethical encounters. This means underlining the importance of a continuum in hosting and guesting (Rosello 2001, 18) – welcoming the other and being welcomed by the other.

2.4 Unlearning the privilege to enter

> Let me just show how you looked to us. You came. You took things that were not yours, and you did not, even for appearance's sake, ask first. You could have said 'May I have this, please?' and even though it would have been clear to everybody that a yes or no from us would have been of no consequence, you might have looked so much better. Believe me, it would have gone a long way. I would have had to admit that at least you were polite.
>
> (Kincaid 1988, 35)

This is how Jamaica Kincaid explains Western colonialism's and imperialism's connections to the modern tourism industries in *The Small Place*. One of the many shared elements of colonialism, global tourism and development is the mobility where 'West visits the rest' and 'cores visit the peripheries', which makes it essential to acknowledge the postcolonial discourses in the theories and practices of tourism and development. In postcolonial debates the desire to arrive and help the other in the previously colonized countries is typically referred to as the 'white man's burden'. The idea was originally based on the 'backwardness' of the colonized and the position of the colonizer at the top of the evolutionary ladder. Hence 'the white man's burden' was seen as a duty to fix the colonized in a perpetual otherness (Bhabha 1994; Eriksson-Baaz 2005, 37, 45). However, later on, the white man's burden – and also the 'white tourist's burden' – have been interpreted as the guilty conscience for the past and present exploitation of the 'other' which takes place in the world. As Vrasti (2013, 4) writes about volunteer tourism, carrying the white man's, woman's and tourist's burden is normally perceived as an admirable sign of unselfishness that *demands* applause (see also Mostafanezhad 2014).

Ultimately global tourism and development interventions – and especially the search for emancipatory solutions that bring progress – are based on the hegemonic discourses whereby self helps and guides and rescues the other. In these discourses the 'North' and the 'cores' maintain the position of superiority, agency and the role of an adult, while the child-like 'South' and 'peripheries' are taught and helped to follow linear, Western-style development as the norm (Teivainen 2004; Li 2007; Escobar 2012; Seppälä 2013, 11; Alt 2016). Despite the call for multiculturalism and acknowledgement of local knowledges, the problems and challenges are continuously found in 'peripheries', while the visitors from the 'cores' are perceived to be capable of providing the needed solutions (for exceptions, see Chambers and Buzinde 2015, 11; Holmes et al. 2016). This mind-set allows subjects from the West and industrialized cores to be conserved. Here it merits mentioning that the same kinds of unequal power relations tend to exist between 'cores' and 'peripheries' within countries in the Global South. Kuokkanen's (2007) work on universities' hospitality towards indigenous people and indigenous epistemes highlights the existence of 'internal colonialism' even within what has become known as the Global North (see also Junka-Aikio 2014[19]).

Sandra Talpande Mohanty (1999), the author of *Under Western Eyes*, has argued that the Western feminists who wish to 'save the poor sisters in the South' might also be repeating the same kinds of contradictory interventions as the 'burdened white men'. Feminist postcolonial writers have posed the questions of how to decolonize the mind, and for whom this decolonizing is relevant (ibid.; McLeod 2010, 206; Chambers and Buzinde 2015). Kincaid's narrative above reveals the need for new tools which can help to acknowledge and interrupt impolite or unethical behaviour when visiting other people's home islands. What I suggest here is that taking for granted the welcome *of* the other (subjective genitive) is a sign of a *colonized imagination*, mentality and heightened levels of individualism. The first step in the process of 'decolonizing minds' is to become aware of the ways and the contexts where such perceptions continue to be produced.

The asymmetry of intersubjective encounters becomes evident when the subjects are located in a particular topography and time; or when they are located, as the feminist, postcolonial scholars Ahmed and Spivak locate them, in a gendered body. Although the asymmetries are expected to be in constant change, depending on the contexts and subjects that are encountered, not all subjects have the same possibilities to mitigate these asymmetries. Especially scholars in the field of subaltern studies focus attention on the subaltern subject position, which has no access to the lines of social mobility or to the processes of cultural imperialism. Rather, subaltern subjects are those rendered voiceless and without agency by their social status (Mohan 2004; Mignolo 2008; Junka-Aikio 2014). Spivak (1988, 283–4) points this out in her now-famous question, 'can the subaltern speak?' This question calls for reflection on how the existing asymmetries might be re-constructed and maintained in the intersubjective relations between self and the subaltern other.

Subjectivities are not formed only in physical encounters with the other, but also through representations that are used to describe our encounters with the other (Spivak 1987).[20] In her analysis of the subaltern speech in tourism, Cara Aitchison (2001, 137) calls attention to representations where 'the people in these landscapes (in 'tropical paradises') are frequently portrayed as passive but graceful recipients of white explorers from urbanized and industrialized countries'.[21] However, the ethico-political implications of these kinds of representations are regularly dismissed even in the discourses of ethical tourism. Instead, concerns over practices that silence and de-subjectify the 'other' have mainly appeared on the fringes of tourism research. Those scholars who draw on postcolonial criticism argue that it is not only the phenomenon of ignoring the marginalized, but also the romanticisation and 'inclusion' of the subaltern that reproduces unethical representations of otherness and deepens the binary oppositions between active self and passive other (Aitchison 2001; Hall and Tucker 2004; Ahmed 2012; Higgins-Desbiolles and Powys Whyte 2013; Mostafanezhad 2014; Chambers and Buzinde 2015; Grimwood et al. 2015).

Spivak's (1988, 272–4, 283–4) work can be of help here, as her speciality lies in problematizing the intention to 'give the voice' to the subaltern other. Her sharp critique demands that one must acknowledge, as the very first step, that the combination of Eurocentric perceptions and trivialization of global inequalities might seriously limit the possibilities of envisioning ethically sound encounters within global tourism. In other words, thinking with Spivak helps to understand the various consequences of neglecting the wider structures of disadvantage and oppression (Kapoor 2004; McEwan 2009, 235). This challenges, for instance, the assumption that calling the participants 'partners' instead of 'beneficiaries', 'hosts' instead of 'locals' or embracing the local knowledges would succeed in erasing paternalism and colonial legacy from the visitors' minds (Eriksson Baaz 2005, 6–12). Similarly, in her reflection about the attempts of decolonization and inclusion of the indigenous Laura Junka-Aikio (2014, 206) points out that 'the moment of inclusion can become simply another means of appropriation, exploitation and marginalization'. Consequently, it is essential to keep asking how the colonial past and neo-colonial present might continue to mediate even supposedly emancipatory encounters with the 'other'. In other words, this means acknowledging, as Grimwood et al. (2015, 23) highlight, 'how even good intentions discipline us to ignore certain truths, are never without their silences or modes of othering, and are always ripe for critical dialogue and debate'.

Neglecting the legacy of colonialism and modern forms of economic and political abuse is, as Spivak (1988, 280; see Höckert 2014, 108) puts it, *epistemic violence*, a practice that forms a pertinent part of neoliberal orthodoxy. In consequence, the unawareness or ignorance of inequalities between self and other, and what Suvi Alt (2016) has called as the metaphysics of modernity, allows the maintenance of European theatres of responsibility (Morton 2007). Unfortunately, even the majority of participatory tourism initiatives produce dramas which fit in well as scenes in this theatre. Tourism researchers Gianna Moscardo, Anna Blackman and Laura Murphy (2014) describe tourism projects through the analogy of a Greek tragedy in order to explain how different stakeholders engage in decision-making. A valid question here – and one that has troubled some scholars within community-based tourism studies – is why the role of the protagonists is so often played by the guests (van der Duim 2006; Butcher 2007; Saarinen 2010; Goodwin 2011).

Spivak, who has valuable insights into these kinds of settings, directs her concern especially to the epistemic or conceptual violence that shapes the relationships between the self and the other (Morton 2007, 61). These forms of violence tend to occur when the voices of the other are being translated, written and represented in the ways that support previous imaginaries about the 'other'. According to Spivak, there are two registers of representation which reconstruct these dislocated subject perspectives of the subaltern other. She criticizes our excessive zeal to *speak for the other* in a political sense, and *speak about the other* in more aesthetic and philosophical sense. In Spivak's view, this double act of representation leads to a situation where the other is not 'speaking'. What Spivak (1988, 280), Derrida (1999) and Levinas (1998) all seem to agree on is *the impossibility of escaping epistemic violence when engaging with the other in discourse*. For them the ethical appears in language. In fact, it was Derrida's approach to conceptual violence in *Of Grammatology* which helped Spivak to situate Derrida's reflections on ethics and violence in terms of the history of European colonialism.

As already mentioned in section 1.3., Spivak herself has been unwilling to provide concrete help on how to represent the 'other' or encounter the 'other' through development projects, academic research, tourism advertisements, and the like. Instead, the main contribution of Spivak's reflections is to point out the dubious character of the privileged position which allows one to enter, master encounters between self and the other and produce representations of the other.[22] In fact, Spivak's proceeding in negative terms makes one doubt whether ethical (non-violent) relations could actually ever flourish in tourism and development projects. However, her scepticism should not be interpreted as pure pessimism. It is clear that Spivak considers Levinas's account (in *Totality and Infinity*) of an ethical relation and an open dialogue between self and other to be impossible. Even Levinas (1969, 215–16; 1985, 98–9) himself describes our interpersonal relations as always asymmetrical. However, Spivak still seems to be driven to understand the impossibility of ethical engagement for collective action. In other words, the impossibility of ethical and unconditional hospitality and ethical singularity should not be seen as a justification to ignore the unequal power relations between self and other. On the contrary, emancipatory interventions require acknowledgement of impossibility and acknowledgement of asymmetry. As I choose to interpret this, Spivak's thinking here calls for acknowledging inequalities in the spheres between self and other, where the risks and responsibilities of welcoming become negotiated.

A valid basis for discussion, in Spivak's view, is to try to expose our blind spots, for instance as Westerners or local 'elite', by challenging two assumptions. The first is that the political desire of the 'oppressed' and the political interests of development experts are identical. That is, we should question the naïve and paternalistic belief that the 'other' is always willing to speak and participate, and is capable of doing so if *I* only listen and want her to speak and participate. The second assumption that must be questioned is that the voices of the 'other' could be recovered from the outside and that scholars can represent these voices as objective intermediaries (Kapoor 2004). For Spivak (1988, 280–4) the problem lies not in the inability of the other to speak, but rather in the unwillingness and incapability of the culturally dominant to listen. More specifically, Spivak takes the view that the privileged position which academic researchers and development consultants, for example, occupy is the reason why the 'locals' cannot be heard. Rather, the other is always already interpreted. As Spivak herself puts it, elite or hegemonic discourses are deaf to the subaltern, even when she or he speaks or resists.[23] The consequences are trivialization and invalidation of ways of knowing that fall outside of the West's, and the local elite's, languages, epistemic traditions and philosophies. According to Sharpe and Spivak (2002, 613; see Kuokkanen 2007, 66–8), these are consequences that can be described as epistemic ignorance and violence.

Going back to Levinas's discussions on totality and infinity, it seems like this kind of representation between self and other resonates with the conventional *said* (totality) instead of *the saying* (infinity). Hence, significantly, the ethical relations that we discuss and explore are not metaphysical but take place in language, as traces of the ethical. In fact, for Levinas Western philosophy in general is preoccupied with the *said* instead of the openness of the *saying* (see Hiddleston 2009, 19, 108, 163; Ladyga 2012, 224–5). This preoccupation means trying to get and represent as sharp a picture of the focal phenomenon as possible. However, Levinas, among other philosophers of ethical subjectivities, argues that getting a sharp picture of the other – knowing the other – is not desirable or possible. The search for ethical subjectivities calls for decolonizing our minds by unlearning the privilege of knowing the other (Spivak 1990, 20), so that the privilege of knowing becomes replaced by infinite curiosity, politeness and wonder (see Despret 2005; Haraway 2016, 124–33). In line with Irigaray's (1994/2000) thought, this wonder goes beyond what is suitable for us, as the other never suits us simply.

In these discussions the most practical instruction for ethical representation might be scepticism and critique of closed ends. For Levinas (1998, 37–8, 45–51), ethical representation would require desiring the omnipresent excess of the *saying* instead of privileging the *said*. At the risk of oversimplifying Levinas's thought, the *said* could be defined as something with totality and limits, while the *saying* refers to openness, to 'the living world', to a gesture towards another human being. These two co-existing facets, the said and the saying, can also be thought of in connection with Derrida's (see Derrida and Rottenberg 1999, 19–29) writings on the conditional laws of hospitality and unconditional welcoming. Just as the law and the ethics of hospitality are not opposites or alternatives to each other, neither are the said and the saying. Instead, the saying expands the potentially reductive and oppressive boundaries of the said. Hence, the 'double session of representation', discussed by Spivak, could be dismantled by a missing (third) sense, Levinas's *ethical saying*. That is, Levinas's ideas suggest that the 'solution' to the situation where 'the subaltern cannot speak' could be found in ethical saying, which opens up new spaces to speak even for the subaltern.

Inspired by Spivak's example, I have modified her question '[C]an the subaltern speak?' to suit tourism scenes and the Levinasian idea of welcoming. My preliminary answer is that the subaltern in tourism rarely speaks, as her or his invitation to the other to visit and intervene is already taken for granted. That is, the subaltern other in tourism is the one whose welcoming is always taken for granted. This means that the other becomes relatively subaltern (Moraña, Dussel and Jáuregui 2008) in the context of tourism. What is more, still following in Spivak's footsteps, the subaltern is never really welcomed – physically or in discourse – which results in the subaltern never gaining access to social mobility. It is the privileged and mobile position of the self which restricts the self's possibility to listen and welcome the other (Spivak 1988, 272–4), including more-than-human others (Haraway 2016, 111).

For this reason, Spivak challenges us and herself to *unlearn our privileges as loss*. The first part of this task requires noticing that one's class, race, gender, ethnicity, nationality, ideology, education, occupation, language, or even access to the Internet can create relative advantage (see Sharpe and Spivak 2002, 617–18; Tlostanova and Mignolo 2012; Vrasti, 2013, 123–4; Höckert 2014, 108–9). Spivak (1988) then asks us to think about what kind of prerogatives we – as individuals and groups – might have as visitors in this particular context. For instance, in tourism and development encounters, these relative advantages as dominant groups can be based on many roles, such as being a tourist, working for development, researching tourism, and so on. In fact, it seems like simply travelling from 'the cores' to 'the peripheries' strengthens the subjectivity of the mobile traveller. Or, as Sara Ahmed (2000, 172) has expressed it, some of us are afforded agency within the global by relegating others to 'local' spaces. The travel itineraries of development workers and volunteer tourists, 'the white men and women with their burden', make sense as long as their hosts remain in the marginal space outside the hegemonic discourses. In other words, guests are allowed to presume the other's welcome as long as the other is 'not quite there yet' (See also Bhabha 1994; Dicks 2003, 52; Eriksson Baaz 2005; Tucker 2010). Hence, looking for a more equal relationship with the 'other' requires, as a starting point, acknowledging how one's own active, privileged subjectivity becomes established through 'freezing' the other.

The second part of Spivak's (1988, 20; McEwan 2009, 68) task of changing one's mind-set by 'unlearning one's privilege as loss' means recognizing one's prejudices, preconceptions and learned responses. To put it in somewhat different terms, our prerogatives have given us only limited knowledge and prevented our gaining new understanding. As a result, we are simply not equipped to understand different ways of knowing (Spivak 1988, 280, 284; Kuokkanen 2007, 3, 103; Junka-Aikio 2014). Spivak's approach means denying the idea of the Enlightenment that the world is expected to be knowable through observation. For her there are certain knowledges, experiences and existences that are closed off from the 'privileged view' (McEwan 2009,

68). As I understand Spivak's thinking, the desire to listen and to take into account, for instance, local knowledge is rather misleading. Notably, paternalistic intentions, unaware as they are of these limitations, can also be seen as a form of silencing, objectifying and trivializing the other (Spivak 1988, 275–6; Seppälä 2013; Navas-Camargo and Zwerg-Villegas 2014; Chambers and Buzinde 2015; Tucker 2016, 38). It means pretending that the encounters between self and other are open and unconditional despite self's limitations in welcoming the other in discourse.

Spivak herself has been criticized for her tendency to silence the subaltern by focusing on the division between self and the other, of reinscribing – rather than disrupting – the authority of the privileged ones (Hiddleston 2009, 163; Hickey and Mohan 2004). While other Gramscian historians have been blamed for their extensive optimism about the possibilities of recovering subaltern agency, for Spivak any attempts to do so appear almost pointless. Instead of laying emphasis on the relational construction of privileged and subaltern positions, Spivak seems to have answered this critique by becoming more cautious about using the concept of 'privileged' as such. It is obvious that *privilege* becomes an uncomfortable concept, especially if it is used for categorizing people as subaltern or privileged. However, these conceptualizations still are relevant when aiming to understand the attitudes and assumptions that shape our encounters with the other.[24] For instance, a study in the USA has shown that people who drive expensive cars tend to drive over crosswalks more recklessly than those sitting in more modest car models (Piffa et al. 2011). This could be interpreted as limited attention towards others and as lack of willingness to be interrupted by other people. The same study indicated how people who win huge sums of money in the lottery tend to adopt superior attitudes towards others, although their relative privilege is based mainly on luck.

In any event, my intention here is to place emphasis on the significance of Spivak's ideas in tourism development schemes (see Aitchison 2001). I wish to propose that the privileged position of guests can undermine the possibilities of promoting more equal and responsible forms of visiting and travelling. So could it be that the pre-constructed categories of what tourism is and how it should help local communities most probably, unintentionally, restrict the subjectivities, choices and voices of the other? Or is it possible that the existing inequalities between the West and the Rest, or the core and the periphery, or haves and have-nots, might lead to settings where guests impose their definitions of development and sustainability in tourism? In essence, if we understand subjectivity as a group of experiences with the others that keep shaping our imaginings, can we say that the imaginings and subjectivity of the mobile, privileged subject have been shaped by the ability to dominate the negotiations about the conditions and risks of hospitality? If the answer is yes, envisioning alternative encounters and decolonizing our minds will require unlearning our privilege of inhabiting a free, mobile, individual, cosmopolitan subject position as a loss, that is, recognizing one's privileged attitude towards the other, and unlearning the privilege to enter without wel-coming the other.

The good news here is that we do not have to stop here. What comes after learning to unlearn one's privilege as loss is the possibility to learn anew (McEwan 2009; see also Höckert 2014). Tracing Levinasian ethics in Spivak, I assume that she has wanted to encourage us to unlearn the individualistic and totalizing subject position and then to learn to learn anew the relational mode of intersubjectivity, based on an openness and receptivity towards the other (see Ladyga 2012). Learning to learn anew through the Levinasian notions of hospitality and welcome is needed here to acknowledge and dis-rupt privileged attitudes and to envision more welcoming ways of being – not as a vision for the future, but as a change that happens in our imaginings at this moment, as a process of decolonizing mind-sets. This means, building on Hannah Arendt's (1982) thought in *Lectures on Kant's Political Philosophy*, to think with enlarged mentality by training one's imagination to both visit and welcome other ways of being. If hospitality is seen as a way of being, ethical subjectivity means not merely entering the other's home, but welcoming and making space for the other in one's own (Jokinen and Veijola 1997, 35–6; Grit 2010, 2014; Germann Molz 2014). It is a desire to welcome the other and to respect the other's welcome. It is simultaneously a polite and curious prac-tice (Despret 2005 in Haraway 2016, 126–7) which allows others to be not who/what we expected to visit, and allows ourselves to be nor who/what were anticipated either. In the following, final section of this chapter I will do my best to draw together these discussions on ethical subjectivities.

2.5   Ethical encounters at home

The purpose of this theory chapter has been to explore the idea of hospi-tality as a call for making space for the other. I have approached this space as a sphere of physical, discursive and metaphysical encounters between our-selves; in essence, it is in these spaces that participation can take place. I have drawn in particular on the ways Derrida, Levinas and Spivak reflect on eth-ical dimensions of encountering the other, and directed my attention on their critique of the Western idea of the individually responsible and masterful subject. However, each scholar posits very different roles in the process of deconstructing and decolonizing different modes of postcolonial subjection and domination. In my opinion, Spivak's work brings into these discussions quite little hope about the possibilities of establishing more equal and open relations with the historically, epistemologically and materially exploited other. However, despite this apparent pessimism, she has proposed that the only responsible thing to do is to keep trying to reduce the violence in the discursive spaces between self and the other (see also Grimwood et al. 2015). By contrast, Levinas's metaphysical thought represents a utopian optimism about the openness of these spaces. He seems to deliberately ignore the histor-icity and materiality of our experiences that shape our desire and possibilities to limit these spaces (Drabinski 2011, 11; see also Oksala 2001, 73). In turn, while Derrida's writings can be read as encouragement to move towards the Levinasian idea of infinitely open welcoming, Derrida (1999, 21) underlines the necessity to negotiate the conditions and ethics of hospitality again and again depending on the case and context (Baker 2010, 89).

The most fruitful context must be a *home* – physical or metaphorical – for it offers many different levels of analysis and abstraction. Thinkers encouraging us to seek more hospitable homes can consider the Earth as our common home (Gren and Huijbens 2012), an entire hemisphere as the home of the 'other' (Truman 1949[25]), or homepages as the home of a virtual community (Germann Molz 2007; 2012).[26] While it is often unclear whether a continent offers a common home for the countries on that continent (Pakkasvirta 2005), most of us consider that we *do* have our own home country. For instance, Drabinski (2011, 189) proposes that home is like a state: a state of exclusion that, on reflection, points to a resulting excessive responsibility for the one who is excluded. As we have experienced ever more strikingly since the refugee crisis began to escalate in 2015, it is at the moats, boundaries and walls of these homes that the problems and possibilities of ethics and politics begin (Derrida 2002, 142–3; Bell 2017, 31). There are also home regions, home towns, houses that offer a home for a community, family homes, second homes, and so on. All these have fallen under scrutiny even in tourism studies. Then there are ontological homes (Heidegger 1927/1972), also called *chora* (Grosz 1995; Wearing, Stevenson and Young 2010; Ankor and Wearing 2012, 180–1; Germann Molz 2014) or *habitation* (Levinas 1969, 151–6, 165), which we imagine either sharing or occupying alone.

Rauna Kuokkanen (2007, 117) uses the concept of doing one's *homework*, drawing on Spivak, in order to make epistemic space for the other. In Spivak's words, the process of doing one's homework implies the need to reflect on and unlearn one's privileges and biases and learn to learn anew. Hence, this homework is not something one could be able to finish. Instead, it is an ongoing task, or an ongoing practice, which calls upon us 'to scrutinize the historical circumstances and to articulate one's own participation in the structures that have fostered various forms of silencing' or exclusion of the other from discursive spaces. This means that for Spivak, according to Kuokkanen (2007, 115), the question of ethics is actually not a question of knowledge, but most of all a question of relationship. Although Spivak and Levinas seem to agree on the relational nature of ethics, they disagree on whether opening self to postcolonial difference would require engaging in conscious work. While Spivak (1995, xxiv) underlines the importance of engaging in 'painstaking labor' when doing one's home*work*, in Levinasian phenomenological thought the ethical relation between self and the other does not denote a similar kind of conscious act of a rational subject. Rather, for Levinas, the responsibility for the other comes from the call *of* the other, which is always prior to the self's knowledge (Derrida 1999, 22–6; Morton 2007, 61–2).

In phenomenological philosophy, thinking about being and becoming is already thinking about the origins of ethics; actually, *ethos* is understood in its original Greek meaning as 'home'. For instance, Heidegger (1927/1972 in Smith, M. 2009b, 628) described philosophy as 'a form of homesickness; as an intellectual desire to find a way of being at home in the world'.[27] For the most part, phenomenology was born of this homesickness and longing for answers and understanding ideal ways of being (Heinämaa 2002, 266). This has included questioning the 'nature' of social life itself – of being at home with and without the others. According to Levinas (1969, 152–5), both hospitality and ethics refer to the dwelling where you receive the other.[28] This is also where Heidegger's and Levinas's thinkings diverge: while Heidegger describes dwelling or sojourning as being at home with oneself, for Levinas (1969, 37, 155–60) the other is the one who 'disturbs the being at home with oneself' (see also Drabinski and Nelson 2014). Hospitality as ontology means making space for the other in one's home and sharing that home with the other. Levinas (1969, 171) explains that 'I welcome the Other who presents himself in my home by opening my home to him'. For him it is a joy in living to receive the 'other' into her or his space. In this sense, ethical subjectivity is not about entering and visiting, but about welcoming, being and dwelling at home with the other. Therefore, according to Levinas's idea of radical inter-subjectivity, we are never home alone as the consciousness is *to be* open to the other, *to be* for-the-other (Derrida 1999, 52; Hiddleston 2009, 20; Drabinski 2011, 95; Lynch 2017, 181).

For Levinas, whose home is primarily a metaphysical one, the subject of the welcome is in his *home* in the home of the other. Home is a place where we are with the others, where we share with the other, and where we are responsible for the other – for all the others. In Levinas's home, being is beyond being – beyond self. It is different from the home of the subjectivist design, where the other is assumed to stay in her or his home. In Levinas's home the self is there for the other to an extent where the roles of the hosts and guests become confused and even cease to exist (Innerarity 2017). It is a radical idea which requires that the host gives away her or his status as a host, which according to Levinas is a prerequisite to a somewhat equal relation between *hôte* and *hôte* (Derrida 1999, 41). However, it is unclear whether Levinas's home has thresholds or walls or whether it is constructed with an unfinished and infinitely welcoming design that allows the other to enter. Levinas is not consistent in this matter. He writes, for instance, '[T]he possibility for the home to open to the Other is as essential to the essence of the home as closed doors and windows' (Levinas 1969, 273).

In any case, it is obvious that the meanings Levinas assigns to ethical encounters are not something that could be located in the history books of previous meetings between self and other. Most likely physical, or even transcendental, worlds do not consist of equal and ethical relations that are based on mutual welcoming and receptivity. For this reason, some might want to claim that Levinas's ethical phenomenological approach is a quasi-theory which is not 'true', or cannot say anything about the 'real world'. However, even though we may not be able to grasp the ethical 'for-the-Other' subjectivity in temporal, spatial and linguistic configurations (Drabinski 2011, 96), for Derrida (2002, 95, 101) the Levinasian philosophy of openness as the fundamental structure of subjectivity is still the oasis that we should aim for. Most importantly, the idea or law of unconditional hospitality makes it possible to move beyond Kantian ethics as conditions of hospitality based on laws and politics (Derrida 1999, 19–20, 48–50). In other words, as political philosopher Gideon Baker (2010, 88; see also Still 2010, 7) proposes, it allows a shift from the universal *accounts* of otherness characteristic of Kantian ethics towards universal *openness* to the other. According to Baker (2013, 3), for Derrida 'it is a condition of all acts of conditional hospitality that they have this unconditional hospitality to aspire and fall short of'.

Yet, opening one's door to all the others, giving away one's role as a host reveals a paradox which is crucial for Derrida's thought on the ethics of hospitality. It leads to a situation where, sooner or later, there will no longer be a home to which the other could be welcomed (Derrida 1999; Baker 2010, 88, 91). In other words, as Germann Molz and Gibson (2007, 5) argue, 'absolute hospitality requires us to go beyond, even beyond the very conditions that enable a state or a person to offer hospitality at all'. This means that although the Levinasian idea can offer a glimpse of a cure to those suffering from homesickness – from longing for the ideal ways of being – it simultaneously creates the greatest anxiety of moral consciousness: we are put out of home with ourselves and others just at the moment we experience responsibility (Drabinski 2011, 166). As a consequence, the binary relationship between unconditional and conditional hospitality is inseparable,

> conditional laws would cease to be laws of hospitality if they were not guided, given inspiration, given aspiration, required, even by the law of unconditional hospitality. These two regimes of law, of *the* law and the laws, are thus both contradictory, antinomic, *and* inseparable. They both imply and exclude each other, simultaneously.
>
> (Derrida 2000, 80–1)

Thus, it is the double law of hospitality – negotiation and calculating between the poles of unconditional and conditional hospitality – where responsibility becomes possible. Between these two laws of hospitality is the threshold, or the space, where 'the conditions, the norms, the risks, the rights and the duties' of welcoming become negotiated (Derrida 2000, 87; Baker 2010, 92). Thus, while unconditional, pure hospitality is never possible as such, according to Derrida (see Derrida and Rottenberg 2002, 14) the choice to *not* negotiate makes hospitality even more impure. It would mean settling for Kantian laws of hospitality based on conditions which maintain the unequal access to mobility and welcome. Clearly, moving towards more ethical encounters, towards ethics of hospitality, requires negotiation.

The situation where the ethics of hospitality must become conditional in order to function leads to what Baker (2010) calls 'undedicability'. In his opinion, drawing always on Derrida, there can be no comprehensive or final answer to the question of 'what to do?'. Baker (2010, 92) explains Derrida's (1993) thought in *Aporias* as follows:

> If the Law of unconditional hospitality could be codified then there would be nothing left to decide and therefore no responsibility. Ethics, understood as synonymous with knowledge, would determine action and apparently responsible decisions would in fact become merely 'technical applications' of some 'pre-established order'.

Instead, reaching towards ethics of hospitality requires constant negotiation and fresh decisions; in other words, these can be seen as prerequisites of responsibility. As Baker (2010, 92) argues, 'Undedicability becomes a condition of ethical action rather than an obstacle to it'. In addition to circumventing any need to create 'codes of conduct' for ethics of hospitality, Derrida denies the possibility of defining general, pre-set rules for the negotiations. Instead, '[N]egotiation is different at every moment, from one context to the next. There are only contexts, and this is why deconstructive negotiation cannot produce general rules, or "methods"' (Derrida and Rottenberg 2002, 7).

In sum, I began the chapter by describing Derrida's reservations about the limitations of Western thought on hospitality, which has been concerned with defining the conditions for invitation. My intention there was to describe how engaging in hospitality between ourselves includes a readiness to share one's home with the other, and a readiness to be interrupted by the other. My suggestion is that these principles are equally relevant in the context of participation; that is, like hospitality, participation is a way of being and doing which means being together and doing togetherness with others. Consequently, envisioning more ethical ways of encountering the other requires not only welcoming the other, but also broadening one's perspective from the issue of invitation towards the issue of visitation. In other words, heightened attention to and respect for different ways the 'other' makes space for the self.

Tourism and mobility scholars Monika Büscher, John Urry and Katian Witchger (2011) have proposed that the temptation to retrain phenomena in order to study them would destroy them. In this study, I have aimed to move and develop with the 'target', the tourism development initiatives in the Nicaraguan highlands. Painting or taking a picture while the target is in rapid motion should also explain the blurriness of representations. In tourism research this blurriness has recently become more accepted, and in some circles even celebrated (see Salazar 2010; Pritchard et al. 2011; Dredge et al. 2013; Veijola et al. 2014; Tucker 2017). We have begun to appreciate those who have dared to publish photos where the artist's finger is partially covering the lens, as it reminds us of the embodied person behind the camera who aims the camera according to her or his personal interest. Although hermeneutic phenomenology and postcolonial critique both call for heightened super-self-reflexivity, the purpose of the following representation of my analysis is not to show 'selfies' of me, taken in other people's homes. Instead I aim to present images of many different kinds of encounters. In order to describe the historical and political context, I start by taking a look back in time, and then move into highlighting more recent encounters. So, while remaining mainly in contemporary settings, my aim is to discuss the encounters in the past might have shaped the imaginings of the present.

Last, I also wish to address a very practical issue concerning the ethics of representation and the researcher's responsibility to protect informants and interviewees. In San Ramón, this question is by no means unproblematic. Although I have carefully asked all my interlocutors for their approval to use the interviews as data in this study, I have chosen to protect their identities by using pseudonyms.[29] However, the villages are still recognizable and changing the names of the villages would not make sense – especially as I have been writing about the same communities in the past. Thus, I hope that the reader of this study treats it as a retrospective narrative and analysis of snapshots. Instead of claiming that entire communities would or would not welcome development projects, or that one should or should not visit rural communities in Nicaraguan highlands, my overall aim in this research project is to heighten attention and respect towards the other's welcome.

Notes

1 Eriksson Baaz (2005, 6–7) argues that calling the other a 'partner' does not make the development encounters less paternalizing (see also Li 2007; Escobar 2012; Zapata Campos 2014).
2 Thanks to Jarno Valkonen for suggesting this idea.
3 In his work, Derrida (1999, 19–20; 2000, 75–81; Raffoul 1998, 213) is especially interested in and concerned about the people who are 'without a home'. The questions of undedicability and inescapability of these negotiations are also discussed in the work of Baker (2010; 2011).
4 First published in 1997, translated into English in 2000. The book is co-authored by Anne Dufourmantelle, who 'invites Jacques Derrida to Respond'.
5 First published in French in 1997 and translated into English in 2001.
6 Quote from Blanchot's (1993, 51–52) *The Infinite Conversation*. First published in French in 1969.
7 See also Cohen R.A. (1998, xiii) in the preface to Levinas's *Otherwise than Being*. However, Levinas has been later criticized for his reductive reading of Heidegger (see e.g. Drabinski and Nelson 2014).
8 Levinas's *Otherwise than Being* (first published in 1974, translated into English in 1981) was dedicated to the memory of the victims of National Socialists and anti-Semitism.

9 Interestingly some of Levinas's commentators, such as Critchley (1999), Hand (2009) and Drabinski (2011), do not seem to pay special attention to the conceptualization of hospitality as such.

10 Please see Veijola et al.'s (2014, 142–7) discussion of 'prepositions and other stories' that focus on the preposition 'with' in particular. I am grateful to Olli Pyyhtinen for training our focus on the prepositions.

11 Derrida (2003) in *Sur parole: Instantanés philosophiques* (French), translated and quoted by Hill (2010, 246).

12 For this kind of interpretation of Levinas's thought, see Davis (1996 in Ahmed 2000, 141) and Ankor and Wearing (2012).

13 For more on global mobilities and immobilities, see for instance Germann-Molz and Gibson (2007), Salazar (2010, 5–16; 2013) and Duncan et al. (2015).

14 On a larger scale, wealthy industrialized countries have helped the unit known as the 'Global South'. This is a common, and fundamental, act of 'othering' – something that forms a firm starting point for postcolonial critique. See Cooke and Kothari (2001), Eriksson Baaz (2005) and Escobar (2012).

15 Chandler (2013, 5) writes, '[F]or Sen, development is no longer a question of material transformation: development is no longer about external world. In fact, development disappears – it has no external material measurement – it is deontologized, or rather assumes the ontology of the human subject itself'.

16 I agree with Judith Still (2010), who points out that Levinas's focus lies strikingly on the self (*même*) despite his idea of ethics that begins with the other. However, as Levinas does not differentiate between self (hôte) and other (hôte) – there are no determinable properties that make these two different from each other – would not it be meaningless to speak separately about self and the other? Nor can we afford to forget the ways in which Levinas's thought builds strongly on his own traumatic experiences of 'otherness' – of being the *unwelcomed* other – in the context of war and the persecution of Jews. So when Levinas underlines the importance of calling in question the freedom of the self, does not he speak to all of us, to each one of the 'selfs'?

17 Drabinski (2011, 2) highlights that Levinas's insight of the other who accuses and obligates without prior experience is necessary when envisioning ethics in postcolonial encounters.

18 Derrida writes about the blindness of the Western episteme or system of knowledge in *The Monolingualism of the Other*. He calls for questioning the self-deluding ethnocentrism by increased attention to the other. Hiddleston (2009, 98) explains further that the object of Derrida's analysis and deconstruction of the Western philosophical tradition was the creation of postcolonial ethics.

19 For discussions on internal colonialism, see Mignolo (2008), Dussel (2013), Ranta (2014).

20 For postcolonial representations and worldmaking in tourism, see Hollinshead and Jamal (2007), Pritchard et al. (2011), Caton (2013) and Salazar (2013).

21 These kinds of representations in travel discourse are also discussed by Simmons (2004).

22 For 'relative subalternity', see Moraña et al. (2008).

23 For another example from Nicaragua, see Anja Nygren's (1999, 267–88) 'Local knowledge in the environment-development discourse. From dichotomies to situated knowledges'.

24 For instance, according to a study done in the USA, people tend to start to believe that they actually are better than others and in a privileged position, even if they have received their position without actually doing anything for it by themselves (e.g. lottery).

25 For postcolonial critique of discourses that categorize 'Third World' or 'Global South' as homogenic units, see Spivak (1988, 271, 291), Kapoor (2004, 634) and Escobar (2012).

26 For discussions on cosmopolitanism and home, see Kant's 'The home and the world' in Jamal and Hill (2002).

27 See also Jamal and Stronza's (2009, 318) article on 'Dwelling in the Peruvian Amazon'.

28 For Derrida's interpretations of home and people without a home, see Derrida (1999, 28, 41–5, 53–5), and for extending one's home through phone lines and internet Derrida (2000, 51).

29 The United States has had a greater mark on birth names in Nicaragua than in many other Latin American countries. See 'Nicaragua-names' on the invisiblecastle. blogspot.se, website accessed on 8 June 2013.

3 Unconditional welcome of tourism to Nicaragua

Nicaragua's capital city, Managua, welcomes its visitors through the memory of Augusto Sandino, the legendary Nicaraguan who fought in the 1930s to send away the 'Yanqui imperialists'. The airplanes land in an airport named after him, the souvenir shops sell t-shirts with his picture printed on them, and his silhouette decorates the horizon of Managua, as a reminder of resistance against foreign oppression, as well as that of the local elites (see Babb 2010, 46, 63). Visitors tend to be surprised by the huge pink posters which celebrate the slogans of the ruling government, the Sandinistas, who carry the name of their hero – and the hero of the entire country.[1] Most foreign travellers leave Managua soon after their arrival and head towards the Pacific beaches of San Juan del Sur, the volcanoes and the volcanic lake Laguna de Apoyo, or the Corn Islands on the Caribbean side of the country. Especially popular destinations are the colonial towns of the *Ruta Colonial*, or colonial route, which snakes through the western side of the country. In these towns the guests can enjoy the memories of the colonial spirit. As an illustration, after a day of walking along picturesque streets and visiting churches, the evening and dinner programme offers travellers a more personal and vivid experience of what earlier colonial encounters were like (see also Babb 2010, 48–51). The programme includes a play called *El Güegüense*, a story of misfortune and suffering under Spanish rule. It was written most likely in the mid-sixteenth century, and is thus one of the earliest and most important pieces of writing about the fusion of the cultures of the indigenous Indians and the colonial Spanish. The masked character, El Güegüense, is a peddler of mixed Indian and Spanish blood – a quick-witted, mischievous and sharp-tongued protagonist. The play expresses the frustrations of a 'mixed-race people', who were looked down on and mistreated by the Spanish colonizers, who held the 'purity' of their own blood in great esteem (Plunkett 2007, 73; Kinloch Tijerino 2008, 83–4).

The story of *El Güegüense* is still regarded as an important expression of Nicaraguan identity and the play is a widely celebrated symbol of the country's culture. According to some, Güegüense was a hard-working, smart and prosperous merchant who did not want to pay taxes to the Spanish crown. To others, he was a small, skilled merchant, but also a rascal and a fraud, who used his many skills to fool the Spanish authorities, not only to evade taxes but also to have his son marry the daughter of the governor. Whichever inter- pretation is the more accurate, the story expresses the resistance of a nation against foreign invaders, and it constitutes one of the most important elem- ents in the cultural heritage of the Nicaraguan people. For many the play is a worthy representation of the stereotype of a Nicaraguan: a rebellious and clever person with a sense of justice and suspiciousness towards authorities (Plunkett 2007; Vianica n.d.).

Even though the Spanish rule brought a brutal end to indigenous cus- toms, traditions and forms of worship, many of the mythical figures and gods revered by the Indians survived and became then incorporated into the stories about the conquerors' cruelty. 'The restless souls of conquis- tadors, headless priests and witch-like women', as Hazel Plunkett (2007, 74) puts it, are among a host of characters who recall the horror of the colonial period and haunt the Nicaraguan imagination. Hence, peculiarly, tourists are welcomed to the country by presenting a play of resistance and challenges related to the arrival of outsiders. This is by no means some- thing unique. For instance, the Maori welcoming ceremony in New Zealand involves performing a Maori war dance, *haka*, the purpose of which is to intimidate and to learn the intentions of the visitor (Kuokkanen 2007, 131; Johnston 2006).

It seems obvious that colonialism and tourism even have other connections besides the colonial towns and plays, not least the acceptance of power relations based on the visitors' privilege to enter when- and wherever they please. In other words, coloniality and transnational tourism development are connected by a phenomenon whereby 'the guests can take over hosting the party'.[2] Nicaragua's history is generally told through the interventions it has endured. Indeed, it has had the role of recipient: Nicaragua has received aid, external economic guidance and Venezuelan oil money, been the object of natural catastrophes, and so forth. At the same time, these narratives tend to neglect the things that Nicaraguans have had to give away to visitors to their country: sovereignty, gold, coffee (Kinloch Tijerino 2008), many of its beaches (Cañada 2013), water security (LaVanchy 2017), and consent to construct an inter-oceanic canal through the country (Hunt 2016). Walter Knut (1993, 3) has described Nicaragua as an extreme case of foreign intromissions and internal anarchy: 'From the days of Spanish conquest itself, Nicaragua was already a battleground of competing expeditions of discovery and conquest which set the basis for the factional conflicts during the centuries to come'. One story told today as an exception to this historical trend – and a tale of gullibility about the country's role in international relations – is the fact that Nicaraguans collected money to be sent to the poor Nordic country of Finland surviving and recovering from the Second World War (*Diario de Occidente* 26 January 1940).[3] This is treated as a somewhat surprising incident in the friendship between Finland and Nicaragua, as for a short moment Nicaraguans had taken the role of helper, instead of passive receiver of aid.

The purpose of this chapter is to sketch a picture of the historical, political and social context in which the encounters that drive contemporary tourism development occur. With a focus on the historicity of experiences, the chapter fosters debate on how contemporary modes of tourism – even the supposedly sustainable ones – might re-open prior histories and experiences of colonial and neo-colonial encounters (see Ahmed 2000, 13; Babb 2010). I will discuss previous visits by outsiders which might keep shaping the subjectivities, 'imaginations' and actions of the hosts. Drawing especially on Derrida's (1999; 2000) double law of hospitality, the chapter focuses on efforts to calculate the risks of welcoming while keeping the door open to strangers. Instead of proceeding chronologically, the chapter is structured in terms of different levels of hospitality and different actors who are as the *subjects of welcome* and *subjects of hospitality*. By approaching 'home' primarily in a political sense, I move from the idea of 'home nation' towards the communities and individual homes where people receive their guests.

The structure of the chapter is the following. The first section focuses on the experiences Nicaraguan hosts had of the encounters that took place before the burgeoning of rural tourism initiatives. The data that I have used for the analysis consist primarily of histories, poems and songs of Nicaraguan intellectuals, policy documents, newspaper articles, and interviews with tourism experts working in the country. The purpose of this section is to approach tourism encounters from different points of view, including the viewpoints of Nicaraguan intellectuals, the Nicaraguan government, NGOs and development aid agencies, as well as those living in, or close to, tourist destinations. By doing this, I wish to point out the obvious that Nicaraguans are by no means a homogeneous group of welcomers. Rather, it is obvious that different actors can give very different meanings to the arrival of guests: in particular the more recent history of tourism development in Nicaragua has shown the ways in which different groups of people experience the impacts of tourism in diverse ways (Cañada and Gascón 2007b; Mowforth et al. 2008; Hunt and Stronza 2014).

Section 3.2 focuses on the recent ambitions of the Nicaraguan tourism ministry, NGOs and international development organizations to democratize tourism development by turning their attention to the well-being of the rural communities around the country. More specifically, the purpose of the analysis is to deconstruct the meanings that the tourism experts give to their encounters with people living in economically marginalized rural areas. The third section changes the scene from urban environments towards the northern highlands. In giving a general picture of the context in San Ramón and the early days of tourism development in the region, I rely greatly on the writings of the local historian Edgard Rivas Chozas and on the stories told by local tourist guides. These accounts, together with the interviews conducted in the communities of San Ramón in 2008, then allow me to re-tell the story of how the people living in these coffee-farming communities have welcomed tourism and have experienced the arrival of tourism experts and tourists into their homes. The ambition of the last section of this chapter is to point out that, in the light of colonialism and more recent interventions in Nicaragua, it is problematic to assume that the others would choose to leave their doors wide open for everything unexpected and foreign (Derrida 2005, 6). In fact, taking for granted that the other unconditionally welcomes self undermines previous as well as contemporary efforts to decolonize encounters between ourselves.

3.1   Exclusive forms of hospitality

Uninterrupted practices of colonialism have marked Latin American history and, despite the long process of decolonization, many would take the view that countries like Nicaragua are still not free from foreign oppression. In fact, it would be impossible and meaningless to analyse Nicaragua's position without an understanding of its encounters and relations with 'outsiders'. During the last five hundred years or so, an increasing number of visitors have arrived in the geographical area now known as Nicaragua. It was sometime in the beginning of the 16th century, as far as we know, when the Niquirano Indians began to receive surprise visitors to their villages on the banks of the lakes of Nicaragua. Soon after the Aztec Indians from the north did so, the Spanish conquerors 'bumped into' the region. Although the locals were not hiding or escaping from anyone, the arrival of the Spaniards is often Eurocentrically and ambiguously described as the *discovery* of Americas, not its conquest, as many especially in Latin America wish to call it. While many in Latin America would term it a *conquest*, the history is largely written based on the visitors' travelogues (Rivas Choza 2008, 19; Dussel 2013, 26–31).

Delores Huff (1997 in Kuokkanen 2007, 130), professor of American Indian Studies, has argued that today it is inadequately acknowledged that the early colonists were actually often 'unconditionally welcomed' by the indigenous peoples. Typically, the hosts welcomed the arrivals, the guests, and treated them according their customs and to their laws of hospitality[4]. According to Kuokkanen (2007, 130) indigenous people were in general eager to welcome the 'other' in order to learn from the stranger – and to share the power and knowledge of their guests. However, and as we know, this hospitality was in most cases turned against the hosts (ibid., 132). The conquered local populations were seen either as inferior and fundamentally different from or as imperfect copies of Europeans, which justified the 'civilizing, emancipatory and developing' missions carried out as part of colonial domination.

Despite the present-day celebration of multiculturalism, the idea of helping the 'other' to follow the development of 'self' forms an uncomfortable part of the development aid discourses (Todorov 1984; Moraña et al. 2008; Dussel 2013, 32–40). This dimension became vivid in the United States' president Harry S. Truman's inaugural address in 1949, which is often named as the starting point for a new era of interventions and development, where Truman 're-discovered' the two billion poor, underdeveloped people in the Global South who needed to follow North America and Europe as models on their development path (Cornwall 2006, 69–70; Easterly 2006, 21; Escobar 2012, 3, 35–6; Alt 2016, 207–8).[5]

The discoverers, conquistadors and guests of the 16th century did not come empty-handed, but with Christianity, slavery, fatal diseases and territorial devastation, to name a few contributions. What is more, the hospitality of the hosts was ultimately abused as the guests stayed until the hosts were exhausted and exploited. This arrangement established a capitalist world order where the newly discovered areas became peripheries that supported the accumulation of wealth in the hegemonic centres of Europe. It is good to point out that the experience of colonialism in Latin America is very different from that of Africa and Asia. Mignolo and other Latin American post-development scholars use the concept of *colonial difference* to call attention to 'the differential time-space where a particular region becomes connected to the world-system of colonial domination' (Moraña et al. 2008, 8). For instance, Mabel Moraña, Enrique Dussel and Carlos A. Jáuregui (2008, 18) use the concept of *colonial difference* in order to emphasize the particularity of Latin American historical, political, social and cultural modes of articulation within the system of domination throughout the centuries. These authors emphasize that although the wave of independence of Latin American countries took place in the 19th century (which was earlier than on the other colonized continents), the wave by no means interrupted the colonial practices imposed by foreign powers: these practices only became different. For many of these scholars the analysis of decolonization and colonial difference seems more meaningful than focusing on scenarios that could be called 'postcolonial' (Ranta 2014, 57).

Just like in many other countries in the region, in Nicaragua the guests started to change after the country gained its independence from Spain in 1821. The United States arrived 'waving' the Monroe Doctrine, promulgated in 1823, which declared and justified the country's influence and control in Latin America and the Caribbean. The Doctrine included possible visits even with army uniforms and band wagons, if necessary. This was the beginning of the continuous tradition of 'Dollar Diplomacy', which included political involvement in other countries' internal affairs, conspicuous interventions and support for political uprisings (Mendieta 2008). The US's presence and control in Nicaragua was allowed by the fighting of two rival factions, the 'Conservatives' of Granada and the 'Liberals' of León (see Babb 2010, 57). Meanwhile, US companies like United Fruit secured great deals on land acquisitions, mining rights, export of bananas and even control of banking and tax collection in the country. To do all this they enacted agrarian reform laws that either pushed Indians and peasants off their land or reduced them to sharecroppers. In the 1850s and 1860s Lake Nicaragua and the San Juan River were important routes for the steamships of Cornelius Vanderbilt's

'American Atlantic and Pacific Ship Canal Company'. Since there were no railways through the USA, steamships were used to transport the treasures found during the Californian gold rush (Kinloch Tijerino 2008). The USA was also closely involved in planning an interoceanic canal route though Nicaraguan territory – a project that has been recently revived, and strongly resisted by many Nicaraguans (Meyer and Huete-Perez 2014; Hunt 2016).[6]

It was Augusto Sandino, the legend whose silhouette decorates the horizon of Managua, who in the late 1920s and early 1930s led the guerrilla war to drive out the US troops and influence from Nicaragua (Palmer 1988; Pakkasvirta 2005). However, Sandino's plan for a free Nicaragua, free elections, peace and agrarian cooperatives had to wait until the 1980s revolution, as he was killed by the Nicaraguan new dictator-to-be, Anastasio Somoza. The Somoza family ruled between 1937 and 1979 and were supported by the US's foreign policy, which favoured right-wing authoritarianism over struggles for social justice. In Nicaragua the Somozas became symbols of power and greed who concentrated development in primary cities while the rural areas and the Caribbean coast of the country remained impoverished. The family ended up owning the vast majority of the best land in Nicaragua, as well as most of the major domestic farms and factories, the airline, construction companies, warehouses, shipping lines and even the cemeteries in Managua. The demand for political change was met with military repression and the National Guard became a form of extortion business. What is more, in 1972 a massive earthquake killed approximately 10,000 people in the capital city of Managua and left 50,000 families homeless. As National Guardsmen looted businesses, Somoza controlled disaster aid, with his personal wealth growing to an estimated $400 million. Following the uprising of the people in 1979, Somoza fled Nicaragua, taking with him the capital reserves in the bank and leaving behind approximately 1.6 billion US dollars in debt (Kinloch Tijerino 2008, 294; Babb 2010).

The four decades of Somocista dictatorship ended with a revolution in 1979. The revolution allowed the revival of the desired 'map of Nicaragua' which Sandino had left behind him (Rivas Choza 2008, 53). Almost 25 per cent of the agrarian land, owned earlier by Somoza and his allies, was now re-distributed to Nicaraguans. However, in the 1980s, US-financed, -trained, -armed and -organized counter-revolutionaries, the *contras*, waged war against the left-wing Sandinista government of Nicaragua (Sklar 1988; Belli, 2002; Ramírez, 2011). Many people in the Western countries showed their sympathy towards Nicaragua by opposing the aggressive and interventionist US foreign policy. The solidarity movement created a form of travelling which can be seen as an antecedent of contemporary models of community-based tourism and volunteer tourism. Young and politically active people arrived to help with the coffee harvest, to build and paint schools and health centres and to live with local families (Mowforth et al. 2008, 68; Babb 2010, 52; McRoberts 2012). In addition to their voluntary work, these international supporters of the revolutionary Sandinista government – also called *Sandalistas* – were interested in visiting, for instance, the Solentiname and Ometepe islands more in the role of a tourist.[7]

According to cultural anthropologist Florence Babb (2010, 52), there are only a few published accounts of tourism in Nicaragua in the 1980s. Nevertheless, the existing writings seem to include contradictory notes about Nicaragua's political openness towards different kinds of guests (see Ramirez 1985; 2011). On one hand, Carter Hunt and Amanda Stronza (2014, 288; Hunt 2011) have suggested that at that time tourism was virtually non-existent in Nicaragua and the government held a hesitant stance towards tourism development. For example, one of their informants from the San Juan del Sur region had argued that 'There was a blockage against investors and they all went away. During the war the president threw them out and closed the door'. Simultaneously, on the other hand, sociologist Paul Hollander's (1986) analysis of 'political hospitality' directed critique towards the Nicaraguan revolutionary government, which was, in Hollander's view, warmly welcoming political tourists who would write 'reverential travelogues' about their experiences in the country. However, it has been agreed that after the electoral defeat of the Sandinistas in 1989, tourism development took a drastic turn: while the visits of voluntary workers diminished, the doors were opened to attract regional and international tourism investors with interest in more exclusive forms of travel (Hunt 2011).

It seems like the Western imaginaries of Nicaragua have been shaped primarily by representations of poverty, the Sandinista revolution, war, natural disasters, political scandals, corruption and aid-dependency. As the majority of the Nicaraguan population lives on less than 2 US dollars per day, the literature and articles tend to begin with the statement of how 'Nicaragua is the second poorest country in the Western Hemisphere after Haiti' (see, for instance, Höckert 2009; Babb 2010; Zapata et al. 2011; Hunt 2016). Hence, the tourism developers have been working hard to change these pervasive images of the country towards ones featuring safety and natural beauty (Babb 2010, 56–7). Depending on the government in power, the country has been sold with slogans such as 'Nicaragua, a country with heart', 'Nicaragua, unique, original', 'Country of lakes and volcanoes' or 'Country of well-being'. Hence, it is easy to understand that the *New York Times'* (2013, January 11) ranking of Nicaragua as the number three tourism destination in the world and the recent reports about the low levels of violence and crime in the country[8] have been received in Nicaraguan tourism circles as great news.

This has meant turning the image of the country from being a place people *escape from* to a place people wish to *escape to*. Besides tourism, international mobility on the Nicaraguan borders has mainly consisted of Nicaraguan migrant workers going to and coming back from Costa Rica. While it has been difficult to know how many people have left Nicaragua to work, the estimate places the figure at around 400,000–800,000 people.[9] Besides mobility of people, this has meant mobility of remittances that the Nicaraguans working in Costa Rica send back home to their families (see Gindling 2008). Nevertheless, while many people from Honduras,

El Salvador and Guatemala decide to look for better living opportunities in the United States, there are only relatively few Nicaraguans doing so. A recent article, titled 'Why Nicaraguan Kids Aren't Fleeing to U.S.', suggested that some of the reasons for this lay precisely in the safety and tranquillity of life in Nicaragua (Replogle 2014; see also PRONicaragua 2017). Nicaraguan tourism authorities have also proposed the growth of the tourism sector as one of the vital ways to prevent emigration from the country (INTUR 2009; 2016).

While some tourism practitioners have predicted Nicaragua's future as 'the Next Costa Rica' with wealth and touristic appeal, some, including Nicaraguan former tourism minister Mario Salinas, have averred that Nicaragua's greatest asset is actually the fact that it is *not* like Costa Rica. Regardless, it cannot be denied that the apparent success story of Costa Rica has affected Nicaraguan visions for the future; that is, as tourism has been growing rapidly in Central America, Nicaragua has been eager to jump onto that bandwagon with its 'big brothers' (Barrera 1998; Hunt 2011; 2016).[10] Since the 1990s, Nicaraguan right-wing governments have succeeded in making more airline companies land in Nicaragua, and in diversifying the demography of foreign visitors in the country. Compared to the 1980s when most of the foreigners were US soldiers, volunteer workers on coffee plantations and representatives from development aid organizations, today there are more than 1.5 million international tourists per year crossing Nicaragua's borders (INTUR 2016).

The most attractive planes have been those carrying investors, speculators interested in vacation and rental home development on the Pacific coastline, potential entrepreneurs, golfers, retired couples and other travellers (Matteucci et al. 2008; Babb 2010). In addition to searching for new possibilities to turn Central American indigenous and colonial history into tourist attractions, the growth in tourism has required a 'race to the bottom'. The foreign investors and tourism entrepreneurs have not been attracted only by the 'lakes and volcanoes', but also by extremely low costs of labour, very attractive tax incentives, privatization of the Pacific coastline and so on (Cañada and Merodio 2004; Bonilla and Mordt 2008). Ratifications of several free-trade agreements have enhanced the Nicaraguan invitations and encouraged international companies to enjoy the benefits of the free-trade zones.[11] In addition to the GATS agreement, which has extended the privatization, deregulation and reduction of trade barriers on goods into the trade in services such as tourism (see Scheyvens 2011; Joppe 2016), Nicaraguan governments have lubricated their open-door policies with several economic incentives for foreign tourism investments. Carter Hunt's (2016) research gives a great and clear picture about the last decade's process of ensuring that Nicaraguan hospitality towards investors becomes as warm and unconditional as possible. He writes,

> the *Ley de Incentivo para la Industria Turística* (Law 306) in 1999 and 2004's *Ley General de Turismo* (Law 495) offered developers and operators complete exoneration from importation, sales, materials, equipment,

vehicle and property taxes for both foreign and Nicaraguan individuals and businesses involved in tourism-related activities.

One of the main actors in this process has been the public-private organization called the Official Investment and Export Promotion Agency of Nicaragua (PRONicaragua), whose main task is to attract new investors to the country and host them. In February 2012, I organized an interview with the representatives of PRONicaragua in their office in Managua. When communicating with the PRONicaragua officials prior to and during the visit, I tried to make it very clear that I was a researcher conducting an academic study on rural tourism development in the country. However, in the actual meeting I was not allowed to ask the interview questions that I had planned; rather, the people I met wanted to focus on a high-quality PowerPoint presentation, which had obviously been prepared for potential investors. It appeared they were receiving me after all as a potential candidate who might become interested in starting my business in Nicaragua. They were proudly describing how in 1992 only five companies were operating in free-trade zones, but that the ratification of several free-trade agreements had made it possible that in 2005 the number was already over 100 companies. The PowerPoint[12] show, and the entire discourse of PRONicaragua, celebrated the beautiful nature, empty beaches, safety, and the Nicaraguans, who were not poor but happy. It seemed that in this context the possible demands for responsibility, equality, sustainability were perceived mainly as themes and conditions that could frighten away potential tourism investors – the guests who even the supposedly leftist Sandinista regime, back in power, hoped would feel at home (Hunt 2011; 2016). However, as the encounters between those with capital are filled with this cosy spirit of 'mi casa es su casa', the critiques of the current regime were openly questioning the possible 'unofficial' gifts that the investors were bringing to their welcomers (Equipo Nitlapan 2008a[13]).

When I left the office of PRONicaragua, I shared a taxi with two other passengers, both in their sixties. During the taxi ride they discussed with the driver about the ongoing demonstrations, where Nicaraguans were demanding that the government would pay them their retirement money as it had promised. After a while they interrupted their conversation to ask me why I had come to Nicaragua and whether I was enjoying my stay. When they heard the topic of my research, they all laughed heartily and commented on how they had never had an opportunity to travel as tourists. One of the passengers pointed out that given the current situation with the pensions, she would probably never be able to take part in tourism in her home country. I thought how I had only twenty minutes earlier watched a colourful PowerPoint performance with great statistics on Nicaraguan well-being and quality of life. While my co-travellers continued chatting about different places that they would like to visit in Nicaragua, I felt thankful for this kind of thought-provoking Nicaraguan taxi ride, which made me painfully aware of the socio-economic contradictions in the country. It was tangible that the impressive numbers in tourism statistics had not translated into reduction of poverty and unequal wealth distribution among the Nicaraguans (see Hunt 2011).

In Nicaragua, just like in many other countries, extensive criticism has been presented of GATS as an instrument which reflects and reinforces the existing unequal wealth distribution in the global economic system. In the context of tourism development, these 'trade restrictive obstacles' would be needed to guarantee that the host regions received benefits from tourism development. However, Nicaragua can be seen as a good example of a developing country which has been suffering from a 'growth fetish' when it comes to tourism industries. Along the same lines as Higgins-Desbiolles (2006, 1200; see also Hall 1994, 12–14; Hunt 2011), I have chosen to use the concept of *suffering*, as this neo-liberal fetish tends to distract the local governments from asking *why*, and *for whom*, tourism is being developed. Why is it considered so crucial to attract visitors into their homes? And *how* does tourism contribute to wider social, economic, political, ecological and cultural processes in the country? Although tourism's potential contribution to development and poverty reduction is the fundamental justification for Nicaraguan governments and aid agencies to encourage tourism growth, the benefits from tourism initiatives do not automatically spread equally around the country. Instead, the attempts to increase the welfare of some may negatively affect the welfare of others, which only exacerbates the existing inequalities between the rich and poor.

Yet, it is not only the free-trade agreements that prevent governments regulating tourism enterprises. One of the extreme examples of internal colonialism and contradictory forms of tourism development in Nicaragua has been a small mega-enclave project called Marina Puesta Del Sol, run by a millionaire US businessman born in Nicaragua and close friend of former Nicaraguan president Bolaños (Mowforth et al. 2008, 86–9).[14] The hotel, which on its webpage promises to 'indulge you with our top quality service and attention to detail in this secret paradise', has a marina, hotel complex, a driving range, a golf course, swimming pool, tennis courts, air strip, helipad, restaurants, shops, and other services and facilities for the guests. While the hotel provides spacious hydro-massage whirlpools for its guests, the residents living by the resort lack access to potable water (see also LaVanchy 2017). The land for building the resort was sold off under dubious circumstances, and the fishing cooperative that owned the land previously was left with only one narrow access point to the bay (Mowforth et al. 2008, 87). Marina Puesta del Sol is unfortunately a typical example of a Central American tourism development, where high expectations of employment opportunities and trickle-down effects from tourism have turned into disappointment (Hunt and Stronza 2011; Cañada 2013).[15] Martin Mowforth, Clive Charlton and Ian Munt (2008) have described the development of this enclave resort as a case where local people are left with few alternatives. Even the scenario presented by Barnett (2008, 34) 'When the tourists come, the fishermen learn to be waiters' sounds rather optimistic.

Allan Bolt described the case of Marina Puesta del Sol in the Nicaraguan newspaper *El Nuevo Diario* (quoted in Mowforth et al. 2008, 89) in this manner:

> Everybody (in the local community) welcomed the new tourism project enthusiastically because it meant work and prosperity for all. But it seems that this investor has his own vision of what he wants the countryside to look like and what type of people he wants to see there, for example he has closed the public right of way to the shore (which is unconstitutional, but which the authorities have allowed), he has prohibited his employees from making purchases in Garay's *pulperia* [mini-store], he has tried to throw them off the Island of Aserradores (despite their land titles), and he has been supported in this dirty game by all the powers of state ...

Although the people had felt positive towards the new development initiative at the outset, they had not been welcomed to participate in it; quite the contrary. As the locals were excluded from tourism development, they cancelled their previous welcome. I barely need to lean on Levinas (1969) or Derrida (1999, 15–16) to articulate the immorality of a situation where guests, by abusing the welcome of the local hosts, have occupied the space, and taken over the position of host. While the fishing community had not welcomed these tourism investors unconditionally, the playing-field where the rights and responsibilities of welcoming become negotiated is obviously very uneven.

Researchers and activists such as Ernest Cañada and Jordi Gascón (2007a; Cañada 2013) and Alejandro Bonilla and Matilde Mordt (2008; 2011) have sought to draw public attention in Nicaragua to the problems and myths of enclave and residential tourism.[16] Even though there also are more positive examples, these quotations seem to reflect experiences common in tourism development encounters along the Pacific coast-line:

> They take your land for a few devalued dollars and then you can no longer get to the shore or to the land that you sold because these people privatize everything, this is the entrepreneurial vision of the foreigners.
> (*Poblador* 2009 in Bonilla and Mordt 2011)

> There are more buildings. Before it used to be populated with fishermen's houses or tradesmen. Now there are buildings up to the hills. The people have sold their homes only to end up far away where there are no jobs ... they didn't know anything about it. If they had realized what it was all about, they would not have sold their land.
> (resident from rural San Juan del Sur in Hunt 2011, 272)

It is important to notice that most of this critique has not been directed towards daily tourism encounters as such, but towards those forms of tourism development that lead to social exclusion and inequality. Critics have turned attention to the contradiction that while some hotels on the Pacific beaches prepare their gourmet buffets for international visitors, food security remains one of the biggest challenges throughout Nicaragua (Knapman 2011; on food security, see Alt 2016, 156–62). Although it has been promised that tourism will bring trickle-down effects to local communities, the Pro-Poor Tourism discourse does not outwardly address the issues of inequality related to tourism. In fact, this proposition underlines the importance of economic growth in alleviating poverty, and accepts that this model of tourism development does *not* aim at promoting equality between different actors (Cañada and Gascón 2007b; Scheyvens 2011, 220).[17] Both Cañada and Gascón have repeatedly described contemporary forms of tourism development in Central America as forms of neo-colonialism and hence call for more radical efforts to disrupt and decolonize the interventions that take place in the tourism sector. Through different kinds of studies, they have called attention to the risks and challenges that many forms of tourism entail. In Nicaragua, as elsewhere, it has become clear that certain forms of tourism tend to lead to a wide range of negative impacts, such as sky-high land prices, land tenure conflicts, increased poverty, exploitation of cultural and natural resources, environmental bulldozing, sexual exploitation of children and adolescents, and criminality. Unfortunately, as tourism research with political economy (Schilcher 2007; Scheyvens 2011; Jänis 2011; Bianchi 2015) and political ecology (Gössling 2003; Mostafanezhad et al. 2015; Nepal et al. 2016) approaches keep indicating, the list is long.[18] Hence, tourism, at least as it appears today, is not different from other industries which operate in the globalized system. It tends to be equally exploitative of natural resources and human populations and is highly vulnerable to external forces and events, such as political upheaval, natural disasters, terrorist attacks and health scares (e.g. Hall 1994, 92–107).

While the development of enclave and residential tourism has in fact been speeded up during the Sandinista rule, there has simultaneously appeared a growing emphasis on the questions of sustainability, inclusion and more equal distribution of benefits from tourism (Cañada 2013; Hunt 2011; 2016). Representatives of NGOs and tourism researchers in particular have been demanding that the Nicaraguan government take a more active role in negotiating and making tourism development encounters fairer for the local communities. Instead of merely enabling the free growth of tourism industries in the country to continue, the Nicaraguan government has been regulating the sector, for instance, by establishing environmental conservation programmes and programmes for more accessible tourism and by aiming to prevent sexual exploitation of children in tourism destinations through cooperating with UNICEF (see Babb 2010, 52). In the context of the Nicaraguan tourism sector, it seems like the negative and unpredictable consequences of tourism development have compelled and encouraged tourism experts working in the public and third sectors to become more active in this space where the negotiations take place.

In the following section I focus on the combined efforts of INTUR, inter-national and national NGOs and development cooperation agencies to find new ways to spread the benefits from tourism especially to the rural areas of Nicaragua. Similarly to other countries of Central America, this has been done by including and welcoming community-based initiatives as well as micro and small tourism enterprises on the new tourism agendas ('San José Declaration of Rural Community-based Tourism', 28 October 2003; Cañada 2014).

3.2   All-inclusive models of rural tourism

In tourism discourses the concept 'all-inclusive' is normally used to refer to hotels that offer packages which enable the customers to stay in the hotel during the entire holiday as everything necessary is *included* in the package. Ironically the development of all-inclusive resorts has contributed to a phe-nomenon whereby the local communities actually become *excluded* from benefits and also from the areas where tourism takes place. Therefore, I have named this section 'all-inclusive models of rural tourism' in order to shift the focus from enclavic spaces (Edensor 1998, 45–53) and all-inclusive services in tourism to the previous intentions of including more people in tourism development. The ways in which the heightened focus on rural or peripheral areas, and on inclusion of previously excluded groups such as women, chil-dren, indigenous groups and Afro-descendants, could be interpreted as active efforts to make tourism more democratic and fair.

A tourism expert from INTUR, Bayola Pallais, summarized in 2012 that 'One of the current challenges in Nicaragua tourism is to design touristic destinations that allow the participation of various actors in each location'. While the current left-wing (at least by name and fame) Sandinista regime has been somewhat surprisingly embracing large tourism projects as a driver for development – and even bought hotels for the government's representatives themselves (Equipo Nitlapan – Envió 2008b, 3–13) – it has also subjected small entrepreneurs and rural areas to scrutiny, unlike before (PNDH 2008, 188; INTUR 2010a; 2017). It is clear that NGOs and international aid organizations have played an essential role in turning the focus of tourism developers to rural areas and finding new ways of distributing wealth through tourism development.[19] Most of all, the promotion of rural tourism has been driven by an interest in finding tourism development which would not lead to Nicaraguan farmers losing their land and becoming uninvited, or abused, guests in their own homes. The process of tourism development in Nicaragua supports the idea of alternative development theory and the participatory approach as the terrain of 'Third System' or citizen politics, which typically takes over following failed development efforts of government (first system) and economic power (second system) (Nerfin 1977 in Nederveen Pieterse 2001, 75; Burns 2004). According to tourism and development scholar David Telfer (2009, 152), the institutional vehicle for this approach 'lies in the realm of NGO's, charities and dissenting social movements', such as the environmental movement and the women's movement. Indeed, as Richards and Hall (2000, 303) argue, a stronger role for the third sector has been seen as a potential solution to promote participation and empowerment in tourism settings. It has been noticed at the global level that unless funds are targeted to assist in community tourism development projects, the potential for community development may be lost amid the pressures of the global economy (Telfer 2003, 160).

In the formal interviews and informal discussions with tourism experts working in Nicaragua, many pointed out that the new opportunities for rural communities could be seen as an outcome of the pressure from different development organizations. In addition to Ernest Cañada, many directed special attention to the role of Harold Ramos, the head of the Nicaraguan Network for Rural Community-based tourism called RENITURAL.[20] Since 2005 this organization has represented the growing number of community-based tourism initiatives across the country. In my interview with Ramos in February 2012, he emphasized the special attention paid by RENITURAL to reducing poverty 'so that tourism development would still have the characteristics of rural tourism'. He described the focus and the accomplishments of his organization as follows:

> RENITURAL succeeded in organizing a conference where INTUR, for the first time, recognized rural community-based tourism as a core activity in order to achieve the Millennium Development Goals and also the four goals in the National Plan for Human Development in Nicaragua (PNDH). The four fundamental principles of the PNDH are protection of nature, gender equality, creation of programmes that support local development, and educational. We claim that if the government cannot come all the way to the communities, with help from international cooperation we can.

According to Ramos, the main goal of RENITURAL has always been to make rural community tourism visible and include it in the Nicaraguan legislative framework. Representatives from INTUR invited Ramos to cooperate closely with other tourism experts and the regional tourism committees across the country in order to sketch the first official rural tourism strategy for the country. Finally, in 2010, INTUR published its first *National rural tourism strategy* (Estrategia de Turismo Rural). The strategy was then supported by a new law on rural tourism, *Ley de Turismo Rural Sostenible de la Republica de Nicaragua* (Law 835), in order to guarantee the needed attention to the growth and the well-being of this economic sector. Although Ramos deeply lamented that the preparation processes of the strategy and the law had not included direct encounters and co-planning with rural tourism entrepreneurs, he was still pleased to reach this important milestone.[21] While listening to Ramos, I became mesmerized by his commitment to make sure that the new rural tourism strategies included the values of *sustainability*, *equality* and *solidarity*.

In line with Ramos, tourism consultant Fransisco López[22] explained in a newspaper interview that for the ministry and its supporters the strategy represents a new kind of political initiative in Central America. Its novelty was seen, in López's view, in its aiming to promote alternatives to the free-market-driven development of tourism. Instead of focusing only on community-based tourism, the alternative forms of rural tourism – listed by INTUR (2009, 24–8) – included agrotourism, cultural tourism, ecotourism, adventure tourism, sport tourism, scientific tourism, educative tourism, tourism events, health tourism, gastronomic tourism, ethnic tourism and religious tourism. INTUR's project document for rural tourism development explains that as all of Nicaragua is essentially considered *rural*, there exists plenty of space for different kinds of rural tourism activities. The strategy for rural tourism highlights the need to expand tourism from the Pacific beaches to the volcanoes, coffee-cultivating highlands up north, lakes, and also to the Caribbean side of the country. Hence, the new tourism routes around the country, such as *Ruta del Café* and *Ruta Colonial*, had been established in order to make new kinds of actors – such as local organizations, communities, families, indigenous groups and handicraft associations – interested in joining tourism development in the country (Cañada et al. 2006, 7; INTUR 2011a, 112–26).

Along with the strategy documents and interviews with the people involved in creating them, rural tourism development was expected to diversify the incomes of rural families and to improve the quality of life locally. Rural tourism initiatives were thought be small in scale, to employ and benefit locals through the use of local resources and to promote gender equality. The products offered to visitors were hoped to value the local cultural traditions, history, tales and folklore and may also include activities such as horseback riding, hiking, walking and appreciating nature in general. Most importantly, rural tourism projects are seen to integrate the richness of domestic and rural life, with the tourism product becoming 'personalized' through *local hospitality*. In fact, one of the key factors in rural tourism development seemed to be rooted in the idea of Nicaraguan hospitality. That is, Nicaraguan tourism developers and tourism strategies emphasize the special character of Nicaraguan hospitality as one of the main attractions and resources in the future expansion of rural tourism. These discourses repeat and reconstruct the picture of Nicaraguans, of the entire nation, as a social, open and loving population among whom one finds a special 'culture of hospitality' (e.g. SNV 2007; INTUR 2011b, 62–72).

In my interview with tourism consultant Josue Flores, he pointed out the importance of the solidarity movement in the 1980s as an antecedent to contemporary tourism development:

> People know how to have contact with actors from outside. You can go to any community and people receive the visitors openly – not with

suspicion. The Nicaraguans are naturally good people, and the theme of amicability is very important in community-based tourism. People here are very wise and, for instance, old people are very knowledgeable as they have a lot of life experience. This is something that could also be called as farmers' knowledge, *sabiduria campesina*.

Like some of his colleagues, Flores argued that the Nicaraguan hospitality was something very particular in peripheral areas. He proposed that in the rural communities where people earlier did not have access to education 'people do not look at outsiders as strangers, or as threats, but as people who you can treat well and to whom you can offer something'. It seemed like the idea of Nicaraguan hospitality was connected, on one hand to the idea of what hospitality scholar Elizabeth Telfer (2000) calls 'moral virtue and source of pride', and on the other to the somewhat patronizing perceptions of special innocence of people who do not have frequent contacts with outsiders (Pratt 1986; 1992; Länsman 2004).

Although the new rural tourism strategies highlighted the special nature of Nicaraguan hospitality, they also indicate the challenges that the rural tourism projects can have. Those working with the planning and implementation of tourism projects saw that their primary role was to help small rural enterprises to develop their capacities and create much-needed new contacts (INTUR 2009). Consultant Flores had been one of the experts actively involved in defining and developing the rural tourism strategy with the Nicaraguan government and donor organizations. During that time he was working at the Swiss development agency COSUDE with a development programme that included a tourism component. Flores emphasized the importance of the efforts that they had been making: first in creating a system of quality assurance for rural enterprises and second in enabling small tourism enterprises to register themselves. Flores explained the benefits of their project in this fashion:

> Another achievement of this project is the creation of registration in order to legalize the rural tourism enterprises. This kind of system was lacking earlier. ... This project is focused on strengthening the regulatory framework, in order to improve quality and to help rural tourism initiatives to become rural tourism enterprises. The aim here is that they will be able to develop themselves into rural enterprises.

Flores pointed out that the support to new enterprises did not only mean registration, but also creation of business plans and maintaining facilities. However, he considered the possibility for registration very important as it enables the tourism initiatives to take out loans to develop their business.[23] According to his estimation approximately 70 per cent of the country's micro and small enterprises were informal. The president of RENITURAL, Ramos, also cited the access to finance as one of the main challenges in rural tourism, but estimated that the number of informal enterprises could be as high as 90 per cent. Ramos pointed out that in addition to the issue of financing, non-registered enterprises faced difficulties in selling their services to official tour operators.

During my second fieldwork in 2012, a representative of the Nicaraguan tourism ministry INTUR welcomed me to their 'roundtable for sustainable tourism development' – in the role of an observer. The purpose of these roundtable meetings was to enhance dialogue between public servants and consultants from the ministry, functionaries of international development agencies and representatives of the private sector. In addition to the lack of official status and access to finance, the members of the 'space for dialogue' in INTUR determined that the small rural tourism initiatives often lacked the necessary knowledge and skills, promotion, entrepreneurial vision, management leadership and so on.[24] When I was observing the discussions in the 'space for dialogue' in INTUR, my perception was that despite the numerous lacks and challenges, tourism as such was always perceived as something good. To put it differently, the space for dialogue did not seem to be the right space to question tourism development as such. In short, to make the farmers and rural communities realize the great potential of tourism, the experts perceived their role as agents offering financial and social encouragement and motivation, and helping the farmers and rural communities create entrepreneurial visions.

Perceptions of rural hospitality

It is not a surprise that the marketing of Nicaragua to tourists includes many promises of 'exceptional hospitality'. A traveller who plans a trip to Nicaragua can read how:

> In our country you can find hundreds of species of flora and fauna which makes Nicaragua a natural paradise ideal for rural tourism and community-based tourism. Add to this the colonial towns, archaeological treasures, folkloric richness and most of all the warm and hospitable people ... what characterizes the 'NICAS' is their innate hospitality and friendliness.
>
> (EduTourism 2009, 3)

In my interview with tourism expert Pallais at INTUR, she also described Nicaraguan hospitality as something unique. She presented their new tourism marketing plan that built on the idea of well-being: or as the slogan goes 'Well-being of a person, harmony with eternity' (*Bienestar de la persona, armonia con el entorno*) (INTUR 2011b, 137–44). Pallais explained that visitors can enhance their well-being by combining different features that Nicaragua can offer: its nature, natural thermal waters, calmness, tranquillity, security, local friendliness, hospitable treatment of the visitors, gastronomy, handcrafts and folklore. Pallais had played a central role in the creation of the national plan 'Sustainable Tourism Development in Nicaragua' (INTUR 2011a, 51), which highlights the Nicaraguans' open attitudes towards tourism and tourists:

> The local population is, obviously, one of the components of the destination – an attraction and a productive factor. As an attraction, the essential element is hospitality, which means that the local population shows their friendliness towards tourists and visitors. This includes the quality of the local populations' reception, the eagerness of the residents to facilitate information to tourists and their attitude towards the tourism industry.

As I brought up in connection with the traditional dance of El Güegüense, the colonial encounters are smoothly brought together with contemporary tourism development; that is, it is not perceived contradictory that the 'hospitable population', 'colonial past' and 'unique history' (including the revolution and war) are used side by side to welcome visitors and investors to the country.[25] Instead, tourism experts and marketers presented Nicaraguans as always happy to receive all potential visitors in their homes. This has led to a situation, which I will deal with in more detail later, where scepticism or resistance towards tourism development has become trivialized. What is more, promising hospitality and an open welcome *on behalf of someone* can be quite ambiguous.

While I was collecting data for this study, I found these representations of Nicaraguan open hospitality curious in the light of the political situation, where the Nicaraguan government was throwing international donors out of the country. It seemed like such an open invitation existed mainly outside the political spheres of welcoming – or that the Nicaraguan politicians felt that their 'innate and natural' hospitableness had been abused by foreign aid agencies, amongst others. As a result of international actors' open critique of the Sandinista government's ways of centralizing power, President Ortega considered it timely to remind the country's guests who were the ones actually hosting, and ruling, the party in Nicaragua. Although I cannot take the discussion here to the rich debates in development studies on the conditionality of aid (Sachs 1992), it merits mentioning that Ortega's actions can be seen as rather noteworthy in the history of development aid. This behaviour showed that the hosts had stopped caring about the conditions and rules for participating, which for a long time were shaped and defined by the guests. With tears in their eyes, after three decades of 'cooperation and friendship', many of these guests began to realize how they were no longer welcome – that they were no longer feeling the Nicaraguan hospitality. Or, more precisely, the political welcome was then directed towards another club of friends, including especially the member countries of ALBA in Latin America.

Moreover, although tourism is traditionally developed for and sold to the foreign visitors, the current Sandinista government has also used tourism as a political tool to promote nationalism inside the country.[26] Indeed, rural tourism, domestic tourism and social tourism have been treated almost as the star products of the ruling government and the two biggest national newspapers, *El Nuevo Diario* and *La Prensa*, regularly publish news about the triumphs and promises of more accessible forms of tourism (Medina Chavarria 2017).[27]

Returning now to the rural tourism development encounters, it is uncertain who were actually welcomed to the rural tourism programmes, and in which ways this welcoming took place. That is, based on my analysis I argue that the possibilities of participating in tourism were experienced in various ways. Despite the government's emphasis on 'citizen participation', many experienced that the right to participate was reserved to those who supported the Sandinista regime. In general, the strong air-conditioning in the offices of Managua seemed to have a cooling effect on the otherwise so warm Nicaraguan hospitality. This became clear, for instance, in my communication with rural tourism consultant Nora Hernandez in May 2013. From the very beginning of our discussion, she expressed her frustration towards the lack of transparency and cooperation between different rural tourism actors working in the country. Her recent experiences came from working in the evaluation of a pilot project called Fincas Agroturisticas (Agrotouristic Farms) (see INTUR 2012a). The project was run by INTUR, it received financial and technical support from the Swiss development cooperation agency COSUDE, and included many counterparts amongst Nicaraguan organizations working with rural development. However, during the evaluation process Hernandez had found that none of these organizations were interested in talking to her. In a highly politicized and polarized atmosphere there can be many different reasons for this kind of behaviour. In our interview, Hernandez claimed that the representatives of these organizations had avoided talking to her because the actual implementation of this particular rural tourism project had been so difficult.

Although the evaluation of the pilot project had been rather challenging, Hernandez thought that she and her colleagues were finally able to form a general picture about the project. She explained that the tourism experts who worked in the programme had been looking for potential farms and communities around the countryside, and invited them to participate in the initiative. Hernandez criticized especially the ways in which the tourism experts had exaggerated the potentialities of rural tourism and recommended people to take out micro-credits to finance their tourism initiatives. She pointed out that, in her view, the idea of tourism development should not be 'sold' like this to anyone. In the evaluation report she and her colleagues argued that a more viable option would be to let the farmers and the representatives of rural communities approach INTUR and its associates by themselves. I agree that recommending loans for tourism is highly questionable especially when interest rates are sky high and many rural tourism projects and businesses are struggling to stay alive.

After my discussion with Hernandez I contacted the officials of COSUDE and INTUR and asked about the possibilities of seeing this evaluation document. However, I received a polite refusal – they were not interested in discussing their experiences or sharing the evaluation report with me. In fact, I was told that the tourism consultants had already left the organizations when the pilot programme ended. It would have been interesting to hear whether they agreed with Hernandez's estimation that fewer than half of the initiatives that had received money from this particular project were actually working with tourism. According to Hernandez, the money from this project had been used for something other than developing conditions and services for tourism. She argued that instead of having real intentions to welcome tourists to their homes and communities, many had taken part in the project in the hope of receiving a grant or a loan.

In my study, Hernandez was amongst the few interviewees who openly questioned the meaningfulness of developing tourism everywhere in the country. She pointed out that in the cases where 'the roads are bad, there are no real tourism attractions and the locals are not really interested in developing tourism; there should not be tourism'. In her view, it was mean-ingless to develop tourism if the locals were not interested or capable of doing that. Well, similarly to Hernandez, her colleague Flores also found it problematic that tourism projects had been set up with no real intention of turning them into functioning entities. Flores argued that in rural tourism projects that are started by international development agencies there is a ser-ious problem of paternalism:

> In many places you can find a building for 'tourist information' financed by this and that project. But they are no longer working after the project has ended. These kinds of things are one of the main challenges in rural tourism.

Flores claimed that in many cases the local actors did not feel that tourism development was their own project. In development jargon this is often described as 'lack of ownership' among the local actors. According to Flores, a better way to proceed would be to implement projects where the local communities were also actively participating in tourism development. His comment underlined one of the paradoxes in the idea of participatory development; that is, the most active actors in community participation might actually be those who come from the outside keen to help the locals to partici-pate in initiatives that have been already planned for them (e.g. Butcher 2012; Sammels 2014; Wearing and Wearing 2014).

While few tourism consultants were highly critical towards the existing 'paternalism of partnership' in these projects, as Eriksson-Baaz (2005) puts it, many blamed local actors for their lack of capabilities and interest in joining the 'joyride' of tourism development. In an interview with Zenayda Delgado, director of a chamber organization for small tourism enterprises in

Nicaragua, CANATUR, she expressed her disappointment with Nicaraguans who did not have 'the right attitude or aptitude for tourism development'. She explained that people were not taking advantage of the help that her organization was offering. Another tourism expert, representing the US development aid organization USAID, clarified to me in a more informal discussion that most of the people in rural areas were lacking the 'right spark for developing tourism and being an entrepreneur'. Thus, despite the strong trust in Nicaraguan hospitality, and even stronger trust in the promises of tourism, one of the underestimated challenges appeared to be that the locals were not interested in participating in 'rural tourism'. While there must be communities that perceive tourism and tourists as a real blessing, this is not something that should be taken for granted (Sammels 2014; Wearing and Wearing 2014). Despite the principle of what Jarkko Saarinen (2006) has called the 'social construction of sustainable tourism development', the goals and means for tourism and well-being come from the outside.

In sum, as suggested in section 1.2, in tourism literature and in Nicaraguan tourism discussions alike, the challenges of local participation are often presented in terms of the limitations and difficulties that the local people have. This challenge has been explained in tourism literature by referring, for instance, to the 'cultural remoteness of host communities to tourism-related businesses in developing countries' (Tosun 2000, 630; see also Aref 2011). Some have taken their ethno- and Eurocentrism as far as to state that '[t]ourism is difficult to grasp for the people in developing countries' (Strasdas, Corcoran and Petermann 2007, 154). In the light of experiences from Nicaragua, it seems possible that people living in economically marginalized rural areas in fact do face difficulties in understanding not only *how*, but also *why* outsiders want them to engage in the growth of the tourism sector. However, if the guiding principle of rural tourism is to promote local participation, could it be considered contradictory to interpret local resistance as a lack of knowledge and understanding? That is, has it been acknowledged and considered that some might resist tourism initiatives as a conscious choice?

This observation corresponds with Spivak's (1988, 280) thought of silencing the 'other'. Although tourism experts from tourism organizations or donor agencies wish to help rural communities, their planned agendas and special knowledge about the tourism sector hinder them from reflecting on different reasons *why* the projects do not have outcomes that they wish for. In my view, these kinds of situations indicate the inadequacy of the notion of 'local knowledge', or the responsibility of 'listening to the local knowledges' (Nygren 1999). Even where an expert arrives with an interest in listening to the 'other', the experts' ability to hear might be limited to tourism as she or he knows it. In other words, an expert who arrives to implement a tourism project might trivialize the voices that would jeopardize the entire planned project. Nevertheless, it was curiously only after thinking and travelling with Levinas (1969; 1998) when I realised that this form of helping reflects an intention to act as a responsible individual, instead of approaching the encounters in a relational way.

After considering tourism experts' understandings of the nature of tourism development encounters, it is time to adopt and examine the perspective of the local communities. In the following section I move the focus from the air-conditioned offices in Managua towards rural settings where tourism has been developed. For the sake of the narrative, I take the bus, again to San Ramón – one of the pioneer sites of rural tourism development in Nicaragua.[28] San Ramón's tourism initiative is formed of four coffee-cultivating communities which receive guests, and of a cooperative union which organizes and manages tourism development. There are also other kinds of tourism initiatives in the same area. Many tourism developers from Managua have visited San Ramón at some point; and if not, they have at least heard about the destination. Yet, it is worth pointing out that many tourism experts are peculiarly reluctant to stay in rural tourism communities. Rather, their evaluation visits tend to be as short and effective as possible. Although the idea of the hospitality of the Nicaraguan people paints a welcoming picture of the nice rural people who always have their doors open to visitors, those who have worked with the communities of San Ramón would most probably *not* describe them as an archetype of unconditional hospitality.

3.3 Cautious words of welcome in rural communities

El único pensamiento original del hombre Nicaraguense es el pensamiento mitico, lo cual puede explicar la pródiga cosecha de imaginación entre nosotros.

The only original thought of the Nicaraguan man is the myth-ical thought, which can explain the abundant harvest of imagination between us.

Eduardo Zepeda Enríques in Rivas Choza (2008, 8)

With these words, author and musician Edgard Rivas Choza describes the shared history of people living in the skirts of the mountains in San Ramón. I interpret it simultaneously as a critique of the many influences and thoughts that have come from the outside, and as a celebration of a special way of life and togetherness in the region. In his book *San Ramón, Indigenous and Fertile*, Rivas Choza (2008) writes about the oppressed, humble, intelli-gent, hardworking, confrontational and strong people living in these moun-tainous villages. Here, in the highlands of Matagalpa in the northern part of the country, still live a small number of indigenous communities, but whose native languages are long since dead (Plunkett 2007, 73). For Rivas Choza the history of San Ramón, and especially of the indigenous *Abai*, is a story of exploitation by foreign conquistadors who came and violated indigenous and human rights. The author describes how a variety of guests have visited the farming town of San Ramón since it was established in 1800. As discussed in section 3.1, these guests have mainly come for coffee, gold and development interventions – and now recently – also for tourism. According to Rivaz Choza (2008, 21), many people in San Ramón feel that the exploitation has not yet ended, which makes it essential to keep alive the same spirit of fighting, dignity and love for the land that their ancestors had.

There have been, amongst others, colonizers, North Americans, those who took the land for coffee cultivation, those who emptied the gold mines and those from former dictator Somoza's National Guard. Rivas Choza (2008, 7) argues that those two valuable resources, coffee and gold, have 'ironically distorted the lifestyle of the people and made them slaves, sick and beggars'. After gold was found in San Ramón in the 1820s, gold mining reached its peak in the 1940s by a company owned by English and North Americans, and ended then as unprofitable in the beginning of the 1950s.[29] Today gold mining belongs to the past, and coffee – red, new gold – has become the real pride of San Ramón.

In San Ramón, the very first coffee plants were cultivated in 1852, and by the beginning of the 1900s large parts of the land were occupied for coffee cultivation. The coffee haciendas, owned by people with 'foreign names', offered low-paid work for the locals and hence formed an important part of economic life in San Ramón (Rivas Choza 2008, 40–1). However, local historian Rivas Choza (2008, 49) has reported that while the coffee plantations created economic wealth, the owners of the plantations 'forgot' to share these benefits and to improve the basic services of their workers. Sharing the benefits would have been an intelligent investment, Rivas Choza argues, to ensure that the workers would have had dignified living conditions, education and health. When reading the history of San Ramón and literature on coffee tourism, I have noticed that there occur only implicit acknowledgements of the ways in which the *history* of coffee cultivation has been based on the violation and abuse of the local farmers' hospitality. However, some authors have quite recently drawn attention to the growing interest among tourists in the *present* situation of disadvantaged coffee farmers (Jollife 2010, 14; Goodwin and Boekhold 2010; Harvey and Kelsay 2010).

The Sandinista revolution in 1979 meant significant changes also in San Ramón: during the following years, local communities took back the lands and replaced the haciendas with cooperatives. Like the war in the 1980s, the occupation of lands is a sensitive topic that the locals discuss only with caution. Although the experiences of the violent encounters from the war can be read from detailed descriptions by Nicaraguan artists and authors (Belli 2002; Ramírez 2011), the reoccupation of land is a less-discussed theme in general. While I want to respect people's decisions to remain silent, I find it acceptable to make a reference to a study on the history of San Ramón, one written by a local tourist guide. In the study he expresses his lingering fear that the family who owned the coffee lands before the revolution will someday return to San Ramón and try to claim the lands. The author of the study describes the current sentiments in his home community as follows:

The cooperative feels that it would be impossible for the former owners to take back the property, because every year that passes by the cooperative becomes more legalized, the families keep growing, and the people gain more rights to possess the land.

The local land has changed owners under dubious circumstances, which many of the locals would understandably like to forget. However, it is apparent that the possible return of these 'guests' continues to haunt the imaginations of the local farmers.

As I mentioned on the first pages of the book, the story of tourism development in San Ramón also goes back to the 1980s when the international solidarity movement began to bring the first international travellers to the area. These visitors were interested in helping with coffee cultivation and learning about the formation of coffee cooperatives, and they stopped coming when the glory of the Sandinista revolution began to fade. However, in San Ramón the cooperative movement was kept alive and the Union of Cooperatives, UCA San Ramón, was founded in 1992. Ever since, this union has played a significant role in the local production of coffee and, for instance, vegetables and basic grains.[30]

During the past thirty years or so, the life of the local communities has been anything but stable. Soon after Hurricane Mitch, an even bigger catastrophe arrived in the area in the form of the global coffee crisis. Between 1998 and 2001 coffee producers were selling their coffee at a price that was barely sufficient to cover the production costs. Many farmers in San Ramón were forced to reduce their farming, or to even abandon their coffee production altogether, and seasonal plantation workers headed towards Costa Rica (Vakis, Kruger and Mason 2004; Valkila and Nygren 2009). In this situation, in the middle of the Fair Trade Coffee certification process, there emerged the idea for more organized tourism development. The Central of Coffee Cooperatives in the North (CECOCAFEN) had suggested the idea to the local cooperative union, UCA San Ramón, and likewise to an international NGO working in the area with social projects. In addition to providing supplementary income from tourism, it was hoped that the new initiative would promote gender equality by bringing new opportunities especially for women and young people (UCA San Ramón 2008). Tourism was perceived as one of the few possibilities to decrease emigration from the area. First two communities, *El Roblar* and *La Corona*, and then two others, *La Pita* and *La Reyna*, were elected to participate in tourism development. The size of the population in these four communities varies from one hundred to two thousand. The closest community, La Reyna, is located only a few kilometres from the town of San Ramón. The bus ride to the furthest community, El Roblar, takes around one and a half hours. A couple of years later, these four communities were connected to the wider *Ruta del Café* touristic route programme, financed and coordinated by LuxDevelopment and INTUR. The route runs through the entire northern highlands coffee region.

In 2003, when the representatives of these two coffee cooperative unions introduced the idea of tourism development to local communities, people's reactions had varied greatly. In my first interviews in 2008, many interviewees brought up how sceptical and cautious they had been about this proposal. Taking into account the history of these communities helps to understand the variety of reactions. Doña Hilda, who had accommodated visitors during the solidarity movement in the 80s, had been among the most optimistic ones. She said in our interview:

> We thought that tourism could help us a lot. We wanted most of all to include the young people and the adults and families. We wanted to develop the community and to bring in extra income as economic help was needed.

In general, the people who had previous, positive experiences of receiving foreign guests received the idea for tourism development with more open arms than those who did not have such prior experiences. People told me that they had been doubtful about the real potential or advantages in the tourism project and found it unlikely that any tourists would be keen to learn about the local ways of living and cultivating coffee. Some of my interviewees explained how they had imagined that tourism would exist only by the beaches on the Pacific coast. But most of all, many were frightened by the idea of inviting strangers to their homes. In analysing and interpreting my interviewees' narratives, I noticed that the resistance towards the idea of tourism development appeared to be a combination of two elements. The first was the fear of welcoming unknown people and ideas to one's home, and the second had to do with the confidence in one's possibilities to be able to welcome and please guests.

This appears as something that Derrida (1999, 18–21; Derrida and Rottenberg 2002, 2, 14) could call negotiations of hospitality and responsibility – or calculations of the risks of saying welcome. While many tourism scholars and practitioners perceive small-scale, locally based tourism development as a responsible and sustainable alternative for developing tourism, this perception might trivialize the possible risks that exist in this kind of tourism. Although these risks might not include heightened levels of criminality or pollution, it does not mean that the locals would feel engagement in the so-called community-based tourism projects as risk-free. The risks can be, as I will explain in what follows, destructive dependency on external tourism practitioners or conflicts within the communities or families (e.g. Pleumarom 2012; Trousdale 2001, 251; Zapata et al. 2011; Salazar 2012a; Cañada 2014, 11; Nunkoo and Gursoy 2016). Generally speaking, the possibility of choosing *not* to participate in tourism does not seem that popular in the academic debates on local participation in tourism.[31] Or as Butcher (2012, 104) puts it: it is normally already decided that there will be tourism, which only allows people to decide whether or not to participate in tourism development.

Dianne Dredge and Rob Hales (2012) have likewise argued that participatory strategies in general tend to ignore the heterogeneity of local populations. Different reactions towards the tourism proposal in San Ramón correspond to the well acknowledged fact that rural communities are rarely homogeneous places where the actors share identical interests or values. Moreover, tourism might not be as interesting and appealing as we tourism researchers, teachers and practitioners tend to assume. In an interview with a Finnish tourism consultant, Mirka Sarajärvi, who worked in Nicaragua, she pointed out the absurdity of expecting that suddenly an entire village of people would start to work with a new initiative such as tourism. As a thinking exercise, she encouraged me to try to imagine that this would happen in a small rural town in Finland. While it surely was difficult to think about this happening, it brought to my mind Hakkarainen's (2009; 2017) longitudinal research on community and tourism development in a peripheral village in Finnish Lapland, where she analysed the real-life fragmentations and variations of interests among the local hosts.

In order to kick-start tourism in San Ramón, local families were offered the possibility of visiting other community-based tourism initiatives in the northern area of Nicaragua. The local hosts described in our discussions how the visits had helped them to realize what they could offer to the tourists, and even more that they did not want to lose the opportunity to work with tourism. Ultimately, five to eight families from every community decided to commit themselves to the new tourism programme. Each community also selected two or three young guides to represent them.

Many of the interlocutors experienced the beginning of the tourism project as a rather bumpy, scary and exciting road. Although tourism scholars often claim that the host-guest relationships in tourism settings tend to lack spontaneity and serendipity (Wall and Mathieson 2006, 224; Grit 2014), according to the participants in San Ramón this was certainly not the case. I listened to several stories of how excited and nervous the local families and guides were when the first 'official' tourists arrived. In addition to excitement, the narratives were also filled with expressions of awkwardness and embarrassment. Many mentioned that at that time there were no separate rooms or beds for tourists and some of the families had shared their own bedrooms with the guests. It sounded like the primary challenge had been the unexpected intimacy with the guests for which the local hosts had not been able to prepare themselves.[32]

Even though many hosts remembered the first tourist arrivals as rather challenging situations, most of my interviewees emphasized that when some time had passed, they learned to enjoy the visits. The San Ramoneans sounded grateful that the cooperative unions and NGOs had invited them to different kinds of training and capacity-building sessions during the first phases of the tourism initiative. It seemed like the experts had offered training and courses which had helped the local hosts to gain more confidence in their skills and possibilities of being 'good hosts'. This was particularly heartening to doña Hilda, who told me that after her first child was born almost twenty years ago, she had lost her right to be a member in the local cooperative:

Earlier I could not be part of almost anything. But when the coffee price went down my husband came and asked if I would like to start to work as a lodger for the tourists. I said 'Yes'! It meant that I was able to go to official meetings and workshops and training sessions with the other women. Before that I had never been able to do so. I have also been able to visit other communities when there have been these workshops.

Yet, becoming a tourism entrepreneur was not the only challenge for the hosts. The new tourism programme had caused internal conflicts within local communities, likewise within the host families. As men have traditionally represented the families in the rural areas of Nicaragua, some of the husbands did not want their partners to participate in encounters or training that took place outside of their home community.[33] A few women voluntarily decided to stay at home in order to avoid conflicts. However, in 2008 one of the young guides gave tourism development encounters a positive meaning for this specific reason:

Now the young men already know and understand that the women can go to places even by themselves. Tourism has changed things here as the Nicaraguans have seen that our culture could be different.

The guide noted that young men in particular had changed their attitudes in favour of more equal relations between men and women. This perception was later confirmed by three local experts working with issues of gender equality at the UCA San Ramón. They agreed that after women began to participate in development projects and meetings, power relations had started to change inside many families. In my interaction with the local women, I also heard these kinds of stories more than once:

At least what happened in our family in the beginning was that the loan was in my name, but my husband took the money that I received from the tourists. Then we discussed in the workshops that we do not have to give the money to the men, but it is actually for our children and for us. This has been a problem for us. ... We have been fighting and now the situation has improved. Today I can keep the money.

Several women brought up how their husbands had earlier been in charge of the economic and other matters that affected the lives of their families. However, the women found that the membership in the tourism project, and availability of micro-loans for tourism development, brought women more alternatives, flexibility and mobility.[34] The increased social and economic mobility, which especially tourism scholars Stroma Cole (2006) and Regina Scheyvens (1999, 2002) interpret as a central part of empowerment, had helped the women to gain confidence about their possibilities and rights to interrupt abusive relations. In order not to fall into a trap of romanticizing the change, it merits mentioning that the change had meant serious and series of power struggles within the families. Besides the conflicts inside the families, tourism caused clashes inside the 'host' communities. There had been disputes regarding the unequal opportunities to participate in tourism development, to use local resources, to access the community's pool or to use the walking trails. As Murray C. Simpson (2008) stresses, tourism can create serious conflicts and jealousies at the local level when different people and interest groups disagree with each other about the control of local resources and the fair distribution of benefits from tourism. These kinds of conflicts caused by tourism activities can make it more difficult for the community members to cooperate with each other in the future (see Quesada 2014).

While the number of tourists kept growing during the first five years of tourism development, in 2008 the tourists were suddenly no longer coming. Most of my interviewees suspected that the sudden decline of travellers was a consequence of bad coordination and tourism marketing at the UCA San Ramón. The situation made the local hosts worried (as I will discuss in more detail in Chapter 4): they did not know how to pay back the tourism loans if there were no paying tourists. The passive waiting for tourists made them painfully aware of their own incapability of being in charge of the local tourism development; that is, it was not them – the 'hosts' – who were actively welcoming visitors. In this situation the local tourism entrepreneurs felt themselves uncomfortably dependent on the local coordinators, who, what is more, seemed to favour only one of the tourism communities in the area.

Especially people from other, smaller communities were disappointed with the coordinators who were supposed to represent them and to work for their best interests. Since 2008 the situation has remained nearly the same. During my last field visit to San Ramón, in 2013, many people told how they had nearly lost all their interest and motivation to wait for the tourists. When I interviewed one of the local guides, Gabriela, she claimed that the coordinators were merely focused on welcoming grants and development projects, instead of paying tourists and tour operators. According to her, this was one of the fundamental problems that they had. The fact that in 2013 the same tourism coordinators had started at least one completely new tourism project in the region supported the guide's claim.

During the course of my study, many of the San Ramonean hosts became rather discouraged about continuing with tourism. At the same time, the local tourism coordinators seemed to feel intimidated and irritated by the growing critique directed at them, and were consequently avoiding direct encounters with the hosts. In Levinasian (1969, 39) terms, as discussed in section 2.3, it could be said that they had begun to avoid proximity and 'the faces' of the people that they were supposed to be responsible for. That is, engaging in a face-to-face encounter would have required a different kind of responsibility on the coordinators' part. The role of local tourism coordinators in San Ramón can be used as the most palpable example of tourism actors who are not clearly hosts *or* guests: the young guides and local tourism entrepreneurs were perceiving the coordinators as guests who were not interested in paying a visit. However, as I will discuss in more detail in Chapter 4, there had previously been coordinators who had taken a more active role of host and leader in tourism activities (on local leadership, see Kontogeorgopoulos et al. 2014).

3.4   The risks of welcoming

The purpose of this chapter has been to demonstrate that while Nicaraguan tourism strategies and marketing brochures celebrate the special sincerity and openness of local hospitality, these narratives are problematic in the light of previous colonial and neo-colonial interventions that have taken place in the country. According to Derrida (1999, 70):

> Unconditional hospitality implies that you don't ask the other, the newcomer, the guest to give anything back, or even to identify himself or herself. Even if the other deprives you of your mastery of your home, you have to accept this. It is terrible to accept this, but that is the condition of unconditional hospitality: that you give up the mastery of your space, your home, your nation. It is unbearable. If, however, there is pure hospitality, it should be pushed to this extreme.

In this chapter I have considered to what extent previous and current hosts and guests have pushed Nicaraguan hospitality to this extreme. By starting from the guests who arrived long before the actual tourists, I first moved towards the neoliberal practices of welcoming tourism investors, and again towards more regulated forms of welcoming guests. By doing so, I have sought to propose – drawing always on Derrida's 'double law of hospitality' – that hospitality at communal coffee tables is rarely pure or unconditional but include negotiation about the risks and responsibilities of welcoming.

Importantly, approaching tourism development as a relational phenomenon means striving to explore ways by which it affects and is affected by various entities, ideas and experiences (Jóhannesson, Ren and Van der Duim 2015, 3). Celebrating the ease of tourism development, along with the unconditional hospitality conventionally ascribed to rural areas and Global South in general, means overlooking or silencing the historical, political and social entanglements and experiences of the hosts (see also Alt 2016). Nevertheless, tourism development is not only based on and shaped by the narratives of welcoming nation, but it also affects the host-guest relations beyond tourism settings. In his recent, fascinating research on political ecology and tourism in Nicaragua, anthropologist Carter Hunt (2016) draws connections between the open-door policies of tourism and the current inter-oceanic canal project across Nicaraguan territory. Hunt describes how *tourism* has transformed the government's development discourse by displacing the previous anti-imperialistic discourse that condemned foreign involvement. This means that tourism has become discursively linked to both foreign investments and the country's economic, social and environmental well-being and, as a result, 'facilitated the hegemony necessary to move forward with HKND's (Hong Kong Nicaragua Canal Development Investment Company) canal' (Hunt 2016, 164; see also Hunt 2011; Cañada 2013). Furthermore, the canal plans include drafts for several tourism resorts along the path of the canal, from the port in Monkey Point on the Atlantic Coast to the beaches on the Pacific shore, and will most likely lead to dramatic growth in the cruise tourism industry in Nicaragua. While there is a scientific consensus that the social and environmental consequences of the canal will be disastrous, the scientists' and local residents' objections have been silenced or dismissed as anti-nationalists and as something that stands in the way of the Nicaraguan progress (Watts 2015; Meyer and Huete-Perez 2014 in Hunt 2016).

Although for Levinas politics do not supplement ethics, politics and ethics both draw on the same source: the responsible subject. Thus, while Levinas's work represents the mobility between ethics and politics as a highly challenging feature, it is obvious that the question of politics and the political cannot be separated from the question of responsibility towards the other and, in fact, all others. Perhaps the idea of a democratically chosen government comprises the very essence of what Levinas calls being 'for-the-Other-subject' (Drabinski 2011, 166–7). According to his suggestion, ethical solidarity is not an obligation just to the 'other', but also to the 'Other' harmed by the 'other others'. Drabinski (2011) proposes that the Levinasian third party tends and seems to function primarily as a phenomenology of how the political is signified in moral consciousness, rather than as an actual clarification or exploration of the meaning of political responsibility. Despite its limitations, I wish to submit that the Levinasian suggestions of ethical solidarity helps one to grasp, describe and open both ethical and political spaces where the conditions and limitations of hospitality are negotiated (Fagan 2009).

Although Levinasian spaces are mainly transcendental, and Derrida's spaces are located primarily at the frontiers of nation-states, I argue that spaces exist likewise within tourism strategies, practices and theories. And while the spaces for negotiating hospitality and responsibility always exist, the accesses to these spaces are very asymmetrical. For instance, the representatives of the Nicaraguan tourism ministry INTUR had opened a physical space for dialogue – twice a month – for the organizations working with rural tourism. However, as the director of the network organization for small rural tourism enterprises RENITURAL said: the rural entrepreneurs' voices were not heard in these spaces. Similarly, many voices have been missed in the planning processes of the inter-oceanic canal – despite the regime's populistic slogans of participation and solidarity. The new rural tourism strategies had seemingly not opened a dialogue *between* tourism officials and rural tourism entrepreneurs. The director of RENITURAL found the exclusion of those whom they were trying to help to be quite contradictory. I agree, not only because I think it would be lovely if everyone could speak and participate but also for a more pragmatic reason. The exclusion of the 'other' from the spaces where the risks and responsibilities of hospitality are being negotiated had in this case meant that there were no discussions about the *risks* – in both tourism and canal projects – that the 'other' is expected to take.

As I have brought up throughout this chapter, the discussions on 'sustainable rural tourism' include very little explicit consideration of the possible challenges and risks that farmers and rural communities might face and take when welcoming tourism projects, development experts and tourists. When I followed the discussions in the 'space for dialogue' in INTUR, the issue was not brought up in any way. However, my analysis of tourism development indicates that the local families were continually estimating the risks of opening their doors to new guests and to their new ideas (see Jamal and Stronza 2009). More specifically, these estimations were clearly shaped by people's previous experiences of receiving guests. I agree that the local actors' inadequate knowledge about the 'Eurocentric' definitions of tourism surely can make it difficult for them to participate in tourism projects in the way they are expected to. However, instead of pointing to the lack of knowledge as a limitation on participation, it could be seen as a factor that the locals take into account when they consider the risks of welcoming new projects. The idea of calculating risk encourages one to deconstruct the tourism experts' assumptions that the locals would 'not have the right attitude, aptitude or entrepreneurial vision for tourism'. These kinds of assumption neglect the active subjectivity of the 'other' who calculates the risks and might take a conscious decision of *not* engaging in tourism development.

The recent decades of tourism studies, and especially the cautionary platform in the 1970s (Jafari 2001), have provided a great variety of studies about challenges and risks in tourism development. Rather than demanding that tourism experts should carry an extensive list of the dangers of tourism – from tsunamis to terrorism to volcanic eruptions in Iceland – the experts who believe in rural tourism development could ask, for instance, 'would *I* be happy to start this kind of tourism business in my own home?'. The purpose of the next chapter is to contribute further reflections on this question.

Notes

1 Palmer (1988) on 'Carlos Fonseca and the construction of Sandinismo in Nicaragua'.
2 For criticism towards the growth of tourism industries as a form of new colonialism, see *Turismo Placebo*, edited by Macía Blàzquez and Ernest Cañada (2011).
3 The story was also told at the Finnish Embassy's goodbye party in Managua in May 2013. Source of information, articles in newspapers in Central America: 'El Ejemplo de Nicaragua. Porque no Ayudamos A Finlandia?' Editorial, *Diario de Occidente*, Sta. Ana, El Salvador, 26 January 1940.
4 Nicaraguan historian Kinloch Tijerino (2008, 50) reports that the indigenous people gave gold to the conquistadors and received clothes as exchange.

5 The majority of development historians have agreed that the process of 'bridging the gaps' between 'traditional' societies and modern, developed nations began after the Second World War, when the more industrialized countries became concerned about the problems of 'underdevelopment' (Berkhöfer and Berkhöfer 2007; Cohen and Upphoff 2011, 36). US president Harry S. Truman's inaugural address in 1949 is often named as the starting point for a new era of interventions and development. By declaring the Southern Hemisphere an 'underdeveloped area', Truman 'discovered' the two billion poor, underdeveloped people who needed to follow North America and Europe as models on their development path. Above all, the homogeneous group of the 'underdeveloped' living in the Southern Hemisphere needed to be helped with Western technical solutions. While material advancement was viewed as the only way to achieve cultural, social and political development, alternatives were left out of the development discourse.

6 The project has been revitalized by the Hong Kong Nicaragua Canal Development Investment Company (HKND).

7 Thanks to Jussi Pakkasvirta for this information (personal communication).

8 See INTUR (2011b, 83). See the article by Jill Replogle (2014) 'Why Nicaraguan Kids Aren't Fleeing To U.S. It is Central America's poorest country, but its kids aren't heading north like those in El Salvador, Guatemala and Honduras' (published 29 July 2014).

9 I recommend the song 'Rios de gente' by Nicaraguan artist Perrozompopo.

10 For research on tourism development in Costa Rica, see for instance Matarrita-Cascante (2010), Quesada (2014), Hunt et al. (2014).

11 See PRONicaragua. These advantages are, interestingly, offered equally by the supposedly leftist Sandinista government.

12 See for example PRONicaragua 2017 www.pronicaragua.org (website accessed 20 September 2017).

13 For this kind of critique towards Ortega's government, see the articles by Equipo Nitlapan (2008a); for discussions on the ways in which gifting and counter-gifting can create and destroy social bonds, see Mauss (2008/1924), Derrida (1995), Länsman (2004), Pyyhtinen (2014).

14 For Bolaños's fight against corruption, see Kinloch Tijerino (2008, 345–6).

15 For more similar examples, see the edited volume by Blàzquez and Cañada (2011).

16 Cañada and Gascón (2007a) illustrate in a provocative cartoon-like book that instead of creating good jobs tourism gives locals only temporary, low-paid employment; instead of only creating new activities tourism also threatens the traditional sources of income; instead of creating better infrastructure for the local community the infrastructure is modernized according to the priorities that the tourism enterprises have; instead of adding value to local assets tourism tends to raise the living costs; instead of helping governments to pay their foreign debt, tourism dollars end up in the pockets of foreign investors; instead of protecting the environment, tourism contaminates and exploits natural resources and uses the local resources in an unsustainable way; instead of promoting intercultural understanding, tourism repeats the prior representations and ideas of the local culture and society; instead of being the key to development, tourism creates a dependency on the international markets; and instead of reducing poverty, tourism tends to create more problems than solutions amongst the most vulnerable groups.

17 For research on Pro-Poor Tourism, see Ashley and Roe (2002), Hall (2007), Schilcher (2007), Scheyvens (2011, 118–39).

18 In her book *Tourism and Poverty*, Scheyvens (2011) argues that the interconnections between tourism and multiple dimensions of poverty have remained largely understudied. The same argument has been made by scholars such as de Kadt (1979,; Viswanath (2008), Carlisle (2010) and Kalisch (2010). Scheyvens approaches the interconnections between poverty and tourism development from different theoretical perspectives, including that of political economy. Throughout her indepth analysis, she explores the ways in which neoliberal tourism policies can lead to economic growth without translating into benefits for the poor. While doing this, she deconstructs the artificial dichotomy between supposedly responsible forms of tourism and conventional forms of mass tourism; thus, Scheyvens (2011, 71) highlights that alternative forms of tourism, such as community-based tourism, should also be subject to the same kind of critical scrutiny as other forms of tourism.

19 For the significant role of NGOs in tourism development, see, for instance, Jamal and Getz (1995), Pérez (2003), Burns (2004), Butcher (2007), Cañada and Gascón (2007a, 85–91), Schilcher (2007), Scheyvens (2011), Goodwin et al. (2014), Jamal and Dredge (2014, 199–200) and Wearing and Wearing (2014).

20 *Red Nicaragüense de Turismo Rural y Comunitario*, RENITURAL. See SNV (2007) Linea base de RENITURAL.

21 For benefits and challenges of collaborative planning, see Jamal and Getz (1995), Tosun (2000). For different forms of tourism planning, see de Kadt (1979, 265), King and Pearlman (2009, 419–28).

22 López (17 December 2010) interviewed by Alberto Mora.

23 Small tourism enterprises' access to micro-credits is discussed in detail in Fleischer and Felsentein (2000), Hossain et al. (2014) and Geleta (2015).

24 INTUR's *Grupo técnicos de Trabajo* included representatives from INTUR, international development cooperation, tourism education and the private sector.

25 For one example of ambiguity of mixing these discourses, see INTUR (2011a, 83).

26 In addition to the Caribbean region, one of the campaigns has focused on the Rio San Juan and it is called 'Yo ya conosco Rio San Júan' ('I already know the San Júan River').

27 For instance, according to an article in El Nuevo Diario (14 January 2012) 'Approximately 17 percent of the Nicaraguan population participates in national tourism, and of this number, 12.5 percent prefer rural tourism". According to RENITURAL's baseline study (SNV 2007, 22), in 2006 approximately 20,000 national tourists and 9,000 international tourists visited rural community-based tourism initiatives in Nicaragua.

28 La Pita in San Ramón is mentioned in the first Nicaraguan guidebook for rural community-based tourism destinations in Nicaragua, published by Fundación Luciernaga. The communities of San Ramón can also be found in the 2009 issue of *The Lonely Planet, Nicaragua*.

29 As a matter of fact, mining in general does not belong to the past: Canadian mining company B2Gold's plan to open a gold mine in the region has faced broad resistance in the region because of the risks of contamination of water and other environmental impacts.

30 See also McRobert's (2012) research on and description of the cooperative unions in San Ramón. La Pita was one the first members in UCA San Ramón;

while they began with five manzanas of coffee, today there are approximately 600 manzanas of coffee amongst the cooperative members.

31 Schilcher (2007, 59), Stronza (2008) and Jamal and Dredge (2014, 195–7) are among the authors who have brought up the question whether people can choose *not* to participate in tourism development.

32 For more on intimacy in home-stay tourism, see Hultman and Cederholm Andersson (2012), Brandth and Haugen (2014).

33 For more discussion on gender equality and inequality in coffee cooperatives in Nicaragua, see research conducted by Alejandra Ganem Cuenca (2011).

34 For more diverse analysis of women's empowerment and microcredits, see Hietalahti and Nygren (2014), Geleta (2015); for analysis on continuity and change in gender relations in the course of rural tourism development, see Heldt Cassell and Pettersson (2015).

4   Negotiating the conditions for rural hospitality

As discussed in the previous chapter, some of the development officials in Nicaragua described tourism not only as one of the few alternatives for the people living in rural areas, but as a simple and easy activity enabling them to earn extra income and develop communities. The enthusiasm in some officials' voices made it sound like, to reformulate Spivak's (1993, 284) words here, the rural communities simply 'cannot not want tourism'.[1] This approach is also reflected in a cartoon booklet which summarizes the Nicaraguan 'Policy and Strategy of Sustainable Rural Tourism' (INTUR, 2012b 6–7)[2] in an easily accessible form. One of the cartoons includes the following dialogue between two farmers:

- Have you heard about this thing called sustainable tourism?
- Yes, I have … Soon you will see that it is something that will change the future of our community … They say that there are many tourists who come and want to experience something new. And in Central America tourism has been growing.
- Exactly, Juana told me that she had seen many 'cheles' ('whities') around here.

In my interview with tourism ministry representative Bayola Pallais, who had played an important role in the process of planning a rural tourism strategy, she explained that rural tourism was by no means complicated. She clarified that, in her opinion, the people living in rural areas must only learn how to be entrepreneurs and 'to show who they are'. Pallais argued that rural tourism entrepreneurs must

> look after things, make the bed, serve the food, make coffee, show how to milk a cow, and to do it all with style. It is not more complicated than that. You wash your pig, dog and hens and put the things in the right places because this is what the visitors come to see. The tourists come to see your home, so the only thing you have to do is to organize and show it.

It is true that welcoming tourists includes a great deal of cleaning; in fact, Michel Serres (2007, 145), another French philosopher, has also described 'purifying one's space as an act of welcoming'. However, in the light of tourism development in San Ramón, and as discussed widely in tourism and hospitality studies in general, the idea of showing your home and yourself to the visitors is quite misleading. Soile Veijola et al. (2014, 1) suggest that hospitality would actually mean 'opening up one's private property and transforming it into something public and accessible to others'. Levinas (1969) and Derrida (1999) too approach hospitality and welcoming as making space for the other. Applying Levinas's description of social relations in general, rural tourism encounters are instances of welcoming the other to one's home – to the place of intimacy. However, instead of claiming that this is simple, both philosophers draw attention to the ethical and risky dimensions of opening one's home to a stranger. While Levinas refers to the act of welcoming the Other as a fundamental task of 'the subject of welcome', Derrida (2000), as mentioned in the previous chapters, wants us to think of how opening the door to the unexpected always includes a risk of losing mastery of one's home.

Although the phenomenological tradition directs the focus primarily on the metaphysical ways of 'making space for the other', postcolonial critique denies the possibility of discussing these spaces as separate from the historical and material contexts (Spivak 1988, 272–4; Dussel 2008; 2013). Similarly, the meaningfulness of detaching the material from the social has been profoundly questioned in the contemporary sociological paradigm (e.g. Bennett and Joyce 2010; Valkonen, Lehtonen and Pyyhtinen 2013; Kinnunen 2017; van der Duim et al. 2017). Consequently, it is necessary to admit that this kind of home-stay and rural tourism is to a high extent based on the inequalities between wealthy, mobile guests and impoverished, immobile hosts. Annelies Zoomers (2008, 979–80) writes, much like Regina Scheyvens (2011, 219), that 'promoting tourism means creating a world of extremes. It is an encounter of two opposing worlds: poor rural and indigenous groups in their daily routines and well-to-do gringos in their time off – each with their own expectations and cultural orientations' (see Dicks 2003, 48–50; Gmelch 2012; Sammels 2014; Bianchi 2015, 292–4). Thus, paradoxically, in the context of rural tourism development the abundance of space without luxury has been increasingly perceived as a potential environment to attract visitors who could help in filling the space with material benefits. One might also ask whether the scarcity of materiality in rural homes becomes interpreted as an 'empty space' for the guests to enter, where- and whenever.

The purpose of this chapter is to describe and analyse the meanings that the local hosts in San Ramón gave their encounters with tourism developers as guests. The main sources of data that I have used for the analysis are the interviews and field notes from participatory observation that I conducted in four tourism communities between 2008 and 2013. I focus on the locals' experiences of the ways in which the conditions, risks and responsibilities of welcoming have been negotiated throughout the process of tourism development. The main argument here is that while external tourism developers aim to help rural hosts to prepare their homes for tourism, as described in the previous chapter, many of the local hosts have become exhausted by the continuous demand for improved material conditions. Realizing this has encouraged me to shed more light on the ways in which the expectation of material wealth mediates the social *and* limits the possibilities of participating – in these kinds of tourism encounters. Interpreting the locals' expressions and actions, I suggest that tourism experts intend to or end up dominating and controlling the liminal spheres between self and other – even when the encounters take place in rural homes.

I elaborate my argument in the following four sections. In the first, I place the emphasis on the ways in which local hosts have described the help from development officials and representatives of cooperative unions in the early phases of tourism development. The second draws attention to the ways in which the assets and conditions needed for rural tourism development have been continuously negotiated in the encounters between local hosts and their guests. By 'guests' I refer here not only to tourism developers but also to tourists and tourism entrepreneurs from other rural communities. The third section introduces an international tourism development programme called Moderniza, which can be seen as an extreme example of a participatory tourism initiative in which the guests pre-design and pre-define the material requirements needed in tourism. The participatory character of these development encounters, in my opinion, is minimal, as the local hosts are nearly silenced in their own homes. In the last part of the chapter, I bring up a common issue in rural tourism initiatives: dependency on middlemen with mixed roles of hosts and guests and the scarcity of paying guests.

4.1   Commodification of domestic hospitality

I begin the analysis here from the tourism developers' flawed perception that tourism is an easy activity, consisting merely of tasks such as washing your pig, dog and hen and showing who you are. These kinds of accounts of the simple character of organizing tourism in rural homes differ drastically from the local hosts' experiences in San Ramón. In the beginning of tourism development, around 2003, most of the families did not own a pig which they could wash, or a cow that could have been milked. In fact, many families were facing problems with food security and struggled to put three daily meals on the table (WFP 2008, 2). And there are families where the the struggle continues. Although nowadays there are more pigs and cows and hens, thanks to loans from Venezuela that allowed the Sandinista government to continue with its clientelist politics (Teivainen 2014), most of the families seldom eat chicken and almost never meat or fish. Instead, basic foods like corn, beans and rice cover the biggest part of the local plates. This includes the staple of the Nicaraguan diet for at least 1,000 years: a tortilla made from dried, ground corn mixed with water (Correa Oquel 2006, 18). The houses in the communities are made of wood, adobe or cement bricks and often have a dirt floor; in the kitchens the food is prepared on an open cooking fire and in many houses the smoke can only escape via a gap between the wall and the roof, leaving smoke in the kitchen. Most of the families do not have fridges or other household appliances; houses close to the main roads have better access to electricity, while others do not. A clear change that has taken place in recent years is the arrival of mobile phones, which have helped not only farmers, but also those coordinating tourism activities. At the time of writing the last lines of this book, most of the young people were very active in social media such as Facebook.

Nearly all the people I interviewed during my first period of fieldwork, in 2008, emphasized that the process of developing services and conditions for tourists was not a job that could be taken lightly. The hosts pointed out that since the very beginning of the tourism initiative, the new guides and people responsible for tourism accommodation had been participating in different kinds of training programmes in order to upgrade their domestic hospitality, and to be able to put a price tag on it. The focus of the courses had been to make the 'holy trinity' of manageable hospitality – food, drink and accommodation – meet the expectations of potential visitors. The hosts had gone through courses on how to cook and serve food for tourists, how to make natural juices, how to make beds, how to clean and, in general, how to be a good host. The people working with accommodation had also received mosquito nets, water filters and sheets for tourists – all donations from international NGOs. This all meant, I argue, learning to understand what the services and milieu 'should' look and feel like in order to be recognized as tourism settings (Urry 1990; Dicks 2003; Salazar 2010). In many hosts' opinion, the first years of tourism development had proceeded in a positive and promising ambience. Edmundo, one of the guides, stated 'The more we learned about tourism, the more tourists there were coming'.

During the solidarity movement in the 1980s, the international guests brought their own food, stayed in the same rooms with the families and often left some kind of 'regalito', a kind of small gift, at the moment of goodbyes. Hence, a concrete difference between these first visitors in the 1980s and the tourists who were coming in 2000 was that the former were not expected to pay for their stay. Actually, despite the later improvements made for tourists, some of the hosts told me that it had still felt uncomfortable to ask for money for their services. It sounded like charging 3–5 dollars per plate for a meal, 10 dollars per night for accommodation and 15 dollars per group for a coffee tour had caused mixed feelings of pressure and excitement. The questions of accommodation and bathrooms were central ones, as doña Hilda and other hosts explained. In doña Hilda's opinion, the local families had felt badly ever since the 1980s that their visitors had to use the latrines and outdoor bathing areas. Consequently, the hosts found it important to offer paying visitors private rooms and better bathrooms. Ever since, the lodging offered to tourists has continued to cause a wide range of feelings from pride to anger. The negative feelings have been caused, as some of the hosts explained in our discussions, particularly by the dubious process of financing and buying the raw materials for the cabañas.

Local hosts felt that the initiative for taking a loan for improving tourism development had come from a group of actors that included the local cooperative union and international NGOs. Representatives of the Fair Trade Coffee Organization, as part of their social project in the area, contributed to the process by helping local women to apply for the financing alone, without their husbands. Veronica, one of the women accommodating tourists, described the process to me in 2013 as follows:

> First they told us that it would be just a small amount of money, and that we could receive part of it as a grant. They said that with every visit, and with our coffee, we could pay the loan. But they told that it would cost much less. They sent the material and they sent the carpenters to show how to build the cabañas. But when we heard that the actual price was so high, 24 000 cordobas (approximately 1000 dollars), we did not want to have them. However, we could no longer say no. And we thought that at least part of it would be a grant, but it was not. They made us pay it all. So, since then we have been cautious about taking loans or receiving grants.

Gabriela, a guide who had been involved in tourism since the beginning, agreed with Veronica that the rooms had proven to be very expensive. Gabriela claimed that 'with this amount of money we could have done something more – made houses that would have been bigger, higher, better made, with more ventilation, and so on'. In some cases, the huts or the rooms were more expensive and stable than the homes that they were attached to. While it is prohibited to cut down trees in the local forest, Gabriela and Veronica were outraged that they had not even been allowed to use their own sand to make bricks. Instead, the sand, wood and material for the roofs were all bought from outside and then delivered, with the bill, directly to their front doors.

There is certainly something to be said about a situation where external development experts and local coordinators recommended to local families living below the poverty line – two dollars per day[3] – that they build the cabañas by taking out 'micro loans', and helped them get the loans. These families, normally careful about how they spend their money and, for instance, constantly trying to save money to be able to send their children to school, all of a sudden had an entire holiday cottage brought to them from the nearby town. According to some of my informants, the situation with the loans became even more problematic after the rooms were built and furnished. In 2008 one woman, doña Thelma, summarized it like this: 'But when we got all this finished – the tourists were no longer coming. That is weird, and it has left us with the loans'. (This is an example of a quote that I did not pay enough attention to when I conducted my first analysis in 2009 as it would have disrupted my positive pre-narrative of community-based tourism.) As described in Section 3.3, in 2008 the number of tourists suddenly began to decline. While many of the local hosts blamed the local coordinators for their incompetence in running the project, there were most probably other reasons as well for the downturn. For instance, tourism scholars and consultants Harvey and Kelsay (2010, 220), who have studied similar kinds of coffee-tourism projects in Costa Rica, listed the economic downturn in 2008 and even the war in Iraq as the principal reasons for the struggle of rural tourism in Central America.

In 2011, when there were only a few tourists coming and the revenues from tourism no longer covered the loans, the families and cooperatives ended up paying the loans with coffee beans. This was possible thanks to a particularly good coffee harvest (*El Nuevo Diario* 2012, July 6). The possible benefits that the office of UCA San Ramón received for brokering these loans have remained a mystery to me. In any case, according to those hosts who dared to bring up the topic, the entire process of recommending loans and helping people applying for them did not include open discussion about the risks and conditions involved. As a consequence, the subsequent development caused mistrust between the local communities and the tourism coordinators and experts. In other words, the 'host' communities were now seeing both local tourism coordinators and external experts as quite bad guests. This meant that both effective individual leadership (Kontogeorgopoulos et al. 2014) *and* trust among different actors (Mair 2014) were missing. Needless to say, the communities of San Ramón were no longer perfect target groups for the Nicaraguan strategy for rural tourism development, which included providing access to microcredits.

Another cartoon describing Nicaragua's new strategy for rural tourism presents a discussion between two Nicaraguan women working in a field (INTUR 2012b, 22–23):

– Have you heard that they are giving loans for improving rural tourism? Emilia told me that this loan has helped her a lot.
– It is true, the government is paying attention to the farmers who want to develop. Even we can apply for this credit.

While access to credit might guarantee successful tourism entrepreneurship, the entire topic – with its connections to risks, dependency, possibilities of corruption and mistrust – seems to be among the overlooked ones in rural tourism debates (Mair 2014; Nunkoo and Gursoy 2016). It is a relevant theme in the participatory tourism paradigm, for these kinds of loans are considered as the best ways to guarantee local commitment to participatory projects in practice. At least this was an argument that I heard in my interviews with tourism experts in Managua. The discussions about the importance of the micro-credits in tourism development have perhaps primarily proceeded from the perspective of the structural limitations which marginalized communities face in community-based tourism development (see Timothy 2002, 162; Moscardo 2008; Scheyvens 2011; Jamal and Dredge 2015). However, it merits mentioning that recent research within development studies has taken a more critical look at these kinds of micro-loan projects (Hossain et al. 2014; Hietalahti and Nygren 2014; Geleta 2015).

Perhaps the project world depends on families and communities who are convinced, excited and willing to participate in new initiatives – those who want to participate in putting into action the plans that are planned for them. On the other side of the coin are those who do not dare or want to participate. These people are described in the harshest development narratives as ignorant, lazy, passive and lacking entrepreneurial vision, as not willing to take advantage of the possibilities offered them. These are more palatable explanations, from the point of view of those who arrive with the plans, than admitting that local actors might in fact be sceptical, doubtful and not willing to take the risks that the projects require (see Eriksson-Baaz 2005, 76, 132; Escobar 2012, 192–9). Amid the claims that local communities do not understand the possibilities of tourism development, it becomes timely to ask, as discussed in the previous chapter, whether the tourism developers are aware of, and understand, the risks of rural tourism development.

In saying this, I do not want to categorize tourism developers as a homogeneous group; this is by no means my intention. I can see that the developers' assumptions about the 'other', and about the risks and possibilities of tourism, vary greatly. These assumptions are, hopefully, continuously reshaped through encounters with the local hosts. For instance, in 2012 I interviewed one of the tourism experts from UNDP who knew the case of San Ramón well. In our discussion she shared with me her worry about the stagnation of tourism activities in these particular communities. She brought up how tourism is often recommended to rural communities, misleadingly in her opinion, as an 'easy business'. She admitted being actually surprised and impressed by the courage and faith that the local families have shown when they make the decision to get involved with tourism development. She described tourism as a risky business for small farmers, and admitted that she was often amazed by those families who believed in tourism and were willing to take the risks and invest all they had – and even more – in it.

Her observation reflects Derrida's idea of calculating the risk of welcoming; it is about welcoming the wide range of unpredictable changes, possibilities, uncertainties and guests that enter their lives with the ideas and imaginings of tourism. It is clear that as there are risks in opening one's door to a stranger, welcoming and offering hospitality is actually a risk that many of us are not willing to take. In participatory tourism development, the encounters between local hosts and experts as guests do not take place only on the thresholds of rural communities or rural homes. Instead, tourism developers are often already inside people's homes when these discussions take place. In these settings, playing down the risks of taking a loan, or comparing tourism to other rural sectors, means trivializing the constant negotiations between the risks and responsibilities of welcoming. More specifically, it means excluding the other from an equal and open dialogue in the other's own home. This can be seen, I argue, as something quite contradictory to the very idea of participation.

One of the central issues here is the harmful image of tourism work as something easy and simple. Although it is not only the Nicaraguan tourism officials who construct this image, we should stop and ask what kinds of representations or imaginings discourses such as 'just wash your pig and show who you are' paint of the locals, of tourists and of tourism as work. To me they are simplistic and patronizing representations of tourism settings. Such discourses describe tourism sites where the main attraction would be a newly washed animal, where the tourists want to see how a cow is milked and where tourism entrepreneurship is an activity of 'just showing who you are'. The assumptions about the simplicity and ease of tourism activities are not a new phenomenon, and I am by no means the first one frustrated by such representations. Sociologists and tourism scholars have been deconstructing in detail the manifold and demanding dimensions of tourism as work (e.g. Hultman and Andersson Cederholm 2012; Salazar 2010, 111–38; Andringa, Poulston and Pernecky 2016; Hakkarainen 2017).[4] Perhaps the image of tourism providing mainly low-skilled jobs allows low wages and other forms of exploitation of tourism workers to continue (Schyst Resande 2015; Buades 2009). In the context of Nicaraguan rural tourism development, that image has meant that the rural hosts who are perceived as good candidates for doing the 'low-skilled jobs' are *not* seen as equal partners in negotiating about the circumstances of and compensation for welcoming. This has led not only to relatively low prices for rural tourism services, but also to a range of risky social projects.

Tourism researchers Berit Brandth and Marit Haugen (2014), who have studied farm tourism in Norway, have shown how work with tourism does not become easy simply because it takes place in people's homes – a place that is considered a site of privacy and intimacy. In fact, it can be quite the opposite (Hultman and Andersson Cederholm 2012; Gyimóthy 2017). The questions of emotional work in private domains – the work of *hostessing*, as Veijola and Jokinen (2008; Jokinen and Veijola 2012) might call it – have been closely examined especially in feminist research. The process of combining the private and commercial domains of hospitality (Lashley 2017) by constructing and making tourist spaces in homes completely alters the idea of keeping one's home as a place only for family and close relationships. Not only is the concept of work considered challenging when it takes place in homes, but the commercialization of domestic hospitality entails particular expectations of what this hospitality should include. This is the topic that I will discuss in more detail in the following.

4.2   Reaching the readiness to welcome

If hospitality is seen as making space for the other, it would mean that you would not have to have that much in order to receive – in fact the opposite. Nevertheless, tourism researcher Johan Edelheim (2013), a Finn like myself, points out that the etymology of the Finnish word for hospitality – *vieraanvaraisuus* – includes two words 'guest' and 'assets'. Literally, as Edelheim continues, it denotes affording, having the assets, to welcome and receive visitors. Perhaps hosts are expected to do their all for visitors, even where it means that they themselves would end up with less.[5] This means that hospitality, and welcoming, would be not only about making space for the other, but also about giving something to the other. But how much of our 'assets' we are willing to offer to a stranger, to a guest, can obviously vary to a great extent. While it is true that in the tourism business the hosts try to match the quality and quantity of their assets to the price guests are willing to pay, this is a quite simplistic picture.

Today, when the tourism and hospitality sector has grown expansively, it has become commonly accepted to use someone else's assets to attract guests (Mowforth et al. 2008; Bianchi 2015; Nepal et al. 2016). One of the most striking examples of this is the use of indigenous cultures, pristine beaches and coral reefs, or non-existent laws against sexual abuse of children or other human rights violations. While there are international NGOs addressing these issues, tourism enterprises are normally not asked to justify why they do *not* use their *own* assets to attract visitors. And if they *are* asked, the demands for 'corporate social responsibility' can be easily fulfilled by launching a recycling system (Pakkasvirta 2010, 3), acquiring a green-tourism certificate (Hunt and Stronza 2011), or putting together a fund-raising campaign for malnourished children in the country called Africa. My suspicion is that during the era of neo-colonization and global trade, we have simply become inured to a business being done and profits made using someone else's assets. It is perceived mainly as brilliance, intelligence or good entrepreneurial vision, to come up with new ways to use such assets. Unfortunately, as discussed in Chapter 3, this has often meant that hosts, who are expected to offer the best they have, might be asked to participate in 'a race to the bottom', for example, to use their low wages and limited labour rights as an 'asset' that visitors can take advantage of (Dielemans 2008, 149–64; Buades 2009; Cañada 2015).

The hope has been expressed that rural tourism, and especially community-based tourism, might offer an alternative precisely to these unethical dimensions of the tourism industries (Telfer 2003, 253–5; Smith 2009c; Cañada 2014). Community-based tourism has been considered an ethical form of tourism especially because it aims to guarantee the local communities the right to define, control and take advantage of their own cultural, social and environmental assets. In other words, those who advocate community-based tourism aim to help local communities to decide whom they wish to welcome into their homes and what to offer. As a relatively rare example in tourism worlds, the communities in charge of tourism development are expected to receive fair and direct compensation for their hospitality. I fully agree that the beauty of community-based tourism lies in the fact that there are only a few middlewomen and middlemen between the service providers and consumers; this is rare not only in tourism, but in global trade between the Global South and North and between cores and peripheries in general.

As the example of San Ramón indicates, it might be difficult for local communities to act independently, without any intermediaries. In fact, when thinking with the idea of participation as making something together, it is somewhat contradictory to strive and lobby for tourism development that would remain detached from entanglements and networks beyond the local communities. As tourism scholar Gunnar Thór Jóhannesson (2015) has argued, entrepreneurial practices in tourism are always based on diverse forms of relationality. Hence, instead of dreaming of community-based tourism where the intermediaries and brokers would not have an important role, it becomes interesting to explore how these actors participate in the negotiations of hospitality. However, among tourism scholars the opinions about the responsibilities of these development intermediaries vary greatly and many have argued that in addition to mediating financial support to rural communities, development practitioners should provide rural communities with technical assistance (e.g. Briedenhann and Ramchander 2006, 124). In their analysis of brokers' behaviour in relation to residents, David A. Fennell and Krzysztof Przeclawski (2003, 47) went as far as stating that the brokers' responsibility is not only to inform the local hosts about the culture, customs and behaviours of tourists, but also to 'help inhabitants in developing an attitude of hospitality and tolerance'. Other tourism scholars, such as Carlos Maldonado (2005, 14) and Michael J. Hatton (1999), have summarized that the brokers' role is to support the communities in valuing their social capital, which can prepare them to take advantage of further opportunities.

The communities of San Ramón have been helped in various ways. Not only did the initiative for tourism come from the outside, but so did the recommendations and evaluations regarding the 'best local assets'. This is not a surprise as such. In fact, it resonates with the basic ideas of relationality and intersubjectivity – the impossibility of separating the actions of individuals or communities from their encounters and entanglements with others (Jóhannesson, Ren and Van der Duim 2015). Indeed, it is impossible and meaningless to demand that communities should come up with the idea of tourism totally on their own – or that they should be able to define their assets without simultaneously interacting with their intended guests. The acts of preparing and assessing one's local resources for tourism are continuously negotiated, not only amongst the hosts, but also between the hosts and guests. These negotiations can as well be seen as an ongoing process of evaluating one's readiness and capability to say 'welcome'.

On the hillsides of San Ramón, this process of evaluation has played out through various encounters, and lost encounters, between the local hosts and their guests. Needless to say, different guests tend to emphasize, and expect, very different assets. In my interaction with the local families and guides, I have seen how the hosts themselves perceive their everyday life, and their green mountains, as their main resources in tourism. The important things that they were offering to their visitors, according to one of the guides, Gabriela, were 'the opportunities to interact with the families, the mountains, the environment, the preparation of coffee and the cultural differences'. Fernando, another local tourist guide with many years of experience, explained:

> In rural community-based tourism quality is something intangible because you cannot give stars (as in hotels) for friendliness. The idea is that the visitor can have the experience of living as part of a family, but without having to know or worry about the problems that the farmers have.

In the guide's opinion, everyday life is supposed to look as normal as possible when visitors are there. Perhaps we could say that the hope was that the settings would look as 'authentic as possible', despite the fact that the guests were sleeping in rooms that the locals had invested a great deal of money in. The local hosts wanted to offer their visitors an experience that included various aspects of their domestic life. They wanted their guests to wake up in the early morning hours to the slapping sound of women making fresh corn tortillas in the kitchen. During the days the guests could enjoy cooking and eating the local food, participate in cleaning the corn, listen to the radio, play football with the children, and so on. The hosts also decided to offer travellers the possibility of visiting the community centre, local schools or a baseball game. Depending on the time of the year, the guests were invited to experience the entire process of sowing, planting, composting, collecting, washing, drying and roasting coffee beans – and finally enjoying a cup of coffee on the patio. Besides the activities related to coffee production, the local guides organized hikes on the trails around the communities, which included observation of birds, flowers and animals, visits to specially constructed outlook points, swimming under a waterfall and the like. One of the communities also encouraged its guests to take a dip in the pool which the residents had built in the middle of the community. What is more, the women accommodating tourists had revitalized the local tradition of making natural medicines in order to teach these skills to their guests. Sometimes a group of local musicians would organize a concert. And at night, as described on the tourism promotion site 'Vianica', the visitors had the unique opportunity to enjoy 'the fireflies, stars and sounds of nature'.[6]

During my stay in the communities of San Ramón, the people involved in tourist accommodation wanted to emphasize that they were always offering the visitors 'the best we have'. There seemed to exist a consensus among the local hosts that quality in this context meant above all 'working well and doing it better'. Many of the women were interested in the possibilities of cultivating different kinds of fruits and vegetables in order to add variety to tourists' plates. Doña Hilda, one of the local hosts, described the process of receiving tourists as follows:

When tourists come, we meet to decide who will accommodate them. We discuss how to receive the visitors. First of all, the room has to be clean, the sheets must be clean, and everything must be clean. We who accommodate tourists know this as we have received different kinds of training about hygiene. After that, we talk about the food. The guides help us out here as they know whether the visitors eat meat or are vegetarians. We have learned how to do the work well, and how to value it. This is our work and our business.

In my interviews the hosts assumed that the tourists had enjoyed their stays and generally found the tourism accommodation and food sufficient. Their assumptions were corroborated by the feedback and comments that the tourists wrote in a guestbook at the office in San Ramón, gave to the representatives of tour operators such as Matagalpa Tours, or posted on Internet sites such as Trip Advisor. Most of the visitors described their experience in 'real rural Nicaragua' with adjectives such as 'great', 'absolutely amazing', 'excellent' and '*perfecto*'.[7] The local hosts seemed to underline how the positive feedback from tourists made them feel good and confident in what they were doing. However, as doña Hilda explained, there were also negative experiences with the tourists:

Once there came a group from El Salvador and they made us feel really bad. They left here and were saying bad things about us. We felt so bad because we do not have money and this was the best we could offer. The hotels have their refrigerators and everything but we do not. So we cannot prepare the same kind of food as the hotels serve! We make rice and beans and typical food here. So they left here very unhappy.

The families had received, in their opinion, a relatively small number of these kinds of 'less flexible customers'. It seemed as if after several years of working with tourism, the hosts became more aware of the kind of 'product' they were offering. I was told that it was easier to receive travellers from the Western countries who, in contrast to Nicaraguan and Central American tourists, did 'not want luxury'. However, the very positive feedback from the Western tourists is not a surprise as such. In her research on volunteer tourism in Guatemala and Ghana, Wanda Vrasti (2013) argues that tourists' happiness and satisfaction with the rustic accommodation is in fact part of the romanticized view of poverty and of the other. Drawing on Sara Ahmed's work, Vrasti (2013, 83) explains how living in relatively modest conditions is perceived as a sign of 'flexible subjectivity that can live fully in the global moment, bypassing the difficulties and constraints that govern the lives of racialized and impoverished bodies'. As part of their privileged, mobile position, the visitors also have the possibility and flexibility to *be* someone else for a while. In my discussions with tourism professors from the University of Matagalpa, they quite aptly pointed out how the locals might perceive domestic tourists as more critical, observant and straightforward in their comments about the problems that their local hosts are having. At the same time, the national travellers most likely have less interest in friendship with the locals or in learning about coffee cultivation.

While many of the domestic tourists and tourism developers had been sceptical about the local level of material conditions, the hosts in San Ramón remembered how the success of the first international visits in the 1980s did not depend on the material conditions.[8] Doña Hilda expressed the following view:

> We think that this kind of tourism is something where we want to offer the visitor the best we have – our friendship and kindness. Before, the tourists did not have their own special room and they still liked this experience. They come here to learn about coffee production, to enjoy the nature and peace and to exchange and share experiences. The tourists normally know better what this kind of tourism is about.

In my opinion, her frustration and need to defend the villagers' tourism services can be seen as a consequence of her encounters with tourism officials who demanded different kinds of improvements in material conditions. One of the checklists that the tourism experts filled out during their visits in San Ramón was designed to help the rural communities to meet the 'minimum requirements for hospitality'.[9] These evaluation visits, which I also had a chance to observe, focused on the conditions and existence of shower curtains, sinks, mirrors, soap, refrigerators, beds, trashcans, chairs, toilet-paper holders, curtains, floors, decorations, sheets, pillows, duvet covers, language skills and so on – on far more things it would seem than 'washing your pig and making the bed'. While the local hosts had acquired most of these things through donations and with the income from tourism, they faced difficulties, for instance, in buying the sinks. The criteria for 'minimum levels of hospitality' were adjusted in 2013 in a project of INTUR, *Lux-Development* and *Agencia Española*, the purpose of which was to make them better fit in with the realities amongst micro, small and medium enterprises.[10]

In 2012, Fernando, a local guide and community activist in San Ramón, was outraged by all the different kinds of requirements that they had faced during the past years. He cursed the various demands for shower curtains, warm water and fire alarms, as these all were things that they could not afford. Nor did he see them relevant to rural lifestyle. He was outraged when he stated that 'the tourism officials did not seem to understand what this kind of rural tourism is about'. It is worth mentioning here that Fernando also had a degree in tourism from the University of Matagalpa. Carter Hunt and Amanda Stronza's (2011) research on local perspectives on ecotourism in Nicaragua has addressed this kind of prescriptive 'check-list approach' to sustainability. The authors argue that while previous research on sustainability and ethics in tourism has generally addressed the role of industry operators, there has only been an indirect concern for local hosts' perceptions on ethical performance and certification schemes. While Hunt and Stronza raise the issue of greenwashing in small-scale projects, the case of San Ramón draws attention to other kind of resistance towards quality programmes and certificates.[11]

Moreover, it was not only the official criteria that guided the negotiations about the assets needed in rural hospitality. During their visits in San Ramón, the experts came up with different suggestions of their own, which included, for instance, decorating rooms with paintings, planting more flowers, buying a refrigerator, improving the road, providing hot water for the guests, and so on. Another local guide, teacher and community activist, Edmundo, told me that one tourism consultant had warmly recommended that the locals should make menus so that visitors could choose what they wanted to eat from several options. According to Edmundo, the hosts decided to turn down the idea of menus, because they required ingredients for different options and preparing different meal alternatives would have been too costly and stressful for the local families.[12]

One such encounter between local hosts and tourism experts took place in 2008, when I had the possibility to join a small group of development officials on their visit to San Ramón. While we were walking around the community, a representative from an international NGO, Rainforest Alliance, posed questions about the locals' readiness to take care of their guests should they become ill or get hurt during their visit. She was giving a local guide a hard time and the guide admitted their difficulties in ensuring that guests could get professional help – just as the people living in the communities had very limited access to medical services. In response, the same development official wagged her finger at the guide and insisted that 'all the real tourism destinations *must* arrange possibilities for a helicopter to come and pick up the guests in a case of emergency'. Instead of categorizing different proposals as 'great', 'good' or 'bad' or, even less, claiming that the locals do not need these things, it seems like many of these requirements reflect ethno- and self-centredness among tourism experts. Although the guests wish to help the locals to find the missing elements of hospitality, they simultaneously question the local hosts' possibilities and capabilities of saying 'welcome'.

The first time I visited the communities of San Ramón, most of the interviewees pointed out how important and positive it had been for them to get involved with tourism. What seemed to be significant for many was the status of officially participating in tourism planning and development (Höckert 2009, 74; McRoberts 2012, 101). This bears out work by Thomas Lea Davidson (2005, 26), who notes how such recognition by the local tourism industry, and new possibilities of contributing to the family economy, can enhance the self-identity of those involved in tourism, for their work is taken seriously. In my first analysis in 2009, which was published in the same year in a research report and in 2011 in an article on social and cultural sustainability of community-based tourism, I interpreted this positive change in the local hosts' lives as what Cole (2006; 2008) and Scheyvens (1999; 2003) have called social and psychological empowerment (Jamal and Dredge 2015, 182–98;

Hashimoto 2014, 223–5; Strzelecka 2015). However, at that time I had not noticed the many ways in which the recent decline in the number of tourists had caused feelings of powerlessness and frustration among the hosts.

This is something that I became painfully aware of only during my later visits: although the hosts felt well prepared to receive visitors, guests were no longer coming, and the women ended up in a difficult situation with their business and loans. Simultaneously, the variety of suggestions from tourism experts had made the local hosts insecure about the quality of their homestay accommodation. It was unclear whether the success of their project still hinged on dealing with the inadequate material conditions. A local guide, Gabriela, whose mother had been working with tourism accommodation, summarized the situation aptly:

> Well, two tourists in a month is not enough. The women cannot make it like that. Tourists need to come regularly because this is a job. The women have been trained, they have prepared everything and it is work that needs to be practised. It is not fair that the women have paid so much but receive so little.

In 2013, in a situation where the entire cooperative had participated in paying back the women's loans, many of the women felt that their skills and the possibilities of running the tourism business had been questioned by their own family members and neighbours. In a talk by a coffee table, one man told me that in his view his wife had been 'tricked' into tourism. Those who were not actively involved in tourism were now sceptical as to whether working in tourism was a real job.[13] Doña Hilda lamented that some of her neighbours undermined the women's efforts, 'They say that we're not making any money and that they have not seen any tourists coming here. There are many who do not value tourism as work'.

During my stays on the hillsides of San Ramón, I noticed the ways in which the local hosts valued the peer support among those who were committed to tourism development (see Miettinen 2007). The encounters with other hosts had helped people to recognize their own resources as tourism entrepreneurs. What is more, working together in tourism had led to new kinds of initiatives. The most significant initiative was probably a coffee-roasting project, organized by a women's coffee cooperative in the community of El Roblar. Besides the cooperation between the local hosts in San Ramón, there had been few special occasions which had strengthened their confidence as hosts. These had been cases where people from other places in Nicaragua had come to San Ramón to learn from the local experiences with tourism. These visitors had plans to develop tourism in their own home communities and were hence interested in asking for advice from the hosts in San Ramón.

In these encounters, I argue, the arrivals recognized the local hosts as professionals in tourism who had lots of experience of rural tourism development. When I asked doña Hilda about the advice she had given to these kinds of guests who came and asked for help, her answer was a mix of optimism and caution. Instead of accentuating the hope that tourism would bring a steady income, doña Hilda described tourism in the following way:

> When there are no tourists coming, we focus on the work on the fields. We cultivate corn and beans and there also are other plants that we can cultivate. So, if the tourists do not come, it really is not a problem: if they come we receive them, when they do not come we have to look for other options. I appreciate it that we have several jobs and not only tourism.

In the light of the tourism literature, it is no surprise that people's attitudes towards tourism and tourists change. Often this change means moving from positive to negative or from euphoria to antagonism (e.g. Wall and Mathieson 2006, 54–5; Jóhannesson 2015), although many scholars have found that residents' attitudes have improved with involvement in small-scale eco-tourism and participatory projects (Hunt and Stronza 2014, 280). Despite various challenges, the majority of the guides and families with tourist accommodation seemed interested in continuing with tourism because they had put so much effort into it. One of the participants captured this senti-ment when she said, 'It is nice to work with tourists, but it is quite boring to wait for them to come'. While it is common that rural tourism entrepreneurs need to combine various sources of income, we cannot overlook the fact that engaging in tourism accommodation means, thinking with Derrida's (1999, 25) words, putting in question one's freedom. It means committing oneself to continuous readiness to receive the stranger; that is, readiness to interrupt self at the moment the guest arrives. In rural tourism this stranger comes relatively often with a gift that includes help and guidance for the local hosts.

4.3   Visits of the tidy guests

In San Ramón there have been many different kinds of tourism experts arriving with cosmopolitan empathy (Mostafanezhad 2014, 70) and enthu-siasm to help the locals to *improve* their tourism initiative (see Li 2007).[14] For a tourism researcher the phenomenon looks like an interesting jungle of ideas and *tourism imaginaries* (Salazar 2010; 2012). Simultaneously, from the local hosts' point of view, the same phenomenon appears as an ongoing invasion of advisors, teachers, volunteers and researchers, who all have their own visions of what is good for the locals and how to develop the tourism business. Most of all these guests offer guidance about the ways in which 'the tourist' wants to visit these communities. I call these experts here 'tidy guests' – self-confident and neat guests with superlative skills for organizing the lives of the others. This concept was developed in the aforementioned pro-ject on 'disruptive tourism', where it contrasts with the notion 'untidy guest'.[15]

I have argued that the 'tidy guests' tend to arrive with radar that detects things that are missing or distracting; besides, these guests are not shy about making explicit comments about these shortcomings. On the contrary; their visits are often justified by the need to give feedback, which makes them appear to be quite altruistic acts of helping. In other words, the guests are able to express their sympathy by offering *help* to the locals – although as visitors they lack understanding of the local context (see Mostafanezhad 2014).[16]

The idea of 'tourism imaginaries' refers to the means by which individuals understand their identities and their place in the world. In Salazar's (2010, 6) words, tourism imaginaries are 'representational assemblages that mediate the identifications with self and Other'. Salazar (ibid.) clarifies the idea, drawing on Vogler (2002, 625), that imaginaries can be seen as implicit understandings and complex systems of 'presumption that enter subjective experience as the expectation that things will make sense generally'. In the context of tourism the imaginaries that underlie tourism are so compelling that without them there probably would be little tourism at all. Salazar (2014, 112), quoting Said (1994) and Hennig (2002), explains that these images and discourses are by no means harmless: they tend 'to propagate historically inherited stereotypes that are based on myths and fantasies related to nature, the noble savage, art, individual freedom and self-realization, equality and paradise'. This means that constructed tourism settings can also be seen to mirror different imaginaries that individual subjects rely on.

Hence, in the context of material assets and conditions of hospitality, I understand the notion of 'tourism imaginaries' as referring to the creation of material settings which are reconstructed in order to become recognizable as tourism sites (Dicks 2003). It means shaping the material fabric of hospitality so that it can be recognized as a service with a price tag. This improved visitability helps the locals identify themselves as service providers and the tourists to identify themselves as guests. However, when looking at this from the social constructivist and constructionist points of view, as both Salazar and Dicks do, it becomes obvious that there exist no absolute criteria for what a tourism accommodation, a tourism service or a tourism encounter must look, sound, feel or taste like. Or, even more, there are no requirements specifying what 'The Tourist', theorized by Dean MacCannell (1976)[17] in particular, expects to receive as a tourism service. Having said this, I would like to suggest that many tourism experts base their advice on not only the ready manuals for hospitality management, but also their own preferences as tourists.

However, the desire to help was not the only driving force behind the visits from bilateral aid agencies and the Nicaraguan tourism ministry. Although reaching higher levels of profitability in rural tourism is not up in lights on the cover page of rural tourism strategies, it is a consideration that is presented in the ways tourism developers talk about tourism. In Nicaragua, there has been a growing worry about how little money the international visitors spend in general (Rocha 2008) and the hope is that all new tourism products will attract international tourists who will spend at least 40 dollars per day. In my view this magic line of 40 dollars has encouraged tourism developers to look for new means to raise the prices in rural tourism. In one example, the Nicaraguan Hotel School, Escuela Hoteleria, was chosen as one of the main partners in a pilot project involving rural tourism farms (INTUR 2010b). Teachers and students from the school had engaged in organizing capacity-building exercises in rural areas, including courses for bartenders and courses on how to prepare different kinds of quite luxurious meals for wealthier tourists.

When these kinds of courses were organized in San Ramón, the local hosts participated in them with slight amusement. The local guide Fernando hoped that such 'stupidities' – as he put it – would end when the official law on rural tourism was approved and people became more aware of the different forms of tourism in the country. He clarified:

> We have courses on how to prepare the same food as they prepare in five-star hotels – where they serve plates like 'steak with parsley' or fish. So they had to explain to the people organizing the course that women who work with tourism do not have these ingredients. They told the organizers that it is necessary to serve food that is typical of this region. The people who work with tourism still think that tourism must always be very strictly managed and professional.

During my visits to San Ramón in 2012 and 2013, the local hosts there were concerned about not only the continuity of tourism development, but also the worrisome prospect that tourism projects would completely change their homes and home communities. Were this to occur, the change would not be caused by tourists, but by tourism experts. This fear was expressed most clearly in one of the communities that had been included in many different kinds of tourism projects and courses. Doña Hilda noted that she and her colleagues had recently become more uneasy about the constant flow of visiting experts and consultants pointing out what needed to be changed and improved in order to attract visitors. She told me about a recent visit by a specialist from the development programme Moderniza:

> This consultant came from the capital city, Managua. She looked at the rooms and said that we could not receive visitors in rooms like these. So she wanted to make changes in the place. She said we should have curtains, raise the ceilings and so on. We thought that we do not want to do this. It is too risky to take new loans for tourism development. This was something very strange to us. It seems to me that she wanted to change what rural community-based tourism is to make it like tourism in the cities. Honestly, it left us sad and offended.

This story was one of the most striking examples where the lack of local material assets was interpreted as a lack of ability to receive visitors. Indeed, it was exactly these kinds of stories that encouraged me to look for a deeper theoretical understanding of what was actually happening in these kinds of encounters, where the guests, who obviously feel that they are helping the rural families, feel obligated to teach their hosts how to receive visitors in their own homes.

The background to the consultant's visit was the following: this particular community had been accepted for a tourism development programme called Moderniza, financed and run by a Mexican development cooperation agency. In Nicaragua the project was implemented by the Nicaraguan tourism ministry INTUR, as well as UNWTO and SECTUR (Secretaria de Turismo). Moderniza was based on a management system originally created in 2002 by the Mexican Secretary of Tourism and designed to improve the quality and modernization of micro, small and medium-sized tourism enterprises. The programme was based on successful cases in Mexico and has since been applied to a great number of tourism initiatives, even outside of Mexico. When I was talking to a representative from the embassy of Mexico in Nicaragua, he presented the programme as an achievement that allowed the continuation of the Mexican success story in tourism in other countries as well.[18] When reading the description and strategies of the Moderniza programme, it is easy to recognize the echo of earlier *community development* projects, which were seen as a way to 'transform traditional communities to modernity' (see Berkhöfer and Berkhöfer 2007, 234; Greig et al. 2007, 234; Midgley 2011, 174).

A project based on Moderniza was implemented in one the communities of San Ramón with the goal of bringing local business to the modern, or '*M*', level. In practice, this consisted of Maria, one of the local tourism coordinators, participating in Moderniza course meetings in Managua, the capital city. After every meeting, as Maria herself described it, she was expected to help the local entrepreneurs to go through modifications that would turn rural homes into hotel-restaurants. Maria, in the role of a local coordinator, just like the local hosts in the community, found this process to be both overwhelming and frustrating. The course required fast and expensive changes which were not possible or meaningful in this context. Although Maria had tried to describe the local realities to the consultants responsible for the course in Managua, they experts continued to demand results. She felt that the entire Moderniza system was designed for bigger companies that would have the capital to make the needed investments. That is, the project was not suitable for the people living in the communities of San Ramón, who were still having nightmares about their earlier difficulties in paying back their loans.

The main importance of this project, according to Maria, was the improved contact between the UCA San Ramón office and the particular community in which the project was run. Although Maria was working as a broker between the Moderniza project and rural homes, she had seemingly taken the side of the community. While she tried to adjust the programme to local realities that the families were living, she found this task very difficult. The community members continued to welcome her as a guest, not as 'one of the locals'. Furthermore, some of the local guides openly ridiculed the entire project: the local guide Fernando wondered, with an ironical tone in his voice, whether I knew how high ceilings the tourists were normally expecting. His comment supports my impression that this particular project could easily be included in some of the satires or parodies of top-down approaches to development aid. Such comedies have been recently written, for instance, in the Kenyan context.[19] The campaign 'Radiators for Norway' is another example of this healthy trend of questioning the perceptions of helping 'the-other-in-need' to help him- or herself through planned projects or charity campaigns.[20] The upshot here is that there exists a need to ask in which ways our representations of the 'poor other' continue to shape the future encounters between ourselves.

In San Ramón the visit of the Moderniza consultant sparked a spirited discussion in the community. Doña Hilda, who had told me about her fear of tourism changing her community, summed up the general feeling in the community in this way:

> We have thought that if visitors do not come, we must accept it. And we have now said to our local tourism coordinators that this particular consultant is no longer *welcome* here. We do not want to receive her here.

In other words, the local hosts had decided to explicitly cancel their welcome to this tourism expert. Or perhaps the comment meant cancelling their invitation to all tourism experts who seemed to arrive with the same kinds of attitudes and intentions. Although they had finally received the diploma with a blue 'M' as recognition of 'modernization', the diploma was now hidden in one of the drawers at the office of UCA San Ramón. It seemed like nobody was desperate to receive acknowledgement for participating in this development course for modern tourism enterprises. Instead, the local hosts seemed prouder of their common decision to not raise the ceilings and to declare the 'consultant from Managua' a 'persona non grata'. I was myself impressed by their determination and straightforwardness in this matter; I interpreted it as a concrete step in taking a more active role in the space where the conditions of welcoming were negotiated. In other words, the local hosts had made an active choice to *not* participate in these kinds of participatory projects.

During my last fieldwork in San Ramón in 2013, I noticed that the local hosts talked about these kinds of 'tidy guests' almost as uninvited guests (Höckert 2014; see also Goodwin et al. 2014). An important theme in many discussions and interviews was the fact that the local hosts no longer trusted and respected these kinds of guests in the same way as they had before. One of the guides, Gabriela, explained that they had become more suspicious towards their 'helpers' and seriously doubted whether they could any longer learn anything from the experts. She was furious that the people who coordinated tourism at the UCA San Ramón (and received a monthly paid salary in tourism projects) had, in her opinion, neither education in tourism nor interest in learning about the field. It seemed to me that, just like Gabriela, many people had become tired of the rude guests, who arrived with no respect for the locals either as people who opened their homes or as tourism professionals with knowledge and experience of tourism.

It is good to stop here to reflect about the paradoxes in the host-guest relations between locals and experts. In one way tourism experts tend to take the role of host, welcoming the people in rural communities to participate in development and research projects and in the tourism industry at large. These experts – or maybe I could say *we* – arrive with good intentions to lower the threshold for rural communities to enter tourism markets. It is as if the tourism specialists from the outside were saying '*Yes, welcome to participate in tourism*' but then continually reminding the locals of their otherness and inadequacy.[21] When the critique towards participatory projects in tourism has been growing, many studies have drawn attention to different limitations on participation; that is, to different reasons why local communities face difficulties in participating in tourism development (e.g. Campbell 1999; Hall 2003; Dixey 2008; Goodwin et al. 2014). Cevat Tosun's (2000) research on 'Limits of participation' must be one of the most comprehensive studies that address the variety of limits on local participation in developing countries in particular, and simultaneously sees local participation as something highly desirable. For instance, under the category of cultural limits, Tosun mentions aspects like 'the limited capacity of poor people to handle development effectively', 'apathy' and 'a low level of awareness in the local community'. In Tosun's (2000, 630) view the lack of tourism culture and knowledge on tourism can be explained, for instance, by 'the cultural remoteness of host communities to tourism-related businesses in developing countries'. Moreover, he suggests that the biggest challenge for the poor in many local tourist destinations in the developing world appears to be mere survival, which occupies all the time and consumes 'their' energy (ibid. 625).

In the case of San Ramón, some of the experts even claimed that the locals were not fulfilling the basic conditions for inviting guests into their home and saying 'welcome'. Levinas and Derrida help to point out the unethicality of encounters where, first, one's welcome is based on conditions, secondly, these conditions for welcoming are based on others' difference and, thirdly, the other's right to say 'welcome' becomes denied. It is clear that their idea of unconditionally open welcoming is a utopia that none of the parties here could live up to. However, while the experts sought to help the locals to participate in tourism development, they also kept the locals in the position of guests, that is, the same people who are assumed to be hosts in their homes and home communities. Could it be that the privileged position of an expert can easily lead to her or his claiming sovereignty over the role of the host?

As discussed previously, in the Levinasian idea of welcoming encounter, the roles of host and guest are in constant change, meaning that the host (hôte) becomes also the guest (hôte) (Derrida 1999, 19–21, 41–2). This means that striving for more ethical encounters between self and other would require, again in Rosello's (2001, 18) words, 'a continuum between hosting and guesting'. Although Levinas himself underlines the asymmetry in welcoming, I suggest that the inseparability of hosting and guesting derives from the idea of participation as such. Just like hospitality, participation cannot bloom with one host who always says welcome and dominates the guests. Kuokkanen (2007, 138), in her research on hospitality in academia, puts it well when she writes:

> There are many hosts, and they are all different. There are many entities that can and do say welcome, but the welcomes of these different hosts mean and imply different things. They may all be important, but that does not mean that they are necessarily equal or that they have the same access to institutional resources and discourses. There is the initial hospitality, and there are the initial hosts who continue to be hosts, even if at times it may appear that they have been erased or become the hostage of the *hosti-pet-s*, the guest-master through benevolent imperialism, epistemic ignorance, repressive tolerance, and other mechanisms of control and domination.

I find this to be a good reminder of Levinas's idea that the subject is a host – and a guest. Actually, the way in which some of the tourism experts in San Ramón undermined the local hosts' possibilities of hosting empowered the local women to claim their subjectivity as hosts who could set the conditions for their welcome. As a consequence of the experts' eagerness to take on the role of host in local homes, the local hosts decided to make their welcome more conditional. This decision is consistent with Kuokkanen's claim that the master-guest does not deserve to receive hospitality or to say 'welcome'. Extending this thought to the larger scale of participatory projects, it can be asked whether experts who dominate the hosting deserve to say 'welcome' or to call their work participatory.

In the communities of San Ramón, the encounters between local hosts and their 'tidy guests' became less hospitable when the years passed by. Although in the beginning there had been a promise of a minimum number of conditions and limitations for participating in tourism, in many hosts' opinions the requirements became unreasonable and unbearable as the years went on. What is more, after several years of capacity-building exercises, courses and improvement of material conditions, the participants felt that they were still not treated or heard as tourism professionals. In other words, their experiences and different modes of knowing about tourism and welcoming tourists were silenced in their encounters with the tourism experts. Adapting Spivak's (1988, 281) notion of 'epistemic violence' (see 1.1 and 2.4), this silencing could be called 'domestic-epistemic violence'. It was something that could be named as violence also in Levinasian (1969, 180–2) terms, as the locals felt that they became categorized as something deficient. As a result, it had become more difficult for the participants to enjoy their encounters with their guests in the same way as they had done before. This form of epistemic violence can be even more exasperating as the act of silencing takes place in people's own physical homes where they should be able to feel very safe – not only in the metaphysical and discursive spheres between self and the other. However, an interesting question arises here: can the locals' resistance to external criticism and evaluation be seen as a sign of empowerment?

It is difficult for me to imagine that such a strategy would have been deliberate. At least I have never come across a community-development strategy or gender equality project titled *Empowerment via critique and humiliation* or *Emancipation via domestic epistemic violence*. To put it differently, I doubt that participatory tourism plans include an implicit strategy of belittling the local entrepreneurs until they become empowered to resist the participatory projects. Luckily I had a chance to bring up this question in October 2013 when I attended a conference called *Local communities, promise or burden in sustainable rural tourism development?*[22] Before going to my actual question, I must point out that the title of the conference – and the conference as such – included a rather robust assumption about the role of tourism in rural areas. In this approach to rural tourism, the well-being of local communities is deemed secondary to the aims of developing tourism (see Höckert et al. 2013, 167). I was delighted when tourism geographer Jarkko Saarinen also discreetly challenged the assumption in his keynote speech at the conference.[23]

Another keynote speaker in this conference was Harold Goodwin, who is not only a preeminent scholar in the area of responsible tourism, but also one of the few outspoken critics of community-based tourism.[24] After his presentation I caught myself reaching eagerly for the microphone that was circulated in the audience. I was excited to hear whether Goodwin could consider rural communities as 'empowered' in settings where the local residents openly resisted social projects that had been planned *for* them. In the course of my question I asked whether this kind of capability of resistance could be seen as one of the goals of emancipatory empowerment projects. However, Goodwin rejected the possibility and meaningfulness of such a tactic of reverse empowerment. In his view, the most serious consequence of such a series of actions is that it can harm people's self-esteem, making it more difficult for them to shape the things that affect their well-being.[25] I agree. Based on my observations and analysis of tourism development in San Ramón, I have become convinced of the importance of acknowledging the consequences that might follow if projects 'fail'.

Developing the world through projects includes a risk that any resistance to planned projects becomes trivialized or silenced. In the case of San Ramón, the local coordinators and tourism experts interpreted local resistance as lack of motivation or entrepreneurial vision instead of meeting locals as active subjects who calculate their risks of welcoming. Following

Derrida's (2000, 75–83) 'double-law-of-hospitality', this calculation of risks is an inescapable part of hospitality between self and other. However, in the settings that take place in San Ramón, the locals are set to play the fixed role of passive receivers who are to a large extent incapable of calculating risks and shaping their conditions of hospitality based on those calculations. What is more, the visits of development officials have seemingly made the hosts' attitudes more hostile, or at least less open, towards their guests. I want to make it clear that I am not interested in making statements about who knows more about adequate material conditions in tourism and hospitality industries. Instead, my main concern here is, similarly to Kapoor (2004) and Eriksson Baaz (2005), the ways in which these encounters between locals and tourism experts lack open dialogue about different views. The consequences of this should not be taken lightly, for the preconceptions and opinions that the experts carry with them often turn into knowledge and practices (Sharpe and Spivak 2002). The risk of this happening in rural tourism development is evident, as the 'mobile' guests' openness towards the 'immobile' locals is limited by the guests' imaginaries of what 'tourism is supposed to look like'.

These risks could be diminished if the guests did their 'homework', as Kuokkanen (2007, 117) calls it, prior to heading to the field and to visit the others. The purpose of this homework would be to acknowledge and address the possible limitations on open encounters between self and the other. Drawing on Spivak, Kuokkanen (ibid., 115) describes the content of this homework as 'critical examination of one's beliefs, biases, and assumptions as well as an understanding of how they have developed in the first place'. This sounds like visiting what Bruner (2005) calls prenarratives and then continuing to travel with a questioning gaze. If the homework is forgotten – or eaten by the family dog – engagement in emancipatory projects includes a great risk of unconsciously reconstructing the unequal power relations between self and the other. Kuokkanen argues that responsibility links consciousness with conscience. She underlines the inadequacy of knowing one's responsibilities without being aware of the consequences of one's actions. Lack of such awareness produces an arrogant 'clean conscience', readily seen in a privileged academic, development expert or volunteer worker, all of whom can afford to be indifferent and not-knowing.

Guests who highlight the lack of material resources amongst hosts can worsen the feelings of 'relative deprivation', as tourism researchers express it (Swarbrooke 2002, 73–4; Höckert 2009, 86–90; Scheyvens 2011). However, feelings of relative deprivation are normally seen as a consequence of the interactions between locals and tourists, not of the visits with tourism developers. In fact, the potential for disappointment in crosscultural encounters between development brokers and local people is a widely acknowledged challenge in development studies (Eriksson Baaz 2005; McEwan 2009, 218–24). In any case, in San Ramón it seemed almost like some of the tourism experts had come with a duty-list that included the task of making the locals feel bad about their slow material progress and things that they were lacking in their homes. While my intentions here are by no means to trivialize the material needs that the people living in San Ramón might have, I want to question the meaningfulness of placing the priority on the needs of visitors who might end up never coming.

To conclude, although 'relative deprivation' calls for discussion about the unequal nature of tourism encounters, understanding experiences of inequality requires a wider range of conceptualizations and approaches. For instance, continual questioning and evaluation of hosts' capability to welcome guests can have various consequences. In San Ramón this has led, at least partly, to lack of motivation when it comes to waiting for and receiving guests. Many of the local hosts have experienced the requirements for material conditions as an endless list of demands that they will never be able to meet. In other words, this narrative of tourism development keeps constructing them as hosts and entrepreneurs who are somehow always, if not failing, at least inadequate.

4.4   Missing encounters

In the very beginning of tourism activities, local families felt uncomfortable about receiving money for their hospitality. But when some time had passed, the hosts started to see tourism and hosting as their livelihood and expected visitors to pay for the services. Yet, although the prices for tourism services were clearly presented on the UCA San Ramón website,[26] it was not always clear whether a walk with a local guide was part of a guided tour or just a chat on the way to the town of San Ramón. It also was unclear whether participation in local life meant eating with the families, or also observing how one's host family was struggling to cope with a semi-alcoholic family member. The limits between backstage and frontstage are evidently blurry in tourism encounters that take place in people's homes (MacCannell 1976; Lynch, McIntosh and Tucker 2009). The blurriness between private and professional domains of hospitality can also be approached with Derrida's (1999, 75–80; Baker 2010) idea of constant negotiation between conditional and unconditional hospitality. If unconditional hospitality means allowing the other to enter one's place of intimacy – backstage – conditional hospitality denotes an intention on the part of the host to limit the guests' access to backstage. However, just like in other spheres of hospitality, these negotiations cannot be pre-designed.

Based on my interactions with the local hosts in San Ramón I could say that this constant negotiation between welcoming and closing doors did not bother the hosts particularly much in cases where tourists arrived as paying guests. With time, as some of the hosts explained to me, they learned to handle even difficult questions about gender equality, religion, Nicaraguan politics, war, as well as more detailed inquiries about coffee production, demographics and so on. These answers were obviously not planned but rather the discussions always took on different forms with different guests.

An important issue that had already emerged in my interviews in 2008, and even more in 2013, was the arrival of those guests who were not aware that one had to pay for tourism services, did not want to pay for them or could not afford to do so. For instance, in one of the interviews doña Hilda told me about travellers who came, ate one meal and wanted to sleep on the patio – for free – without occupying the room built for the visitors. In my discussions with the local guides Alexis, Gabriela and Fernando, I heard stories about visitors who refused to pay for what they regarded as relatively rustic accommodation. There were also those who entered a community by themselves, walked on the tracks, took pictures and left. One of the guides, Gabriela, explained:

> We feel bad if people come here without us and without control because in practice the cooperative is the owner of this area. They should respect the fact that this is private property, but they do not show respect to this place and to us. They just march in without a guide and go to the mountains. Sometimes even other guides bring tourists here without our permission.

The most striking cases, in the guides' opinion, were occasions where a group of travellers came into the area with their own guide, had a good look at the local life and nature, ate their own food and left without leaving any compensation to the local community. The local guides told me that after these kinds of experiences they had considered it timely to call a meeting in each community to discuss common *rules for tourists*.[27] In these meetings they had agreed on the principle that tourists should always walk in the communities with the local guides. Gabriela clarified, 'We decided that every foreign person has to pay US$1 and Nicaraguans 10 Cordobas [approximately 50 cents] through here. By doing this we try to control the people who come through here'. Additionally, they defined more clearly those areas in the communities where the visitors were allowed to enter, and which areas were *only* for the people living in the community. For instance, the hosts felt it was important to respect the privacy of those community members who resisted the idea of tourism in their home community. What is more, some of the local guides approached the tourism coordinators in San Ramón and asked them to try to keep away intrusive or unwelcomed guests, that is, guests who did not show respect for the local tourism initiative and the rules by which it worked. The local guides seemed proud of the process where the conditions of welcoming had been decided, and they were also determined to implement their own codes of conduct (see Fennell and Malloy 2007; Holmes et al. 2016).[28]

When thinking with Levinas's (1969) ideas of ethics, the ways in which the local hosts were limiting their hospitality could be considered unethical. However, Levinas's idea of infinitely open welcoming means welcoming in a home that is not a property that could be owned. Hence, opening one's home completely to a stranger would require readiness to become a guest in one's own home. Without the codes of conduct, there is a risk that the locals become guests in their homes. Then, could it be said that the local hosts in San Ramón had seen it as their responsibility to protect their homes from those who did not acknowledge and respect the locals' hospitality? From the guests who had taken for granted that the locals would say 'welcome'? Or, even worse, from those who had not even recognized the local hosts as hosts? In fact, the above-mentioned conditions for unpaying guests were among the first codes of conduct that the locals compiled. Later on they continued to protect the borders of their community, and the thresholds of their homes, from researchers, students, as well as tidy guests, whom they had considered intruding or rude (see 3.3). Interestingly, community-based tourism had turned into efforts on the part of the communities to control access to the their home communities. At the same time, nearly all the local hosts whom I interviewed during my last visit were warmly welcoming visitors who stayed for several days and paid fairly for the local services they used during their stay.

For me the phenomenon whereby tourists and travellers try to avoid paying for the services described above is simultaneously irritating and fascinating.[29] It is by no means a unique phenomenon that takes place only in the Nicaraguan countryside. I will always remember one sustainable tourism workshop where a Finnish ecotourism entrepreneur decided to open her heart about tourism developers and tourists.[30] She told us that she was exhausted and outraged not only by EU regulations and municipality clerks, but also by visitors and neighbours who did not recognize her as an entrepreneur. The visitors, as she explained it, tended to arrive at her farm with their own picnic baskets and wanting to pet and feed the animals for free. When the entrepreneur, this Finnish woman, kindly informed the guests about the services she was offering on her farm, such as food and the possibility of visiting and petting the animals, she got to hear how rude and greedy she was. Rural tourism scholars have also noticed that consumers often expect rural tourism services to be cheap, if not almost free, as 'tourism is something that people do besides their real jobs' (see also George et al. 2009). In their edited volume on tourism in peripheral areas, Müller and Jansson (2007) also draw attention to these kinds of assumptions and challenges. With a clear graphic, tourism researcher C. Michael Hall (2007, 25) demonstrates that in rural settings where visitors do not come frequently tourists need to pay a relatively high price for their visit, not the opposite. This might be one dimension that becomes neglected in projects that combine tourism and rural community development.

In San Ramón the latest decline in visits seriously undermined the community's faith in a brighter future. The people felt that they lacked nearly all support from the middlewomen and tourism intermediaries who could have brought paying visitors to their home communities. The last time I visited Nicaragua, in May 2013, I discussed this issue with local coordinators at the office of the cooperative union UCA San Ramón. The two coordinators seemed to be aware of the expectations that the local hosts had; however, they considered that they were already doing all they could in order to revitalize the project. They underlined that there were still some groups coming to the area, but that the local hosts lacked the motivation and readiness to receive the guests.

In our brief meeting, the coordinators told me that they had succeeded in creating new contacts with some volunteer tourism organizations in the United States. This was not a surprise as such, taking into account the last years' rapid growth in volunteer tourism (Wearing, Deville and Lyons 2008; Vrasti 2013; Mostafanezhad 2014; Germann Molz 2017; Nisbett and Strzelecka 2017). Moreover, families in San Ramón had accommodated long-term volunteers, especially from Denmark, somewhat regularly. Hence, UCA San Ramón's website also included the following option:

> *Volunteering at UCA San Ramón* (3 months): Three meals per day, lodging, talks about coffee, etc., access to Internet, paper, free use of a bike. Price: US$ 1050.

Knowing this, I was surprised and disappointed to hear that the local coordinators had already agreed that a group of volunteers could come and stay with local families *for free*. Young volunteers from an organization called *Amigos de las Americas*, with 'focus on youth leadership training and community development in Latin America', were expected to arrive in San Ramón for a six-week stay during summer 2013. Instead of paying for their stay, they had promised to run social projects in their host communities and to leave a donation of approximately 400 dollars at the time of their departure. It turned out that the local coordinators also had mixed feelings about the meaningfulness of these visits. Even more, they seemed to be afraid of how their member communities would react to this agreement.

The coordinators must have been aware that the timing in asking the local hosts to receive visitors for free was not the best possible. A few months earlier the coffee-cultivating communities had been attacked by a severe coffee plant disease called *La Roya* (Olam 2013; Terazono 2013) and many farmers had lost up to 50–70 per cent of their coffee plants. The scenery in the coffee hills was quite dramatic: the local farmers, just like many farmers around the entire Central America, had to cut away the dead plants and had piled the plants to be used as firewood. It was estimated that it would take from three to four years before coffee production would recover to the level it had been at before this disease. In 2003, the original idea of tourism development had been introduced to San Ramón in order to bring supplementary income and to help communities to survive coffee crises like this.

During my stay in the coffee communities, many farmers and their family members shared with me their concerns about the situation. It was not only that they wondered whether they would be able to send their children to school; the poorest families were also anxious about the possible shortage of food. A few weeks after my visit to the office of UCA San Ramón, I met the other coordinator, Keyling, in one of the tourism communities. She came there for a meeting with the local hosts in order to help them to get prepared for a forthcoming one-day visit by a tourist group. The agenda also included a discussion about the arrival of the volunteers of 'Amigos de las Americas'. I was pleased that Keyling and the local hosts invited me to participate in the meeting.

The meeting took place in the new coffee-roasting house, built for the women's cooperative. In addition to the coordinator and myself, there were six women and one man who were together responsible for tourism accommodation in their homes. The women were happy and proud to present the new building for coffee roasting and to tell that many small coffee shops in the closest town, Matagalpa, were already buying their coffee. In the actual meeting the discussion was led by Keyling, who began by going through the plans for the approaching one-day visit. Thereafter, the participants shared some concerned words about a young Danish volunteer who had been staying in the community for a couple of months. They could not understand why this young man had stopped participating in his only task in the community: roasting coffee with the local women twice a week. After a while, Keyling went on and told about the new groups of volunteers called *Amigos de las Americas*. She reported briefly that there were young volunteers coming from the US; more specifically, these guests wanted to stay for six weeks and carry out an unspecified social project during their stay. They were not going to pay for their visit, but would leave a donation for the community.

Everybody in the meeting remained awkwardly quiet. One stared at the floor, one was looking out the window and the rest were glancing at each other. It was obvious that the people were reluctant to accept even the idea of receiving visitors for free. They had just cooked their lunches using firewood made out of coffee plants! From their point of view, I assume, it must have looked like the coordinator had just encouraged them to forget their various efforts, experiences and expectations as tourism entrepreneurs. At least she had left no room for the local hosts to discuss the compensation they would receive for welcoming these guests. When the uncomfortable silence finally ended, the hosts brought up how expensive and stressful it was to feed, guide and take care of the visitors. It became clear that the guests' presence does affect the family routines, add to their food consumption, make the hosts worry about their guests' health and comfort, and so on. These arguments are in line with Derrida's (1999, 51; Levinas 1969, 82) definition of welcoming and hospitality as interruption of self – as putting into question one's freedom. In this meeting the local hosts discussed and considered their willingness and readiness to interrupt their freedom by welcoming the young volunteers.

It would be naïve to expect that visitors, even volunteers, would not affect the hosts' everyday life. In her research on the idea of sharing a home,

Järvinen-Tassopoulos (2010, 314–23) brings up the need to acknowledge the ways in which the existing social relation between host and guest paves the way for hospitable encounters. In the case of San Ramón, the visitors were young volunteer workers with an interest in learning from and helping the locals. However, it is possible to imagine that the social relation or a social contract between tourism entrepreneurs and these guests who flouted the need to pay for tourism services must have been rather weak. It can even be so that these particular volunteers were not even perceived as guests, which can also explain the hosts' reluctance to express their hospitality. This situation also brought to mind Hazel Tucker's (2003) tourism research on *negotiating identities in a Turkish village*, where she discussed the challenges of shifting back and forth between encounters that appear as visit/hospitality and tourism/profit-making.

The situation was also awkward inasmuch as the local tourism coordinators had seemingly already promised this volunteer tourism organization that they could send their volunteers to San Ramón. The coordinators had already welcomed the volunteers, meaning that the people working with tourism accommodation were not the ones saying 'welcome'; they were not *the subjects of welcome*. After a decade of tourism development, Keyling, in the role of tourism coordinator, tried to assure the local hosts that receiving volunteers would be better than nothing. But was it really? For whom? This was one of the many situations in which I had to seriously question my rights and responsibilities as a researcher.[31] In this case I must admit that I ended up hinting that in my opinion the volunteers *should* pay for their visit as they were actually coming to communities whose residents were professionals in tourism. I was quite irritated by the fact that the hosts who had taken loans to improve the tourists' accommodation were now being asked to accommodate visitors for free. What is more, during this time the visitors' rooms would be occupied and the families would have to say *no* to other possible guests. If the tourists stayed with the families for six weeks, the costs (according to their official price list) would be approximately 840 dollars, that is, 140 dollars per week for six weeks. According to the special pricelist for volunteers, the price could be a little bit lower. It might be relevant to mention that each volunteer paid 5,850 dollars for his/her experience to the organization *Amigos de las Americas*.[32]

Without questioning the possible positive impacts of such volunteer projects, I want to make clear that this particular meeting at the coffee-roasting house did not include any discussion about the purpose and goals of the 'social project' that the volunteers wanted to carry out. In my later discussion with doña Thelma, a woman from another community who had promised to accommodate these volunteers in her home, she said that she did not know anything about the forthcoming social project either. Doña Thelma had been active in constructing a health centre in her community and she was now hoping that the new volunteers would help to build a fence around this centre. Otherwise, doña Thelma continued, there were no real social projects that they would have needed help with. Listening to the earlier meeting in the coffee roaster and then the thoughts of doña Thelma, it sounded like the local hosts were receiving young volunteers as kids who needed to have some activities during their vacation. Vrasti (2013, 89) succinctly states that in these kinds of volunteer programmes it often remains 'a mystery what exactly is so problematic about the country that requires the urgent intervention of white vacationing youths'.

Vrasti (2013, 65) also points out that these volunteers are rarely sent to the poorest areas or poorest homes. This corresponds well with the arguments presented in the meeting in the coffee toasting house. In fact, during the meeting one of the women proposed that the volunteers could actually stay with families who were *not* involved with tourism. In response, her peers considered this impossible as the volunteers needed their own rooms, better toilets and carefully prepared meals. In addition to this, they ended up agreeing that by accommodating these young visitors in the tourists' rooms, the rest of the community could develop a more positive attitude towards tourism. They felt that with volunteers somehow helping the entire community, the act of accommodating them would make the hosts appear unselfish. To borrowing from the latest business jargon, it seems like these entrepreneurs saw this as a good chance to market their 'corporate social responsibility'. However, their wish to look like responsible community members and ethical hosts does not vitiate, in my opinion, the dubiousness of the volunteer organization and local coordinators asking the local hosts to put up volunteers.

It must have been convenient for the volunteer organization to send its customers to rural communities that had a great deal of experience in receiving tourists. In these homes visitors even get their rooms cleaned every day. As this study focuses especially on the encounters between tourism experts and rural communities, I have not found it relevant to contact the volunteers who came to San Ramón between June and July 2013. However, if I had had an opportunity to pose a few questions to the 'amigos', I would have been curious to hear whether they had acknowledged the extensive efforts that the locals had made to turn their homes and home villages into 'visitable' tourism sites. Or whether had they experienced the communities as a huge 'backstage' where they had had an extraordinary chance to experience authentic local life. How had they experienced and interpreted the welcoming signposts, hostel-like rooms and, not least, webpages that inform visitors? Had they noticed that while they were using a flush toilet and taking showers, their hosts went to an outhouse and used water from the buckets? Or perhaps the volunteers felt that they deserved better conditions as they arrived with their project and donation, that is, with their gifts for the hosts.

Taking into account the previous tourism encounters in San Ramón, it looks like many guests had valued the help they offered as the best gift the local hosts could receive – even better in fact than paying for the tourism services that the hosts were offering. Could it be that these gifts function like 'backstage passes' which separate the tidy guests from tourists? Often these gifts come wrapped, if not in the white woman's or man's burden, at least in assumptions about the local needs. These gifts bring to my mind Anni-Siiri Länsman's (2004) research on host-guest relations between Finnish tourists and the indigenous Sámi minority in the northernmost part of the Finnish province of Lapland. In her research, Länsman, using the concept of the gift by Marcel Mauss (2008 [1924]; see also Pyyhtinen 2014), discusses the discourses and traditions relating to a bottle of liquor as a gift. The bottle is here seen as a gift which makes the local hosts more receptive and ready to invite their guests onto their lands. However, as Länsman (see Codelier 1999 in Länsman 2004, 187) argues in her research, 'viewed from the theory of the logic of giving, *land* (home) is an object that Sámi cannot give away without losing their identity'. As in Finnish Lapland, in San Ramón the local hosts have different opinions about the symbolic or real meanings of the gifts that their guests bring.

Not only do gifts call for a response from the host, but they can also challenge and question the hosts' right to define their conditions and limits of hospitality. In other words, the hosts can feel obligated to receive the gift, which comes in different forms of projects and studies. Although it is uncertain whether the visitors will come with something helpful, or even with something harmful, the rural communities are expected to be receptive towards these guests. If hospitality is about interrupting self and suspending one's ego (Levinas 1969, 82–4; Derrida 1999, 50–1), I argue that asking the hosts to say 'yes' unconditionally to strangers and their gifts means demanding that the hosts question their own ego. Or, as in the research by Länsman (2004), Finnish guests are asking their hosts to question their identity. Particularly in the case of volunteers, this might mean that the hosts in San Ramón have to question their identity *and* ego as tourism entrepreneurs – and even as adults who are well-off without the help from young, foreign volunteers. While Derrida and Levinas define the act of questioning one's ego as a precondition of ethical subjectivity, responsible encounters would require both parties, host and guest, to be ready for this interruption.

After ten years of tourism development in San Ramón the local tourism entrepreneurs still feel that they are not recognized as tourism entrepreneurs. Many of their guests have openly or indirectly pointed out how the hosts are continuously in need of assistance in order to improve their homes or their lives in general. These settings reconstruct the hosts as those who are always 'not there quite yet'. It is this subject position of 'being a subject which is not quite there yet', which is interpreted as a need for more experience and practice – and more help from the tidy guests. I will now move on to conclude the thoughts presented in this chapter.

4.5 Responsibilities of welcoming

Various examples from San Ramón indicate that developing tourism in rural communities might be more complicated than, as stated in section 4.1, 'washing your pig, dog and hens and showing your home'.[33] I began the chapter with the encounters where tourism developers had recommended to the local farmers and families that they should take loans for tourism development, and then moved on towards the time when tourists were no longer coming. When numbers of guests declined – despite the material improvements – the hosts were expected, on the one hand, to take more loans and, on the other, to receive visitors for free. It seems like during the first years the local hosts appreciated and benefitted more from the help of development officials than they did thereafter: a decade of different kinds of tourism projects had made many local hosts frustrated and reluctant to receive more tourism experts, volunteers, students and even researchers. With this development in mind, the chapter sought to discuss the challenges in establishing open dialogue between local hosts and guests who want to help them. Thus, in comparison to Chapter 3, here I have placed more of an emphasis on the existing and missing face-to-face encounters in rural communities and homes.

In the light of the present analysis, I would argue that, despite – or actually because of – emancipatory intentions to empower the local hosts, tourism experts end up dominating the spheres of dialogue even at the grass-roots levels. In San Ramón this happened, for instance, in the encounters where tourism officials ignored or played down the challenges and risks of taking loans, of opening one's home for strangers, or of combining the traditional forms of income with tourism activities. It seems like the meagre material conditions in local homes might be interpreted as an open and unconditional welcome for the active guests to enter, help and develop the locals. While some travellers and volunteers might be attracted by the modest circumstances, developers tend to perceive material scarcity as a limitation on tourism growth. As Vrasti (2013, 70–5) argues, both of these views are privileged ones which re-construct otherness and silence the other; the first romanticizes and the latter patronizes the local hosts. Putting things in somewhat different terms, I argue that the lack of material conditions in tourism accommodation maintains the privileged position of the visitor, and limits the possibilities of creating open dialogue between hosts and guests (Höckert 2014, 108–11).

When it comes to participatory projects, tourism developers in particular should take seriously the challenge of ensuring discursive spaces for the other. First, this means acknowledging how the others might be excluded from the spheres where conditions of hospitality are supposed to be negotiated and decided. It means acknowledging the ways in which one – based on one's relatively more privileged position – might dominate and host these spaces without welcoming the other to engage in open dialogue. We should avoid assuming, as Spivak's commentator Kapoor (2004) emphasizes, that the other will be participating equally in the dialogue at the moment one wishes to listen (e.g. Grimwood et al. 2012; Wearing and Wearing 2014).[34] Second, after acknowledging the impossibility of completely equal participation in the spaces of dialogue, there remains the challenge of resisting the pre-closure of the space, that is, keeping the doors open to the unexpected (Derrida 1999, 26).

To conclude the chapter, I suggest that, in the context of participatory tourism development, the spaces for negotiation must allow open and informed discussion about the possible challenges of welcoming tourism and tourists. This requires acknowledging how previous experiences of tourism encounters, or lack thereof, shape the possibilities of making an informed decision. However, as Derrida (Derrida and Rottenberg 2002, 31) argues in *Negotiations*, even the decision or action based on this calculation includes a risk. Naas (2008, 26) quotes Derrida's statement 'Nothing can ever assure us that this negotiation will not go terribly awry, either for the host or for the guest'. In regard to social projects, we could expect that dialogue, actions and their outcomes would prioritize the well-being of the rural hosts; that is, they would strengthen the subjectivity of the local hosts – subjects as hosts (Levinas 1969, 84, 299; Raffoul 1998; see Holmes et al. 2016). If this is the case, development experts in the role of guest have the responsibility to bring up the challenges and possible downsides of rural tourism development, even if it would risk the future of a planned tourism project or the arrival of an already welcomed group of volunteers. While I acknowledge the structural problems in the project-worlds that relate to this, it might be always timely to challenge the ways in which participation becomes implemented in participatory projects. I argue that more inclusive forms of participation require a readiness to interrupt self and to question one's ego as an expert, a researcher, a helper. In the following chapter, I go on to envision what these kinds of more welcoming encounters might look like.

Notes

1 In Spivak's (1993, 284) words this task is about engaging 'in a persistent critique of what one cannot not want'. Eriksson-Baaz (2005, 176) uses this quote in her research on *The Paternalism of Partnership*.
2 Original quote: – Ha oído hablar usted de turismo sostenible? – Pues mirá ... esa cuestión se va convertir en el future de nuestra comunidad muy pronto, ya vas a ver ... Dicen que montones de turistas quieren vivir nuevas experiencies. Y en Centroamérica ha crecido el turismo. – Con razon la Juana me dijo que ha visto varios chelés por estos lados.
3 For different national and global poverty lines (PPP 1.90 $ a day) see for example UNDP Human Development Report 2016.
4 See the 'Special Issue on Tourism as Work' in *Tourist Studies* 2010, 9(2).
5 See for instance O'Gorman (2010, 115–26) on offering hospitality to those in *necessitudine*.
6 Vianica, www.vianica.org, website accessed on 8 September 2008. For description of the atmosphere, different activities and attractions in San Ramón, please see Cañada et al. (2006, 85–7), McRoberts (2012, 151–4) or the website of UCA San Ramón, www.tourism.ucasanramon.com.

7 Examples of tourists' feedback can be found on the website www.tripadvisor.com with titles 'Matagalpa tours' and 'Rural Agrotourism – UCA San Ramon'.

8 For a detailed description of solidarity tourism in Nicaragua in the 1980s, please see Babb (2010) and McRoberts (2012, 60–8).

9 I refer here to *Sistema de calidad del turismo rural comunitario* (Quality system of rural community-based tourism) developed as part of *Ruta del Café* (Coffee Route), Nic/022. One version of this quality system was presented by Carlos Santovenia Pérez in *Foro Latinoamericano de Turismo Rural Comunitario* (Fair of rural community-based tourism) 28–30 August 2008 in Catarina, Nicaragua.

10 While the hosts in San Ramón had found the quality indicator documents overwhelming and unreasonable, these documents can simultaneously restrict and limit the requirements that the tourism experts can pose on the locals.

11 For discussions on the role and importance of labelling systems and certifications in indigenous tourism contexts, see de Bernardi, Kugapi and Lüthje (2017).

12 Please see Chalip and Costa's (2012) article on clashing worldviews between tourism development planners and rural residents living in a rural community in Portugal.

13 For reflections related to paid and unpaid work in tourism, see George et al. (2009, 185–7) and Jokinen and Veijola (2012, 39).

14 See Tania Li's (2007) thorough discussion about development encounters guided with the 'will to improve' in the context of Indonesia.

15 I have also used the concept of 'tidy guests' in Höckert (2014). It seems like these visitors are experts knowing what tourism is about – although they have only in rare cases studied tourism. The project research on disruptive tourism and untidy guests, to which I contributed, is written up in Veijola et al. (2014).

16 For discussions about the importance of understanding – or of acknowledging the difficulties of understanding – the local context in tourism, see Wearing and McDonald (2002), Cañada and Gascón (2007b), Höckert et al. (2013), Sammels (2014, 124–40), Wearing and Wearing (2014) and Quesada (2014).

17 For critique of the ambiguity of the label 'tourist' see also Edensor (2009, 543–5) and Caton (2013, 347–8); for the variety of ways of being 'a tourist', see also Veijola and Falin (2014) on mobile neighbouring.

18 For a more critical approach to tourism development in Mexico, see for instance Jamal and Camargo (2013), Balslev and Gyimóthy (2015).

19 See the series of *The Samaritans* on a dysfunctional, fictitious NGO in the Kenya field office, where 'the cosmopolitan staff deal with the strange demands and decisions of UK headquarters and hopelessly inept local bureaucracies, all under the guise of 'Saving Africa'. Source: aidforaid.com, website accessed on 15 August 2015.

20 For an insightful example of postcolonial analysis and action see videoclips such as 'Radi-Aid' and 'Let's Save Africa – Gone Wrong' by The Norwegian Students' and Academics' International Assistance Fund. Their 'Africa for Norway' campaign encourages all the Africans to save Norwegians from dying of frostbite. Their slogan goes: 'You too can donate your radiator and spread some warmth!' Their latest video 'Who wants to be a volunteer' (a modified version of 'Who wants to be a millionaire') offers an entertaining chance to question one's perceptions about volunteer tourism by telling the story of Lilly, who wants to 'save Africa'. Source: www.africafornorway.no/why website, accessed on 14 December 2014. For critique of this kind of 'humanitarian gaze' in tourism, see Mostafanezhad (2014, 5–6).

21 Please see Mireille Rosello's *Postcolonial Hospitality* (2001), where she discusses the refugees who are welcomed and then reminded of their otherness. See also Kuokkanen (2007) on the ways universities remind indigenous people of their otherness.

22 The conference on *Communities as a part of sustainable rural tourism – success factor or inevitable burden?* was organized on 9–10 September 2013 in a Finnish coastal town, Kotka.

23 See also Jarkko Saarinen (2006) on *Traditions of Sustainability in Tourism*. Saarinen's (10 September 2013) keynote in the conference 'The role of communities in rural tourism and rural development'.

24 Goodwin's (10 September 2013) keynote in the conference was titled 'It is not Tourism until it is sold: commercializing community based tourism'. See also Goodwin (2011), Goodwin et al. (2014).

25 For discussions on social empowerment within tourism, see Höckert (2011), Jamal and Dredge (2014, 188–90, 198), Hashimoto (2014); for resistance in tourism, see Jamal and Stronza (2009), Mettiäinen et al. (2009, 226–37), Pleumarom (2012), Sammels (2014, 130–1); for resistance to aid, see Escobar (2012, 215–17), Seppälä (2013).

26 The pricelist that can be found on the San Ramón webpage (accessed 23 March 2014):
   • Lodging with family incl. breakfast per night per person: $12.
   • Lodging at the Eco-Albergue in La Pita per night per person: $15.
   • Breakfast per person: $3.5 / Lunch per person: $5 / Dinner per person: $4.
   • A local tourist guide per day per group: $15 / Tour to Solcafe per person: $5.
   • Entrance to the finca per person: $2 / Using the pool: $2.
   • Workshop to learn how to make traditional food per group: $40 / Workshop with natural, traditional medicine per group: $40 / Cultural activities (games, music, dancing) per group: $60.
   • Prices for volunteering at UCA San Ramón, Package 1 (3 months): Three meals per day, lodging, talks about the coffee, etc., access to Internet, paper, free use of a bike. Price: US$ 1050.

27 For the importance of codes of conduct in local communities, see also Dowling (2003, 214), Wearing and Wearing (2014).

28 For discussions about the roles and creation of ethical codes of conduct, see Fennell and Malloy (2007) and Holmes et al. (2016). The former discusses, for instance, the technical characters of these kinds of codes that are often developed and deployed by industry officials as a tool tailored to modify or manage visitor and operator behaviour (Fennell and Malloy, 2007). The latter tells a story about a participatory research and development process for negotiating and creating an 'Indigenized visitor code of conduct' based on local expectations of respectful visitor conduct within their ancestral territory.

29 Please also see Sammels's (2014, 130–4) analysis on the 'performances of bargaining' in the highlands of Bolivia.

30 This happened at the *Best Practices of promoting responsible travel* workshop in Helsinki, Finland (25–29 April 2011).

31 This dilemma is wonderfully explored in Caton's doctoral research project (2008) and in her article *Between you and me: Making messes with constructivism and Critical Theory* (2014b). Caton discusses her responsibilities as a researcher and teacher to address injustices and work for social change.

32 The prices in 2013 were taken from their previous webpage, www.amigoslink.org. In 2017 this webpage no longer existed and the new website of the Amigos, with somewhat changed programmes in Nicaragua, is https://amigosinternational.org/.

33 This was the comment made by a representative of the Nicaraguan Tourism Ministry, INTUR.

34 See Derrida's discussion on asymmetry of response (1999, 22–5). See also Levinas (1985, 98–9).

5 Envisioning hospitable encounters

It was during my last field visit in San Ramón that I met one of the local guides, Fernando, at the office of UCA San Ramón. He told me that he was there waiting for a group of representatives from the national rural tourism network RENITURAL and from an international tour operator. This group had become interested in tourism development in the area of San Ramón through an international tourism feria called *Fenitur*, which was organized in Managua in April 2013. As a result, the tourism coordinators at the office of UCA San Ramón and the local hosts in Fernando's home community were hoping that these visitors would become interested in sending more tourists to the area. Fernando was calling this visit a simulacrum, which would allow them to show these 'test visitors' how they welcome travellers in local homes. The representatives were supposed to arrive at 8:30 in the morning, but now it was already noon. Fernando was still waiting, wearing a nice pair of black trousers and a 'RENITURAL' shirt. He told me about the detailed plans he had made for the visit; however, now he would have to present San Ramón and his home community much faster than planned.

Finally the group arrived. It was already one o'clock and Fernando had almost no time to give the tour before having lunch in doña Jisenia's kitchen. During what was a quick meal the guests did not talk to doña Jisenia, or ask anything about her experiences with tourism development; instead, they spoke only with Fernando. After this they, the visitors jumped into their minibus and drove away. Later, when I had a chance to discuss the visit with the local hosts, they pointed out that the guests had mainly been interested in checking the quality of local accommodation and food services. Although I knew that working as a guide or with tourism accommodation required flexibility and constant readiness (Lynch et al. 2007; Rantala 2011a), this simulacrum made me annoyed and upset on behalf of the local families who had expended quite a bit of effort in preparing their homes and themselves for this visit. My frustration was undoubtedly mixed with the worry about the difficulties of bringing in tourists to the area. All in all, it seemed contradictory that people who had been interested in sending visitors to this community had neither respected the plans for the guided tour nor started any kind of conversation with the local hosts.[1] Moreover, I knew that the local hosts consider the interaction with the families and tranquil walks on the mountains to be the most important part of their tourism product – more important than food, beds, curtains or showers.

Although some of the tourism practitioners had focused primarily on curtains and menus, this was not the case with all the tourism experts. For instance, I was once there when a tourism consultant from Lux Development took a long and slow walk with the local guide through the coffee fields and other sights. While the consultant also focused on technical issues, the walk offered an opportunity for a more equal discussion about the concerns and challenges related to tourism development. However, instead of dwelling on these kinds of disappointing experiences of unequal encounters – or wondering why the Levinasian (1969) idea of infinite openness between hosts and guests does not seem apply in the rural communities – I would like to try to change perspectives. Rather than focusing solely on encounters without hospitality, I will continue with an exercise that challenges me to articulate what hospitable encounters could look like. The instructions for this exercise, which draws inspiration from Christian Lund's[2] lectures at the University of Helsinki in January 2013, are the following:

> One day when I came home from collecting my empirical data, I thought that 'today I had seen hospitality as Levinas and Derrida would define it'. So what do I think I had seen? What makes me think I had seen hospitable encounters? What were the things that I observed? And, finally, who did I think had hospitality and how?

Answering these questions could also be called 'Sociological Fiction', where the change is expected to happen not in the future, but in our imaginings at this moment.[3] This approach can be weaved together with Donna Haraway's (2016) different variations of SF, those of science fiction, speculative fabulation, string figures, speculative feminism and science fact, which all can help us in learning to be present, and, as the title of her book states, *Staying with the Trouble*.

In order to challenge and question some of the taking-for-granted understandings of tourism encounters, this chapter is dedicated to imagining different modes of being and becoming or, put otherwise, to envisioning alternative ways of being-with and becoming-with (Veijola et al. 2014; Pyyhtinen 2015; Haraway 2016). Accordingly, I have set myself two tasks in this chapter: first, to imagine and describe what an ethical and hospitable space between hosts and guests could look like in San Ramón's context and, second, to discuss how these spaces could be made more open and equal for everyone to participate in. Tourism scholar Alexander Grit (2014), drawing especially from the discussions of Deleuze and Guattari, uses the concept of *hospity* to describe the idea of opening up new spaces of hospitality. According to Grit (2014, 132):

This hospity is an experience within spaces of hospitality which is not defined yet; the host guest relationship and interactions are not pre-given. This space can host different becomings with, on the one hand, creative becomings whereby the virtual becomes actual and, on the other, rather planned becomings whereby the possible becomes real through a process of realization.

In Grit's (2014, 133) view, host-guest relationships can quickly alter, meaning that hospity can be a very temporary space of hospitality. Rather than reinforcing the notion of hospitality as an obligation to prepare people, places and spaces, Grit's call for hospitality prompts an idea of an open and serendipitous encounter between self and others.

Drawing especially on Derrida's and Levinas's discussions on hospitality as 'being-for-the-other', this chapter suggests that opening more hospitable spheres between hosts and guests requires a mutual readiness to interrupt self, that is, to disrupt one's freedom as spontaneous subject. As discussed in the sections 2.3 and 4.4, the idea of interrupting self, as Levinas and Derrida (1999, 51–2) highlight, is necessary in order to allow subject positions, such as self-other, subject-object, teacher-student, host-guest, to become more mobile. This chapter focuses mainly on the local hosts' experiences of successful encounters with their guests. The reason for this one-sidedness lies in the abundance of already existing narratives told by different kinds of tourism experts. The main data used for the analysis are the interviews with the local hosts in the communities of San Ramón. Additionally, the analysis is based on my 'field notes' of my own experiences as a visiting guest in these communities. Doing this exercise made me realize that traces of hospitability are weaker in the encounters between local hosts and tourism experts than they are in other host-guest relations. I do not want to dismiss the ways in which rural community-based tourism development, at large, can be seen as an interruption of large-scale, growth-oriented forms of tourism development. However, this chapter emphasizes hospitable spaces in microlevel face-to-face-encounters between hosts and a wide range of different kinds of guests.

The first section discusses how hospitality could be understood as an idea of sharing time among ourselves – as a readiness to interrupt one's plans and schedules for the other. Hence, I approach the issue of 'making space for the other' with the notions of *time* and *tranquillity*.[4] The second section approaches the question of interrupting self from the perspective of being ready to be taught by the other. The Levinasian idea of welcoming teaching reveals how his primary interest in ethical relations lies in neither teaching nor learning, but in the idea of being taught (Levinas 1969, 180–3; Derrida 1999, 18).[5] Here, the primary focus of the analysis is on the meanings that the local hosts have given to the possibilities for learning from one another (see Dredge and Hales 2012). The last part then takes up the importance of recognizing how the conditions of welcoming become negotiated between hosts and guests. The section is based on local hosts' wishes that guests would respect the conditions, such as paying for the tourism services, when visiting the community of San Ramón. The analysis suggests that basing the debates on more responsible forms of travelling merely on the guests' assumptions of responsibility includes a risk of reconstructing the immobile subject positions between haves and have-nots, those who can afford mobility and those who cannot (Ahmed 2000, 172; Higgins-Desbiolles 2006; Holmes et al. 2016).

5.1   Tranquillity at home

The exercise in changing the perspective – of imagining what hospitable encounters actually could look alike –requires me, peculiarly, to go back in time. As a result, it means putting on the same sunglasses[6] that I had on when I first visited the communities of San Ramón, when I was inspired for the first time by their slogan 'meet, and get to know, the faces behind the coffee cup'. Back then in 2008, I was eager to see the great potential of community-based tourism as a unique setting of mutual respect and responsibility between hosts and guests (Höckert 2009). I saw that community-based tourism included an aspiration to care for each other, mixing happily the ideas of communality and multiculturalism (Vrasti 2013). The visitors would arrive with enthusiasm to help the locals, and the locals would be committed to caring for their guests. However, as I gained more knowledge about these encounters in practice and read more of the scholarly debates on these kinds of encounters, I noticed that the brand of my previous sunglasses was – quite embarrassingly – 'Naïve'. No doubt, this brand has never been cool or trendy in academic discussions. Moreover, many might consider it even strange that these kinds of sunglasses, with small silhouettes of unicorns on both sides of the lenses, come in adult sizes. In any event, I still have mine and I am happy to get to wear them on special occasions like this; that is, in a situation where they help me reflect how and why we consider something as responsible or ethical.

Another good reason to put these glasses on is the way they force me to think about the filters that I have used when drawing on the postcolonial approach. By filters I refer to the special view of the world one gets when travelling – albeit in fiction – with postcolonial writers such as Spivak, Escobar, Mignolo, Pratt or Kincaid. Using these filters comes with a risk of strengthening, instead of deconstructing, the existing binaries between self and the subaltern other. That is, the risk in postcolonial analysis is that the outcomes – such as finding instances of epistemic violence and material exploitation based on colonial conditions – are decided even before engaging with the empirical context. For instance, in my study I have conducted fieldwork and analysis with Spivak's thoughts close by, which has directed my radar towards unethical behaviour among the privileged ones. This makes it difficult *not* to romanticize or victimize the unprivileged 'other' – although this is exactly what Spivak and Kincaid tell critical researchers and travellers *not* to do. In order to avoid essentializing postcolonial encounters, tourism scholars Keith Hollinshead (1998; 2004), Darlene McNaughton (2006) and

Hazel Tucker (2003; 2014, 201) have called attention to the ways in which Homi Bhabha's (1994) idea of *hybrid subject* offers an opportunity to resist the totalizing repression of colonialism. On the whole, I argue that wearing only postcolonial glasses can make one blind to emerging, alternative ways of caring for the other and the multiple others.

Although my study has focused extensively on guests' desire to help the hosts in San Ramón, it is worth keeping in mind that the hosts also care for their guests. While it is true that the tourism practitioners provided different kinds of training and capacity-building exercises to prepare the hosts to offer their *care* in a context of tourism services, we cannot deny that there are also many other forms of caring than serving food and drink and cleaning one's home (Noddings 2002; Puig de la Bellacasa 2017). Doña Thelma, who had been accommodating tourists for several years, explained in our interview:

> One time this one tourist from US got very sick, which really made the family (who was hosting her) worried. The tourist needed to go to the hospital, but she wanted to go there by herself. The family continued to be worried after she had left alone, so they decided to follow her to Matagalpa (a one-hour bus ride away from this community), and look for her because they wanted to take care of her. The poor girl had appendicitis and the family was saddened that she went through everything alone.

Other people whom I interviewed in the communities of San Ramón also brought up the fact that they were often concerned about their visitors' health, whether their guests found their accommodation comfortable, or whether the guests were walking safely on the mountains. People who work with tourist accommodation emphasized the importance of letting guests know that the hosts were there for them. Thus, while many of their guests arrived in the communities of San Ramón to promote the locals' well-being, the local hosts also considered it important to be able to take care of their guests. Perhaps this kind of mutual longing to take *care* of each other could be interpreted as a sign of hospitableness between hosts and guests.[7]

This resonates with Jokinen and Veijola's (2012, 40) discussions in *Reflections on Borderless Care*, in which they propose that tourism and the tourist experience in general is *all* about the care. The importance of mutual *caring* in ethical relations is also present in the theoretical discussions in Mary Mostafanezhad and Kevin Hannam's (2014) anthology *Moral Encounters in Tourism*. Some of the writers in the book share a concern about the ways in which the recent trend of moralizing tourism has turned the question of care into one of the laudable personal qualities of *the traveller* (Butcher 2014; Smith, P. 2014; see also Strzelecka et al. 2017). Thus, the attention is drawn mainly to the guests' desire to be responsible towards the host communities and host environments. As argued in section 1.2, it is necessary to keep asking whether the discourses that search for more ethical forms of tourism assign the role of active subject solely to tourists and tourism developers.

Furthermore, what might be the consequences of co-constructing narratives where ethics and respect in tourism depend primarily on the interests, values and plans of the guests?

During my stays in San Ramón, it became obvious that *time* played a significant role in hospitable encounters. Based on my own experiences, and discussions and interviews with the local hosts, it is fair to say that peacefulness and tranquillity are, in the local hosts' opinion, pivotal aspects of the desired tourism encounters in San Ramón. In fact, 'todo tranquilo' (everything is tranquil) is a common saying which indicates that everything is all right. A good starting point for envisioning hospitable encounters could be to quote doña Hilda. For her hospitality means saying 'Welcome to my home'. She continued that welcoming means hoping that 'the visitors feel like they are part of the family and that they feel at peace'. The same message occurred in many of my interviews: the people accommodating tourists hoped that their visitors could feel calm and at peace. Many highlighted that they wanted their visitors to stay for at least a couple of days. Longer visits would mean more income from the visits; however, the longer stays also allowed the local hosts to present their home community and the mountains at a peaceful tempo, without needing to rush.

Although some of the local hosts in San Ramón wished to receive tourists all the time if possible, many pointed out their desire that their home communities would also remain peaceful. One of the guides, Edmundo, argued that bigger flows of tourists

> could bring positive economic impacts, but this could affect us who have to live our life here, to study and work and do everything at the farm ... If more and more visitors come all the time, it will change the life and the culture here in the communities and inside the families too much. It's good that the tourists come, but with a slow rhythm.

It seems as if the positive attitudes towards tourism could be directly related to this *slow rhythm* mentioned by the guide (see Rantala and Valtonen 2014). This evokes one of the basic topics in tourism literature: how tourism development becomes socially and culturally more 'sustainable' when the growth of tourism is not overwhelming. However, the question of *rhythm* becomes pivotal especially in *rural* tourism development, where tourism activities form a supplementary source of income. In her longitudinal study of rural tourism development in Finnish Lapland, Maria Hakkarainen (2017) addresses the challenges of synchronizing the rhythm of tourists' arrivals and activities with agricultural life and work. Hakkarainen describes how tourism development had become part of the village's livelihoods, when it had been driven by rhythms and task-scales of the village's nature-based livelihoods. Although it would be convenient if the 'high seasons' of tourism took place when there is less work in the fields or farms, it is often precisely that which forms an important part of the tourists' experience. This is also the case in San Ramón, where guests were more interested in coming between October and January so that they would have a chance to engage in the processes of coffee production. However, as the number of tourists had always been relatively low, the local hosts did not seem to experience this as a serious challenge.

In relation to the question of hospitality, many of my interviewees highlighted that while there were guests in their home or home community, they dedicated their time to them. Although many of the local hosts no longer prioritized the different kinds of capacity-building meetings, the tourists' visits were prioritized over everything else. Many used precisely the expression 'to dedicate our time' to describe their commitment towards the travellers. Doña Hilda told me about such a visit:

> A little while ago there was a young traveller who came to visit us. She asked whether we would have time to listen if she played guitar and sang a few songs. And yes, we did have time for her. So, we sat there listening. And later on, she left with tranquillity. This is something that we do with our visitors.

In San Ramón the words *tranquillity* and *happy faces* were vividly present in stories where the hosts described their experiences of successful encounters. Or, to put it differently, perhaps the calmness of the encounters allows the hosts to enjoy these happy faces. A young woman working with tourism, Claudia, explained that in her opinion hospitality is:

> To smile and show your happiness of meeting a person that you do not know (*no conoces*). And you give this person your best. And they look at you with happiness on their face. This is what I think is hospitality. It is the happiness of seeing that these people, the new faces, come to visit us. It is about being kind and about making people feel like this is their home.

I can confirm that throughout my participatory observation as an ethnographic researcher I have noticed that this often seems to be the case. In fact, I am thankful for having had the chance to experience this kind of welcoming happiness on some peoples' faces. For me, Claudia's description of hospitality includes a sight of Levinas's notion of embodiment of ethics and peace in the (here, smiling) *face* of the other. Levinas (1969, 197) describes this situation as the 'welcome of the face'. These are encounters where the happiness of engaging in a face-to-face conversation with the other disrupts the closed monologue of the self (see also Hand 2009, 40). It is the face-to-face encounter which becomes prioritized over other tasks and duties (see also Hales and Caton 2017).

The face ethically fulfils and embodies the whole purpose of Levinas's philosophy, especially his aims in *Totality and Infinity*.[8] For Levinas (1969, 67), the face-to-face encounter is a primordial production of being which helps in tracing the absolute experience of unconditional hospitality, that is, to pursue an absolute ethical experience that is not a disclosure. The face resists possession or utilization, and invites and obliges one to take on a responsibility that transcends knowledge. However, Levinas (1969, 305) explains, somewhat paradoxically, that goodness 'concerns a being which is revealed in a face, but thus it does not have eternity without commencement'. He continues that 'peace must be my peace, in a relation that starts from an *I* and goes to the other, in desire and goodness, where the 'self' both maintains itself and exists without egoism' (Levinas 1969, 306). For me, it is precisely our egos which enjoy comparing difference and otherness to self – to 'same'. Hence, for Levinas, the face emerges as an emblem of everything that fundamentally resists categorization, containment or comprehension (Hand 2009, 42).

With this in mind, it is interesting to take a look at the slogans used for marketing tourism in San Ramón. There are, for instance, different versions which encourage the visitors to *meet* the faces and to get to *know* the faces. UCA San Ramón's website invites the visitors to 'Get to *know* the faces, voices and culture of the people behind your cup of fair trade coffee in San Ramón, Matagalpa, Nicaragua' (see Kalisch 2010; Boluk 2011). From a Levinasian (1969, 194–7, 305; Derrida 1999, 21) point of view, it is quite problematic to utilize faces for tourism marketing; it is incongruous to freeze faces on posters and web-pages, as the face is the sign of ultimate openness and welcoming towards the other. As discussed throughout the study, there is a fundamental difference between *knowing* and *meeting* the other: for the philosophers of ethical subjectivity, the other is not a knowable unit (1969, 84). When testing this thought, at least I personally feel strong reluctance towards being reduced to something that can be known, categorized and 'said' (see Levinas 1969 and sections 1.4 and 2.4 in this book).[9]

It is easy to recognize the desire to know the other, in order to be able to help the other. However, paradoxically the eagerness to know and define the other is often stronger in short-term encounters. In contrast, when meeting the other tranquilly, it becomes less meaningful to categorize and 'to know' the other. The fact that caring and listening requires time has been underlined especially by those scholars who have critiqued participatory development methods such as 'rapid rural appraisal' (Chambers 1983) as rather imperialist ways of collecting information about the other. This methodology, elaborated especially by development experts, includes guidance for studying and understanding the local context in a speedy manner. In other words, by using this approach, a guest-expert can acquire a good overall picture of life in a rural village in a short period of time (Kapoor 2004), that is, understand and evaluate the wishes and desires of the people by going or running around with a recorder, notebook and a pen. A somewhat similar kind of efficiency is also celebrated in tourist hype promising that a true cosmopolitan traveller can absorb the essence of an entire country or a continent during a few weeks' vacation. For instance, The Lonely Planet travel books offer great solutions allowing busy travellers to 'discover' a 'hidden' pearl, for instance Nicaragua, in 14 days. There are also speedy travellers who measure their success – like Phileas Fogg (Jules Verne 1873) – in the distance covered during an adventure (see also Pratt 1992; Germann Molz 2009, 276; Vrasti 2013, 67–9).

The point I want to make here is that the fast visits and appraisals can make it difficult to find, recognize or promote hospitality. Similarly, when we encounter each other stressed or in a rush, there is a smaller chance of meaningful communication and mutual openness. Nevertheless, the appreciation of slower life and tranquillity, or even more the fear of the things that we might miss in the middle of 'multitasking', is something that has become a growing trend in the Western world during the past years. There seems to exist a mass awakening of living mindfully in the present. While the commodified ideas of mindfulness might paint a picture of a new trend, the search for consciousness, just like the search for participation or hospitality, is by no means anything new (see Chen et al. 2017). In fact, following the Levinas (1969) and Derrida (1999, 46) reflections which describe metaphysics as an experience of hospitality, I perceive consciousness, hospitality and participation as something inseparably intertwined.

What bothers me here is not only the tendency of describing mindfulness as a new idea, but also the way in which it has been commercialized to promote the well-being of a busy individual, not well-being between ourselves. These discourses strengthen the individualistic idea that taking care of oneself means closing out the multiple others who might be constantly interrupting us from *ourselves*. In this sense, being-well would mean focusing on one's own way of being and controlling the interruptions in one's own time. Carl Cederström and André Spicer (2015) call this the *Wellness Syndrome*, arguing that the ever-present pressure to maximize our happiness, health and mindfulness has turned against us and provoked us to withdraw into ourselves. Their eye-opening analysis describe how happiness and wellness have become moral imperatives where the visions of social change have been reduced to dreams of individual transformation. Similarly, Swedish philosopher and psychologist Ida Hallgren (see Branner 2016) argues that the demand to be happy, mindful and to think positive – with closed eyes and a hot cup of tea in our hands – has helped us to achieve new records of self-centredness. Nevertheless, making wise decisions that benefit the well-being of all beings, in Hallgren's view, requires ability to face also the negative reality here and now (for discussions beyond happiness, see also Alt 2016).

What is drastically different between the contemporary discussions of wellness and mindfulness celebrated by many 'life-coaches', self-help books and yoga-magazines, on the one hand, and the Levinasian thought of hospitality, on the other, is how the Levinasian (1969, 172; 1987) idea of transcendence reaches out towards the absolutely Other.[10] It means that the beginning of ethical – of ethics as hospitality – is to welcome the other to one's space and to one's time. Likewise, consciousness for Levinas is not first and foremost the practice of representing existence to ourselves, but a moral event that recognizes and welcomes the inexhaustible other. Consequently consciousness, according to Levinas, is inherently social and plural – rather than a

mode of being which is isolated and sacred. Thus, instead of only finding harmony within oneself, Levinas's idea of infinity means being 'beyond being' –
beyond the ontology of isolated subjectivity (Levinas 1969, 305; Hand 2009,
38). This idea goes well beyond the current wellness ideology where 'feeling
good' equals 'being good' (Cederström and Spicer 2015).

Putting differently the Levinasian idea of the face, I propose that
encountering and spending time with 'faces' *do* make us less eager to place
that other into neatly limited categories, such as, annoying, naïve, old, shy,
dupe, successful, lazy, selfish, chubby, rich, poor, and so on. Or when we do so,
it does not feel right. Please go ahead and test this by taking a good, calm look
at someone's (or something's) beautiful face. As a result, if the moment of
meeting the other is the beginning of the ethics as hospitality, then a vision of
a hospitable encounter could be focused more on sharing time with the other
than on knowing that other. In summary, the call for tranquillity in face-to-
face encounters includes allowing the mountains and coffee tables to mediate
hospitality.[11] Unlike capacity-building or individual mindfulness exercises,
these encounters are based on the idea of reciprocity and mutual exchange.
Adopting a well-known saying, I wish to propose that 'just like democracy,
hospitality, too, begins from the breakfast table'. When allowing the coffee
or the cup to mediate the tranquil encounters with the other, it becomes less
relevant to judge, teach and guide the other. Instead, it helps creating an open
space for a mutual sense of caring and responsibility and a desire to engage
in storytelling with the other. This means taking off the 'Naïve' sunglasses
decorated with magic unicorns – but continuing to speak the language of
kindness, care and hospitality.

5.2   Continuum in teaching and learning

Many of the interlocutors in San Ramón gave exceedingly positive meanings
to those encounters that took place during the international solidarity
movement, in the 1980s (McRobert 2012). At that time, as people described
it, visitors were received 'as friends, not as tourists'. I would submit that one
of the main reasons for these positive experiences must have been the fact
that the guests stayed for a longer time, with no hurry to leave. Nor did they
cause an economic burden to their hosts, as they brought food with them. In
those days, there were no third parties involved and the 'rulebooks' for the
visits were somewhat unwritten. Coupled with the interest in learning from
each other, the guests seemed to have few requirements and expectations of
their hosts.

During my stays in San Ramón, I also heard stories about guests who had
been there in the 1980s and then returned many years later. One was told by
doña Hilda:

> I remember this very beautiful experience. In the end of their visit we
> roasted a pig and celebrated, and it was a beautiful experience. And when

they left, and as it was the first time we worked with them, all the families were very sad. (...) And this person who was the guide for this group said that we must learn that the groups come and go and come and go. And that we had to learn to attend to them. And I have had opportunities to meet the visitors again (pride). For instance, there was this one visitor who had been staying here with me around year 1985. Then suddenly one of the local guides said that there would be a group coming. But I did not know that this group had people who had been here before. And she came and said, 'here I come again'. (...) They always remember us.

While such stories about the first guests were filled with tears of happiness and feelings of appreciation, it is quite interesting to reflect on the leap from those visits to more official tourism encounters. This is particularly so because the positive experiences from the previous encounters had encouraged families to commit themselves to the more official forms of welcoming tourists.

Perhaps the following quotation from Gabriela, a local tourist guide, can disclose the differences between the 1980s and now. In our discussions of hospitality and tourism she distinguished the ideas of being hospitable from material conditions and from offering a tourism service.

I would not like to define hospitality as a concept which refers to service. I want hospitality to be a concept of humanity – to be a human. And tourism is how to sell services and quality.

I would be happy to follow this way of approaching tourism. The approach means that tourism as such is not automatically about hospitality, but rather ethical encounters in tourism settings require hospitality between people. This approach denies the possibility of treating the responsibility of welcoming as a responsibility of the host. Instead, it calls for open welcoming and hospitality from both hosts and guests – just like my grandfather in Finland put it (see Preface). This thought is in the same vein as Levinasian philosophy, which suggests that the *hôte* as host is actually also a guest, meaning that in ethical encounters hospitality and openness cannot be expected only from hosts (Derrida 1999, 41). However, while the purpose of the later tourism development projects, in most cases, has been to enhance local entrepreneurs' readiness to work with tourism and tourists, this kind of mutual openness has been somewhat missing from the encounters between tourism practitioners and local hosts. This is obviously a strong and provocative argument to make.

I should point out here that in my interactions and interviews with the local hosts, many people talked warmly about a woman called Heather, whose help they greatly appreciated during the first years of tourism development. Heather worked, if I have understood correctly, for a North American NGO, and she had been coordinating tourism development at the UCA San Ramón for a couple of years.[12] People also told me about Juan-Miguel, who in their opinion, like Heather, had also been a great coordinator and nice person to work with. In the local hosts' view, both Heather and Juan-Miguel had always stayed in close communication with the members of the tourism communities, and especially with the local guides. The expression that was repeated in people's accounts was *open communication*: in the local hosts' eyes, the coordinators had kept the communication and all actions as transparent and democratic as possible. Most importantly, people committed to tourism development had felt that these coordinators listened to them and took their concerns seriously. According to previous research on community-based tourism in northern Thailand, Kontogeorgopoulos, Churyen and Duangsaeng (2014) have underlined the importance of these kinds of 'individual champions' who are willing to shoulder the bulk of responsibility for community-based tourism. Unfortunately, neither Heather nor Juan Miguel gets a bigger role in this book, as Heather left Ramón long before I got there. I did have a chance to meet Juan Miguel, but he left his job as coordinator before I could interview him. All in all, it was obvious that the local hosts were disappointed with the new coordinators, who had nearly stopped having face-to-face contact with the people from the four communities involved with tourism.

In connection to the idea of open communication, one of the recurring themes in the descriptions of positive encounters in the 1980s and then twenty years later was the aspect of sharing experiences and knowledge. In fact, the guide Fernando suggested that through tourism development the local hosts had learned to become better listeners and improved their understandings of other cultures. In our interview in 2013, he explained how the experiences with tourists had taught the host families to eat together and use the time to discuss things with each other in peace and quiet, which was, according to Fernando, different from the times before tourism development. In his opinion, there were also many things that their guests learned and experienced during their visits in San Ramón, such as 'to eat typical food, speak Spanish, work on the fields, take care of nature and to wake up early'. Fernando continued, 'a happy visitor, who learns from us, is like having a five-star hotel'. Similarly, to Fernando, many hosts explained that sharing ideas and ways of doing things formed part of a successful encounter with their guests. These encounters with tourists, different from the encounters with many of the tourism experts, had allowed more mobility between the acts of teaching and being taught (Höckert 2014; see also Freire 1970/2000; McRoberts 2012).

Envisioning more ethical encounters in the context of participatory tourism development could mean mobilization from limitations of participation towards more mobile roles between teachers and learners. The approach where the other is presented mainly through his or her limitations is a limited one; consequently, I do not find it meaningful to list or define any skills or material conditions as requirements for saying *welcome* to the other. Instead, welcoming and hospitality can be found nearly where- and whenever. Or even more, as I have aimed to emphasize here, we all can give our contribution so that open welcoming could flourish in as many settings as possible. The hospitality that Levinas and Derrida encourage us to envision does not rest on certifications, or stars that a hotel or an eco-lodge have acquired, or on the type of coffee cups or silverware on the table.

The material requirements for receiving guests are socially constructed and constantly negotiated, and therefore always due to change. When hospitality becomes commercialized, measured and certified, it also becomes a target of critique and appreciation (Chalip and Costa 2012). Extreme examples from San Ramón had been those cases where tourism experts or tourists had not been able to appreciate the mountains – which are no doubt the source of local storytelling and pride – because a window was lacking a pair of proper curtains or there were no menus on the table. This means, as Spivak (1988, 281–4) could explain it, that in order for the subaltern other to speak (in this case to be able to show the mountains), she must first adjust herself to the expectations of her guests (in this case to purchase curtains for the tourists' cabins). The use of quality indicators which are made by the guests makes it impossible to spot or to find somehow equal encounters between the development practitioners and the locals.

While it is unethical to romanticize or trivialize the material needs of those who are being helped through development projects, it is equally dubious to continuously encounter the farmers and entrepreneurs as people who are 'not quite there yet'. In a longitudinal study on rural tourism in Turkey, Tucker (2010; see also 2003) uses the analytical concept of *peasant entrepreneurship*, which is a great illustration of this condition. Tucker suggests that rather than struggling to change the status of a 'not quite yet' subject to a 'ready' one, the struggle could be re-directed towards acknowledging how actually none of us are 'quite yet there either': in fact, not even the tidy guests who arrive with the emancipatory intentions to help the rural other. In other words, the acceptance of how we all are in an eternal state of becoming could be faced with celebration instead of grief – as an Octoberfest that comes after cultivating moral imagination. At least for me the 'eternal state of becoming' has a more relaxed and kind-hearted undertone than 'never being enough'. Or as Donna Haraway (2016, 4) phrases it referring to all beings on Earth, 'We become-with each other, or not at all'.

The ideas of an 'eternal state of becoming' and 'continuum in teaching and learning' are needed, first of all, to question the chronological idea of progress and the 'stages of growth', which still dominate much of the predominant discourses of development.[13] In other words, these thoughts inevitably disrupt the artificial dichotomy between developing and developed where a developed self takes the role of 'teaching' the other how to become developed. To put it differently, the idea of reciprocity in learning disrupts the colonial mind-set which protects the subjects of the West (Kuokkanen 2007, 113–22). Acknowledging and embracing the unfinishedness of self questions the fairness and meaningfulness of transferring knowledge only from self to the other, that is, to teach the other. Instead, following Levinas's (1969, 51) line of thought of 'welcoming more than I contain', embracing unfinishedness allows self to make space for the other to enter – to say welcome *to* the other.

Even though the local hosts in San Ramón appreciated the different kinds of training in the early years of tourism development, they did not feel comfortable staying in the phase of 'not quite yet'. Just as most of the tourism development experts might see their encounters with these rural communities as a possibility to teach the 'other', the local hosts are also interested in teaching their guests. As an illustration, I go back to my interview with doña Hilda in 2013, when she told about a visit by two women from another tourism community. She was seemingly delighted and proud when she spoke about the topic:

> A little while ago, they came from Jinotega. They will start to work with community-based tourism over there. But there they do not have mountains but just an island. There they are selling their products and food and they have been trained by UNDP. So they came here because we have been working with tourism for long time. They came and stayed with me in order to learn about tourism.

Doña Hilda had told them about the visitors in the 1980s, and how the idea for tourism development had occurred after the difficult coffee crises around 2001. She highlighted that she had wanted to be honest to these women. She continued:

> In the beginning we felt that this was something very difficult, because we had to go to the capacity building meetings and to be away from home a lot. But this is how we begun with tourism. So we shared all this with the women from Jinotega. And they asked me, 'But how are the visitors? As you have received visitors from all kinds of places, how are they?'. I told them that we have had very nice experiences, but also some less pleasant ones.

Doña Hilda described to me that she and the women from Jinotega had stayed up late by the kitchen table and shared different experiences and expectations that they had about tourism. It seemed to me like the meeting had likewise been important for doña Hilda. Unlike in many previous encounters with tourism experts, these guests had recognized the experiences and knowledge which doña Hilda had as a tourism entrepreneur.[14] The visit had given her, I argue, a chance to change her role from learner to teacher. Or to put it better: while she had received and welcomed the guests, the guests had also welcomed her.

Also other face-to-face encounters around San Ramonean coffee tables indicated the ways in which a fair and equal discussion requires both teaching and learning. Indeed, there is much that we might miss if we are focused merely on being ready to teach and guide the 'other'; that is, there are things that we might overlook when we are focused on being readier, and more capable, than others. A Levinasian (1969, 180) radical intersubjectivist perspective reveals how we become ready to welcome life and the others, ironically, at the very moment when we give up on the ambition of readiness (see Strhan 2012). In practice, this means shifting from the protection of the ego and individual projects of happiness towards cherishing the unfinished and messy. Hence, ethical subjectivity, consciousness and well-being could be, as Levinas (1969) forms it, a desire towards infinity.

In contrast to silencing the other, Levinas celebrates the revelation of the Other that takes place in conversation and teaching. Although Levinas talks about teaching, his prime interest does not lie in either teaching or learning, but in *being taught*. For him welcoming teaching means *receiving more than I contain*. Therefore, welcoming teaching refers to openness and infinity – to a soul capable of containing more than it can draw from itself, to a soul that does not take its own interiority for the totality of being. That is, welcoming teaching is receiving from the other beyond the capacity of 'the I', which means precisely to have the idea of infinity (Levinas 1969, 51, 180; Derrida 1999, 18–27). This requires, most of all, a readiness to question one's learned position to guide the other. For me Spivak's call for *unlearning* and Levinas's approach of *receiving more than I contain* sound, when put together, like a continuum of mutual learning and teaching (Kuokkanen 2007, 128–42). In the context of rural tourism, it means rejecting the assumption that teaching is directed only towards 'host' communities; that is, that the flow of teaching would have only one significant direction. Saying this, it is fruitful to trace especially the importance of critical pedagogy and Freire's (1970/1992) thought in tourism education (Belhassen and Caton 2011) and in the participatory paradigm (McRoberts 2012).

The idea of mutual learning includes the possibility of disrupting the legacy of paternalism in rural tourism encounters – the wish to teach the 'other'. The desire to be taught by 'the subject of the welcome' would mean questioning my will to teach, develop, modernize, thematize, speak, theorize, define, correct, enlighten, and so on (see Höckert 2014, 115). It would mean questioning the assumption 'that only if things work do they matter' (Haraway 2016, 4). Following Jennie Germann Molz's (2014, 31–2) work on Freire's notion of *unfinishedness*, it would be necessary to think how to build unfinished design into different kinds of development projects. She suggests that we often mistake fullness and readiness as preconditions of sociability in tourism, when in fact it is unfinishedness and incompleteness that make new moves possible in the first place. In the field sites of development assistance, this approach would, paradoxically, mean that it is the *failure* in planning, teaching, theorizing, developing, modernizing, colonizing, speaking and defining that could be interpreted as *success*.[15] In a way, success can be a failure to force someone to buy new curtains or giving up on intentions of knowing, defining and totalizing the other (Höckert 2014, 115). Or as Spivak (2001, 15) and Kapoor (2004, 644) put it, we should try to think about working without guarantees and about seeing one's failure as a success. The approach likewise resonates with Derrida's (1999, quoted in Kearney and Dooley 1999, 70) thought on being 'unprepared or prepared to be unprepared, for the unexpected'.

5.3   Learning anew the welcome of the other

Although the purpose of this study has been to focus on the encounters between tourism experts as guests and local communities as hosts, in practice the subject categories of guests and hosts – or experts and locals – are tangled and messy (Ren 2010). In fact, it would be paradoxical and epistemologically violent to try to maintain these categories. One of the many situations where this mobility of expertise became clear took place in doña Hilda's home in 2013. Doña Hilda's son, Jason and I were sitting in the hammocks out on the patio and drinking coffee. I had already met Jason for the first time in 2008, and ever since stayed many times with his family. When the guides were busy, and I had no interviews to make, Jason used to take the role of the host, inviting me to join him on the football field and the coffee fields.

I appreciated the fact that we had had many of these kinds of discussions like we were having now on the patio. This time, we were talking, most of all, about the current situation with the coffee disease *la Roya*. Jason told me that he had had to put his university studies on hold, because the income from the coffee was not enough to pay for his education. He was interested to hear how it was going with my study – and pointed out that it had taken an awfully long time for me to finish this study. I laughed and responded that my family back home thought the same. However, I also wanted to tell him that in the course of this longitudinal study, I had become more and more fascinated about different ideas of hospitality and different ways of welcoming guests. As a reaction to that he explained that, in his opinion, there were three different kinds of tourists. He described his categorization of tourists, and although my purpose was not to conduct an interview in this situation, I asked whether I could record his interesting 'typology'.[16] It was fine with him, and with a big smile on his face he repeated:

> Firstly, there are tourists who want to go to comfortable places to have fun. Secondly, there are tourists who are interested in conviviality, learning, teaching, sharing and having a close relation with the locals. Thirdly, there are something that we call 'mochilleros' (backpackers). They are interested in getting to know different places with less money. They like to get to know places, but simply without paying.

Based on our discussion that followed, it was clear that the local hosts in San Ramón perceived the tourists from the second category as their ideal group of guests. However, Jason continued, there had also been many visitors who had chosen, for varying reasons, to ignore the price list for tourism services. According to Jason:

> Here people come normally to learn, to get to know the place, and to meet us. But sometimes, all of a sudden, there are also these backpackers who come here. They have heard about the place and they come without knowing that there are rules. That we have rules here. For instance, that you have to pay an entrance fee. But they enter, take their pictures, walk around without paying for a guided tour or anything.

The *Lonely Planet* travel books have succeeded well in helping the backpackers to 'live and travel on a shoestring'. In fact, a clear sign of a real globe-trotter is to have a story or two about exploring exotic places with a minimum budget. Tucker's (2003) book on tourism in Turkish villages also offers amusing examples of backpackers' quests for cheap or free services as part of colouring their travel narratives (see also Bruner 2005; Stronza 2008, 180). I must admit, although I did not admit this to Jason, how I had also been previously bragging about the cost-efficiency of my own trips. However, this is not a phenomenon that only backpackers could be greeted, or more correctly blamed, for. The chase for cheap flights, hotels, Airbnb lodging, wine excursions, or all-inclusive fitness resorts rarely includes deeper consideration on *why* a trip to Greece or Mexico can actually be so cheap.[17]

Jason's typology reminded me especially of a travel story which a certain tourism researcher once, very proudly, told me and his other colleagues in a Nordic tourism conference. In his story the protagonist, the tourism researcher himself in the role of a traveller, had travelled through the entire Central America by using only one dollar per day. This had allowed him to test and experience the real local life with a budget equivalent to extreme poverty line.[18] The thrilling adventure had been possible, because of, what many like to call, the local hospitality. He had hitch-hiked, stayed with local families for free, enjoyed their meals and celebrated their holidays. The story included no information about possible compensation for this hospitality. Although he in his own research acknowledges the importance of tourism revenues for small tourism enterprises in the European context, this aspect was peculiarly missing from the story that took place far away from home. He seemed to neglect the fact that in Central America there are thousands and thousands of tourism services which have been developed for foreign visitors like him. And what is more, some of these services have been developed in a way which can help the others *not* having to continue to experience their everyday lives under the poverty line: and one day even have a possibility to choose their own ways of travelling.

Salazar (2010, 8) writes 'the global space is often thought of as the 'flow' of people, objects and ideas across national borders and geographic regions'. However, Salazar continues, this trendy imagery of flows is badly chosen if we wish to describe how people, objects and ideas move around the world (see Hall 2013; Duncan et al. 2015). That is, taking Salazar's discussion on cosmopolitan mobilities to San Ramón, the image of cosmopolitan travellers neutrally flowing through rural communities trivializes economic privileges, political implications and the history of previous encounters. In my opinion, Fernando, one of the local guides in San Ramón, puts it quite well:

> Tourists come here because they get bored at staying at their own places. The same happens here: the farmers also get tired of their own place and want to get to know other places, but they cannot do that. They do not have money.

The distortion of cosmopolitanism masters the other to allow the flow to keep flowing – at least in one direction. To put it differently, it is hoped that the other participates in encounters that permit free mobility without clashes, misfires, confusion or unnecessary entrance fees. No doubt the encounters between the hosts and guests could be seen as fluxes that the visitor, depending on their travel purposes, might choose to 'have'. And when they do, the locals are expected to engage in these encounters with open homes and open hearts.

Instead of denying the existence of open doors and hearts around the world, I have serious doubts that this would be a special quality of the people living in the rural areas in the Global South (see also Szczesiul 2017). However, an over-myopic view on the local neglects the fact that a wider scale of global inequalities in wealth, power and mobility limits the possibilities of many of these rural communities to *not* open their homes. The idea of a flowing movement of cosmopolitan travellers becomes interesting at the very moment when these flows are imagined on our own backyards. In fact, the members of the campaign 'not in my backyard' obviously have already dedicated much thought to this. As did the people living in the touristic quarters in Barcelona, Lisbon, Amsterdam, Venice who in 2017 organized anti-tourism protests to express their irritation towards excessive tourism and ever-growing flows of badly behaving tourists.

Hence, I wonder whether engaging in hospitable, face-to-face encounters with the other could be first practised in one's own homes before widely demanding it from the others. While I acknowledge the difficulty of this, I suggest that we can find the welcoming, smiling faces from our everyday encounters. Especially if you are sceptical about this suggestion, give it a try. Most of all, this practice might reveal the awkwardness of searching and longing for conviviality, open hospitality and authentic smiles only when leaving home and travelling abroad (see also Kippendorf 1989; Gmelch 2012; Caton and Santos 2009).

While some of the tourism destinations might suit the idea of 'flow' of visitors, there are increasing numbers of those which do not. Although a Nicaraguan tourism consultant expressed in our interview the view that community-based tourism in rural areas has great potential as, 'people are not suspicious towards visitors but receive them happily', the unconditional welcome of the guests cannot be taken for granted. I see that the imaginaries and narratives of always-welcoming rural communities is what Spivak calls 'epistemic violence', which denies the voices that resist or set limits for welcoming. This violence trivializes the questions, such as 'Why did you come here?', as Julia Svanberg (2014) wonders in her book on tourism encounters in the impoverished communities in the Colombian countryside. In Svanberg's story, this is what a young Colombian woman asks from tourists who arrive in her home community that she herself desperately tries to escape from. Hence, especially the encounters where the 'local attractions' are based on economic marginalization and expected immobility in time and space, it is contradictory to promise hospitality on behalf of someone else. Now, instead of opening a new stream of discussion about slum tourism, I try to stay on the topic.

What I am trying to argue here is that the local hosts in rural communities, in my opinion, often are expected to be unconditionally hospitable and social, as rural people always are, amongst themselves and towards their guests. Interestingly, and conveniently, as rural communities are always open and welcoming, the travellers are offered an opportunity to try and celebrate the lost forms of human warmth during their holidays. That is, while the travellers are open-minded and happy during their holidays, the local hosts are expected to wear an eternal smile (Gmelch 2012). A web-page which has previously offered educational trips from North America to Nicaragua explained this as follows:

> NSS wants to model a different kind of development in Nicaragua that conserves traditional relationship between people and their land and neighbours as the primary relationship that defines the culture. That, in great measure, is what the developed world has lost, but what countries like Nicaragua still have. For that reason, Nicaragua is a valuable reference for our fading memory of what life used to be before the beginning of the age of mass marketing and alienating consumerism.[19]

Although this description was written back in 2000, Vrasti's (2013) recent research on volunteer tourism suggests how todays' discussions on ethical tourism reflect similar kinds of attitudes about the travel destinations in the 'Third World'. These discourses of responsible travelling tend to neglect or romanticize the inequalities in material progress, and also the social immobility of many of the people living in rural communities (MacCannell 1976/1999; Pratt 1992; Simmons 2004; Mostafanezhad 2014). This narrative co-constructs colonial imaginings where the authentic 'other' is there for the self to be discovered (see Caton and Santos 2009, 194); what is more, this kind of romanticization of 'traditional ways of life' contributes to a mind-set in which it is seen almost damaging to 'give money to the locals' (McEwan 2009, 301; Vrasti 2013, 84; Sammels 2014, 130–3). As the travellers who 'look around at their own country and bemoan the problems that false prosperity has brought to them' (as expressed on the same website) might become convinced that the local communities in the 'developing world' are better off without this harmful prosperity. As an outcome, it is again the guest who has the active agency and who interprets and knows what is best for their subaltern hosts.

As the purpose of the chapter has been to consider what hospitality could look like, it merits mentioning that hospitality between hosts and guests in tourism settings includes something as simple and banal as paying a fair price for the tourism services.[20] In this kind of context the payment of a fair price for accommodation and food could promote more mobile subject positions in very concrete ways. Even in a way that would allow the people hosting guests to also have the possibility of choosing to travel as a tourist – or choose not to host tourists. Instead of proposing that travelling would require having lots of money, I *do* suggest that a prerequisite for more responsible travelling and visiting is to keep doing one's 'homework' (see sections 2.5 and 4.3).[21] As discussed in the previous chapters, the call for doing homework means engaging in hyper-self-reflectivity, in Kapoor's (2004) words, about one's position and pre-assumptions about the other. In this context the homework would include considering, for instance, how and why the 'other's' welcome to self becomes self-evident. Has it been all tourism advertisement that has convinced us, the wealthy guests, to feel welcome to arrive whenever and wherever (Höckert 2014, 114)? I suggest that engaging in this homework could help to recognize how *choosing* to live on a shoestring is already a privilege as such which does not automatically disrupt the gaps between haves and have-nots. In fact, taking for granted that the other welcomes self, without welcoming the other, rather de-subjectifies the subaltern host. Or, as a matter of fact, whatever kinds of hosts – including grandparents (see Preface).

5.4   Towards mutual welcoming

The purpose of this chapter was two-fold: first, to envision what hospitable encounters could look like, and second, to suggest how more spaces for ethical encounters could be opened. Based on the analysis of those encounters that the local hosts in San Ramón have given positive meanings to, I have focused on the issues of sharing time, sharing experiences and knowledge, and sharing space. While ethical encounters, at their best, can mean the unconditionally open being and flow[22] of ideas and experiences, they can also mean less asymmetrical mobility in the spaces where the conditions and responsibilities of welcoming become negotiated. While saying this, I agree with Derrida that the only precondition of ethical relations is the readiness to constantly renegotiate the conditions and responsibilities of welcoming. In my opinion, the following quote from doña Hilda somewhat summarizes the essence of the hospitable space between ourselves. In our discussions about respectful encounters in one's home, doña Hilda explained,

> when they come, we do everything possible to discuss with the guests. But how to say … we do not know who are the visitors who wish to share,

and which do not … A little while ago there was a couple from Spain. I attended them, they told me that everything is well and the food is good. But what I observed was that they wanted to be alone: so we respected that. And at the moment of their departure, they told us that everything was well. We respect if the guests want to discuss, and also if they want to be alone. There are those like you who we discuss with and eat together with. We have learned to observe and to respect how the visitors prefer to be while they are here.

I propose that hospitable relationality and relations require what doña Hilda calls 'observing and respecting' how the other wants to be in these encounters. They require attention to the other, putting aside one's pre-assumptions about the other and welcoming the other in discourse. Most importantly, these forms of togetherness mean respecting and being attentive towards the welcome, and the *yes* of the other, as Levinasian philosophy submits. Like doña Hilda's reflection proposes, welcoming the other in discourse does not always require actual speaking to each other. This theme of hospitable dwelling in silence has been explored in Veijola's (2014) research, where she elaborates on the notion of silent communities as a form of mobile neighbouring. With the help of a real-life event of reindeer safaris and the notion of silences, she disrupts and revitalizes the ideas of 'the social', community, and hospitality. Veijola (2014, 89) suggests that understanding the social meanings of silence can help us to 'imagine and practise the ethical ontology of social beings as dwelling-nearby' (see also Veijola and Falin 2014; Veijola and Säynäjäkangas 2018).

No matter if we are together speaking or in silence, welcoming others means giving up one's freedom of being a spontaneous subject who enters whenever without asking. To translate this into the theoretical discussions in my study, it means unlearning the privilege of being a spontaneous host or spontaneous guest, when wishing to engage in a respectful relationship with the other. Most of all, as Levinas and Derrida (1999, 29, 52) argue, readiness to be interrupted by the other is a mutual responsibility and risk of both hosts and guests. Hence, the call for this readiness is not only a question of good customer service, tolerance or patience towards the other, but a fundamental question of ethics.

Notes

1 I acknowledge that my view could have been very different if I had had a chance to talk to the visitors.
2 For Lund's work that we discussed during the course, see Lund (2014), 'Of what is this a case?: analytical movements in qualitative social science research'.
3 See also how Veijola and Jokinen (1994), Ronkainen (1999, 14) and Caton (2012, 1907) approach the idea of imagining the change at this very moment. For endless possibilities of different variations of SF (in addition to Sociological Fiction), see Donna Haraway's (2016) *Staying with the Trouble*, which dives into science fiction, speculative fabulation, string figures, speculative feminism and science fact.

4　In addition to the previously given reasons, I have not approached the issue of time from the tourism practitioners' perspective for the reason that the idea of sharing time did not occur in those interviews I conducted with the tourism experts in Nicaragua. In fact, based on my own observations, many of the development practitioners seemed to visit the rural communities as fast as possible – despite the fact that the communities had prepared themselves to accommodate these guests.

5　I have previously discussed unlearning, teaching and being taught (Höckert 2014, 111).

6　Just a note: these are not the same sunglasses that Eeva Jokinen and Soile Veijola were wearing in Mallorca in 1994, but the metaphor of sunglasses is borrowed from them.

7　For the conceptualization of *care* in local-global spaces, see Jamal and Stronza (2009), Jamal and Camargo (2013), Jamal, Budke and Barradas-Bribiesca (2014, 140–80) and Hales and Caton (2017).

8　For 'face as a trace', see Derrida (1999, 53).

9　Thus, it is also questionable whether the locals themselves would write the slogan 'Come to visit me so that you get to know me'. For me it does not sound a very common phrase that people say to their guests.

10　In this case the Other is written with a capital letter as it refers to the absolute Other.

11　For research on the ways in which landscapes mediate the welcome, see Huijbens and Benediktsson (2013).

12　On the role of transnational brokers like Heather, see Helene Balslev Clausen and Szilvia Gyimóthy's research on pueblos magicos of Mexico (2016).

13　Rostow's 'stages of growth' was the predominant theory of economic development after the Second World War. For more on this development theory, see Todaro and Smith (2006) and Telfer (2009; 2014). See also Teivainen's (2004) writings about the reversal in learning. Most recently Teivainen has addressed the context of global economic crises, where the 'West' has failed to learn from the previous crises, for instance, in Latin America.

14　See Valtonen's (2009) research on small firms as agents of critical knowledge. See also Dahles and Lou (2002) on tourism entrepreneurship in Latin America.

15　See also Kapoor's (2004, 641–2) call for 'hyper self-reflexive development'.

16　For alternative typologies of tourists, see Cole (2008, 166).

17　For discussions on labour rights, dislocation and economic inequalities within the hotel industry – in Greece, Mexico and beyond – see Dielemans (2008), Buades (2009), Lovelock and Lovelock (2013), Bianchi (2015), Schyst Resande (2015) and Cañada (2015).

18　Perhaps this took place before the extreme poverty line was raised to 1.25 dollars.

19　Paul Martin in 2000, A New Revolution in Nicaragua: Edu-Tourism!, www. planeta.com website, accessed 4 March 2014.

20　Or in case the concept of *paying* sounds too banal in this context, the exchange of money and services could also be considered as an act of exchanging gifts. For discussions on exchanging gifts, see for instance Länsman (2004), Kuokkanen (2007), Pyyhtinen (2014).

21　See Kuokkanen's (2007, 114–15) conceptualization of 'homework'. See also section 2.5 in this book.

22　Mihaly Csikszentmihalyi (in Veijola 2014, 76) approaches the idea of *flow* as 'the optimal experience' of being completely absorbed in one's being and doing.

6 Conclusion

At the end of my last visit to San Ramón, in 2013, it was not easy to say goodbye to my host family and the local guides. I had received a small bag of freshly roasted local coffee and a warm-hearted note saying my family and I were welcomed to return. For me this was a special gift, which I packed into my backpack with care. I think that this time my backpack had more space than when I first arrived in San Ramón in 2008. Back then, my bag was loaded not only with books on sustainable tourism development and qualitative research methodologies, but also with developmentalism and desire to help. I have been unloading this backpack during the past years in order to make space for alternative ways of encountering the 'other'. Accordingly, the last time I travelled home from Nicaragua I thought about the virtue of 'being welcomed to return'. Although I was facing difficulties appreciating some of the contemporary aspects of the global tourism industries and academic research, I knew that it had been the ideas of tourism and research that had brought me to these communities and given me the possibility to meet 'the faces behind the coffee cup'. It had been these encounters in particular that had made me realize that hospitality and ethics form the fundamental basis of being, doing and knowing with others.

The main question guiding my journey in this book has been: how do self and other, or hosts and guests welcome each other in tourism encounters? I have analysed tourism encounters in the economically marginalized communities where the guests often arrive with an interest in helping their hosts. My analysis suggests that emancipatory intentions to help are quite not enough when what we are looking for are more responsible encounters in tourism settings. Drawing on postcolonial critique and a phenomenological approach, my research process shows that envisioning more ethical encounters between self and 'other' requires active decolonization of the ontologies and epistemologies that dominate the field of tourism development. The first step in the process of 'decolonizing minds' is to become aware of different ways and contexts where our imaginings and ways of being continue to be produced (Spivak 1987; Kuokkanen 2007; Chambers and Buzinde 2015).

My research has located the notion of participation in the intersection of intersubjectivity, hospitality and ethics and in this way aimed to offer an alternative approach to examining the phenomenon of community participation. The research project has focused on exploring how Levinas's and Derrida's notions of hospitality could be used as conceptual tools to acknowledge and challenge the limitations of our imaginings and to envision more ethical ways of encountering the 'other'. My analysis was driven by curiosity about the ways in which the contemporary idea of participation in tourism development might differ from Levinasian idea of ethics as openness towards the other. This has meant training attention to the spheres between *self* and *the other*, where negotiations of hospitality, responsibility and participation take place. In these negotiations the prepositions between *welcome* and *the other* become crucial (see 2.3).[1] Based on my analysis of tourism development encounters in San Ramón, I have suggested that both sides of the Levinasian idea of ethics seemed to be missing: attention to and respect for the welcome *of* the other [subjective genitive] and saying 'welcome' *to* the other. In other words, while tourism experts were failing to welcome the locals within the discourse, the tired hosts had ended up limiting their hospitality towards these guests.

The ways in which tourism experts – including researchers – take for granted the unconditional welcome of rural communities can be understood as a sign of colonized imaginings and heightened levels of individualism. By telling the story of my longitudinal research in Nicaragua in this volume, I have sought to contribute to the processes of decolonizing our ways of knowing and acting where tourism is concerned. The first part of this concluding chapter summarizes how my doubts about the ultimate fairness of community-based tourism have grown during my walks and talks in Nicaragua. I will show here why I have become convinced, corresponding to a growing number of other studies, that the issue of privilege must be addressed within the discourses of supposedly alternative and fair forms of tourism in marginalized communities (Butcher 2007; Scheyvens 2011, 71; Goodwin 2011; Higgins-Desbiolles and Powys Whyte 2013; Wearing and Wearing 2014; Chambers and Buzinde 2015).

The second part of the chapter continues by drawing closer attention to the ways in which local hosts in San Ramón had become silenced in their homes. From the discussions of 'domestic epistemic violence' I move to discuss hospitality as the methodological basis of the present research. I argue that research on local participation should include more reflection on the representations and subject positions that these studies construct. In the closing part of this book I move to another level of abstraction and summarize why I see that participation or participatory approaches should not be overlooked or dismissed. Instead of compiling guidelines for participation, my research highlights the importance of openness between hosts and guests.[2] I finish by asking how this alternative approach to examining the phenomenon of community participation could be used to explore participatory encounters beyond the human community.

6.1   Sandinistas and Sandalistas in Nicaragua

The core focus of my research has been to explore how the notion of hospitality can help to analyse the expectations and disappointments related to community participation in tourism. If hospitality is a desire to make space for the other, for the guest, the ultimate form of open welcoming would be to leave one's home empty for the visitors to occupy on arrival (Derrida 1999). Although this sounds like a peculiar form of hospitality, it is actually almost a standard scenario in tourism. In the Global South, in particular, it is common that beaches, streets and hotels are built exclusively for tourists to avoid the disturbances and dangers of the local life in otherwise pristine destinations (Edensor 1998, 45–53, 150–63; Blàzquez and Cañada 2011; Bianchi 2015).

As shown in Chapter 3, this kind of development has also taken place on the Pacific coast of Nicaragua. Taking a look back in Nicaragua's history, I have argued that tourism can be seen as continuation of the long, colonial tradition of visits, where the guests take for granted the country's hospitality. Large-scale development of residential tourism and other types of high-end tourism has taken place over the past two decades, allowing the guests to take over, displacing local communities and privatizing beachfronts. Since 2007, the previously protectionist Sandinista government has peculiarly sped up the open-door policies to foreign investors with attractive tax incentives for tourism development. Despite the dramatic growth in Nicaraguan tourism, the country has continued to under-perform on economic indicators, including those that measure absolute and relative poverty (Cañada 2013). While the focus of my analysis has rested on describing how the colonial 'discovery' mentality has become materialized in unconditional tourism policies and tourism investments in enclave resorts, the anthropologist Carter Hunt (2016) has taken this assessment one step further. His research makes a strong argument for how the open-door tourism discourses and statistics in tourism growth have paved the way for the new inter-oceanic canal mega-project. Hunt (2016) writes that to welcome and justify the project, which is run by a Hong Kong-based company, the Ortega regime has used the same hegemonic discourse that situates 'the dispossession of lands and displacement of people on the basis of tourism-related economic development as being in the greatest interest of Nicaragua'. Building on Hunt's research, it seems that tourism development is not only shaped by the images of hospitable nations, but that tourism development also shapes the host-guest roles well beyond tourism settings.

Now, in comparison to investments and enclaves which are all-exclusive to unwanted local hosts, community-based tourism can be seen as a radically alternative form of doing development and tourism. As it is based on the possibility or desire to enjoy conviviality with local families, the 'native hosts' do not belong to the scenery, or serve as props, but form a pivotal part of both, the tourism development and the touristic experience (Urry 1990; Dicks 2003, 136–43; Córdoba Azcárate 2014; Veijola 2014). My research journey was originally inspired by a meta-narrative where small ecotourism and community-based projects were used for fighting the villain of mass and enclave tourism. This villain had been mocking and bullying economically marginalized groups and regions for too long (e.g. Turner and Ash 1976; Stronza 2001; Higgins Desbiolles 2006; Hunt and Stronza 2014). In this story community participation was the lead character of 'alternative development', which celebrated people-based, locally owned, grass-roots initiatives for change (Telfer 2014, 54–9). Nevertheless, I then had to admit that this narrative was not as heroic and alternative as I wanted to believe. Instead, it was also filled with pragmatic and instrumental approaches to argue what kind of participation is successful, whether participation can promote further environmental conservation, why communities fail in developing tourism, and so on.

The intent of the third chapter was to show how Nicaraguan government, NGOs and development aid organizations have promoted community-based tourism initiatives in order to spread benefits from the tourism sector into rural areas. These kinds of tourism programmes and projects have been seen to entail more solidarity, communality and equality than the conventional forms of tourism developed on the country's Pacific coastline. Based on my interviews with tourism experts and development officials, I argued that many rural tourism initiatives in Nicaragua have been built on perceptions of tourism as easy and profitable business, especially in the cases where the host families could receive paying guests in their private homes. However, as I have highlighted repeatedly throughout the study, tourism does not tend to become easy simply by virtue of its taking place in people's homes. Experiences from San Ramón indicate that the outcome can even be quite the opposite. More precisely, many of the tourism experts who participated in this study were underestimating the variety of resources that tourism development might require from local families and communities.

Drawing on Derrida's (1999; 2000) conceptualization of hospitality in particular, I have suggested that opening one's home always includes a risk for the host. In fact, one central dimension of coloniality is the way the guests abuse the hospitality of their hosts. However, strong belief in the promise of rural tourism development – especially when held collectively – seem to lead to overlooking challenges. The examples from San Ramón reveal, for instance, the risks and consequences of dependency in participatory tourism projects (Zapata et al. 2011). For the meantime the hosts in San Ramón were hoping that tourists would return to their home communities, representatives from international NGOs, development aid organizations and the Nicaraguan tourism ministry continued planning and starting new, similar kinds of tourism initiatives across the country. While the combination of rural poverty, agrarian lifestyle, Nicaraguan hospitality and rapid growth in the tourism sector were presented almost as a 'match made in heaven', I have considered it problematic that local communities are expected to stay on hold, welcoming unconditionally all the possible guests. I can imagine that my sentiments are shared by the members of one rural community on the Caribbean coast of Nicaragua: after a few years of anxious waiting for tourists and tourists' dollars, they tore down the huts they had built for tourists and used them as firewood.

6.2 Domestic epistemic violence

My research journey has shown that the encounters between hosts and guests in rural communities are shaped by two contradictory suppositions. While the first is based on a romantic idea of traditional forms of hospitality that exist in rural communities in particular, the second highlights the inadequacy of material conditions in local homes. Both ways of giving meanings reconstruct unequal power relations and *representations of otherness*. Thus, although Nicaraguan tourism policy documents promise the hospitality to be found in rural areas, in practice the efforts to commodify local hospitality have regularly turned into a pile of disappointments (see also Chalip and Costa 2012; Sammels 2014). In my analysis I focused on different experiences of tourism developers' aims to modify local homes and communities into tourism sites and noticed that although the hosts in San Ramón had found the experts' help useful in the earlier stages of tourism development, they had later become drained by the continuous flow of advice. Visiting experts had readily commented on nearly anything that they regarded as inappropriate, inadequate, inauthentic, tacky or rustic in comparison to quality indicators which 'measure' the minimum requirements for being able to welcome guests.

The guests' accounts of local hospitality in rural communities, on one hand, and of the supposedly uncomplicated nature of tourism activities, on the other, trivialize the experiences of the local hosts. In practice, many of the guests had overlooked the local hosts' arguments, such as 'We give the visitors our best', 'These are the conditions we have', 'We cannot improve the material conditions for the guests' or 'We do not want to take new loans for tourism development'. In other words, it seems like the experts might take over the role of host in rural tourism projects, and fail to make space for the local voices and choices (see Derrida 1999, 15–16; Kuokkanen 2007, 138). I have suggested that the ways in which many tourism officials and experts (including researchers) overlook the challenges of participating in planned projects can be seen as a form of silencing the 'other'; that is, a form of epistemic violence. In rural tourism settings epistemic violence occurs in people's homes, where tourism developers both encourage and evaluate local families. in San Ramón, the operation of 'domestic epistemic violence' has been most evident in projects where tourism experts ignored local resistance to risky loans, or local resistance to receiving volunteers for free: that is, in a situation where the guests continued to master the discussions of what kind of tourism development was desirable.

I have approached tourism development encounters from different perspectives in order to understand why participatory tourism encounters have caused so much frustration and prompted so much criticism. One of the great contradictions in these kinds of tourism programmes can be found in the different ways marginality and the lack of material progress attract travellers and tourism developers. While some of the guests travel with a concern that the authenticity of local life might be under constant attack by material progress (Vrasti 2013, 84[3]), some take a more active role in advocating material improvement. At the same time, it is obvious that while all the local hosts in San Ramón valued material development, they did so in various ways. In fact, as the author of *Postcolonialism and Development* Cheryl McEwan (2009, 256) has pointed out, it is already a good step forward towards decolonizing imaginings to recognize that individuals and communities hold and utilize a complex multiplicity of identities and values depending on the particular circumstances.

However, engaging in this discussion, as Vrasti (2013, 84) warns, gives rise to ethical dilemmas such as denying the distribution of material assets in order to preserve communities' cultural diversity, or rejecting people's creative agency to adapt their cultural and natural sources to changing social needs. The challenge is to acknowledge and embrace the messiness without falling into a form of multiculturalism that can lead to romanticization and further exclusion of the 'other'. This risk is always palpable in development circles, foreign policies, academic production of knowledge and popular culture; needless to say, the risk exists also in tourism research and practices (ibid.; McEwan 2009, 31; Tucker 2017). Despite the 'perils' involved, it is necessary to consider whose ideas of tourism development and material progress are being heard and followed. Most importantly, when the local hosts are represented through their adequacy – or lack thereof – as tourism entrepreneurs, these representations essentialize local cultures and supersede rural communities' active agency. These depictions then taint future encounters, with the other being met as someone who is 'not quite there yet' – almost as a memory from the past.

Although tourism is often perceived as an effective tool for promoting intercultural understanding and peace (Higgins-Desbiolles 2006; Pritchard et al. 2011; Dredge et al. 2013), it is also what Veijola and Jokinen (1998) call 'a violent narrative'. It is a narrative which tries to keep the other immobile and static for the sake of the self. Tourism practices and tourism research are businesses run by mobile outsiders whose interests, imaginings and representations contribute to the way the world is made – to the worldmaking (Hollinshead and Jamal 2007). In his research on tourism imaginaries, Noel Salazar (2010, 5) argues '[w]e live in imagined (but not imaginary) worlds, using our personal imaginings as well as collective imaginaries to represent our lifeworld and attribute meaning to it'. In his view, the tourism imaginaries and representations of the 'other' are predominantly seducing and romanticizing for the purpose of making the destinations recognizable as visitable tourism sites (see also Dicks 2003, 4–8). Monika Büscher, John Urry and Katian Witchger (2011, 5) have also underlined the role of 'imaginative travel' in which the images of places and peoples appear on and move across multiple print and visual media. Acknowledging the violence of postcolonial worldmaking calls for acknowledging the various ways in which these representations shape our imaginings and encounters with the 'other' (Spivak 1988, 283–5; Caton and Santos 2009, 193–200; Chambers and Buzinde 2015). Hence, rethinking tourism encounters requires more pronounced acknowledgement of the different perceptions and cultural values that guide the visions of what hospitable and ethical encounters consist of (see Inayatullah 1995; Higgins-Desbiolles 2006, 1203; Fennell 2008; Caton 2012; 2014a).

The book at hand suggests that while caring for others is something natural to us, something that we have in us since the very beginning (Levinas 1969), the ways in which tourism experts travel and gaze at rural communities are socially organized and constructed. This means proposing that the myth is not an altruistically caring subject, but instead, as the authors of *The Tourist Gaze 3.0* John Urry and Jonas Larsen (2011) have shown, a pure and innocent eye (see also Mostafanezhad 2014). My research process has helped me to realize that despite – or actually because of – the good intentions that the visiting experts carry, these guests (read: we) are likely to dominate the negotiations between us and the members of rural communities. Spivak (1988, 283–4; see also Chambers and Buzinde 2015) aptly observes that the question in these kinds of settings is not so much one of what the 'other' says, but what the self can hear. The example from San Ramón suggests that tourism experts might erase or trivialize locals' opinions that differ from the experts' previous suppositions. Rather, the encounters are shaped by experts' perceptions of tourism as an easy source of income – as something that economically marginalized rural communities simply 'cannot *not* want' (Spivak 1993, 284; see also Eriksson Baaz 2005, 176). Struck by the nature of tourism development in San Ramón, and elsewhere, I want to call for heightened caution among tourism experts who would recommend to rural communities that they should invest their time and money in tourism projects. Likewise, more focus should be put on different forms of resistance as a way of participating in planned participatory initiatives (see Jamal and Stronza 2009; George et al. 2009, 58–9, 89–93; Mettiäinen et al. 2009, 226–37; Pleumarom 2012, 90–1; Seppälä 2013).

6.3 Knowing with hospitality

The desire to study and know the 'other' is something that becomes visible when formulating research questions and even more when defining the units of analysis and levels of analysis associated with one's chosen theoretical approach. The most typical 'units of analysis' in the social sciences are individuals, groups or institutions, whereas scholars in international relations, for example, often focus their analysis on entire nations or transnational organizations. Although these generalizations might be needed in order to be able to communicate about the phenomenon at hand, such conceptualizations require that we also reflect carefully on the levels at which the explanations and theories relating to these categories are expected to work. Normative studies in particular – the ones that criticize social processes and institutions and point out a way towards better ones – become more fruitful when the units and levels of analysis are kept fluid. This suggestion is based on my own eye-opening experience of changing the units of analysis from *individuals and communities* (the first phases of the study) to *encounters* (the later phases of the study). This also meant broadening my level of analysis from tourism development in San Ramón in two different directions: to more general encounters within supposedly responsible tourism development and to more micro-level encounters between self and other. Moreover, once I had turned my focus on encounters, I became aware that almost every element of life can be treated as a valuable source of data (Vrasti 2010, 85; Wilson 2014, 224). It was no longer meaningful to argue that interviews, field-notes and policy documents alone were shaping my assumptions and interpretations. For instance, the way Cesar Castañeda (2006) describes conducting fieldwork as *being* in the fieldwork encouraged me to reflect on my experiences of shame (Tucker 2016), excitement, happiness, disappointment, frustration, anger and confusion while I was collecting the 'real' data for my analysis.

My search for decolonizing methodologies has been based on Spivak's and Kuokkanen's, amongst others, writings about the ways in which our desire to 'know' the other – or to understand the life of the other – can be seen as an ideology of conquest, control and possession. I have considered this epistemic position as highly contradictory to the hermeneutic task of ethnographic scholarship, which has encouraged me to envision more hospitable methodologies that can disrupt one's privileged position to study and represent the other. During the course of this study, I became convinced that the discussions on the ethics of academic research would gain from explicit acknowledgement of *why* we consider it meaningful to study and represent the other (see Alvesson et al. 2017).

Scholars who apply participatory research methodologies argue that meaningful research agendas should better reflect the balanced interests of all partners involved in the research (e.g. Holmes et al. 2016; Hakkarainen and Garcia Rosell 2018). However, during the course of this research in the Nicaraguan highlands, I had to give up on the goal of finding this kind of balance in this research project.[4] Although I had hoped to be able to promote more open dialogue between different actors *during* my fieldwork visits, local hosts' exhaustion amid the steady flow of new participatory initiatives made me change my plans. Hence, my research project has not led to any significant changes in tourism development in San Ramón, nor does it provide results directly applicable at the local levels. Although I am looking forward to sharing some of the main thoughts of this book especially with the people who contributed to developing them further, it would be, in my view, contradictory to provide any guidelines or recommendations for action for the local families in San Ramón. Instead, I hope that this study could contribute to more open and responsible (tourism development) encounters between self and multiple others in the future.

While my first research plans for my doctoral thesis underlined the importance of understanding 'local knowledges' in tourism development, I subsequently became highly critical towards the ambiguity of the concept as such. The scholarly literature of development studies has helped me to grasp the ethno- and Eurocentrism of this concept (e.g. Nygren 1999; Briggs and Sharp 2004). Indeed, while 'local knowledge' is often sought in relatively remote areas, I have difficulty imagining the opposite scenario, where a researcher from Nicaragua would collect data on local knowledges, let's say, in this Swedish rural village where I am currently living with my family. It is equally challenging to imagine a community-based research project where these same Nicaraguan researchers would call together participatory workshops to develop together, for instance, more respectful and ecological ways of collecting blueberries or mushrooms from our forests. I acknowledge the naiveté of this comment, but consider that in order to decolonize tourism epistemologies we should not accept entrenched relations between those who research and develop, and those who always find themselves in the role of the object of research or development projects. In my view, the search for 'local knowledge' or 'indigenous knowledge' becomes ambiguous when it is driven merely by non-locals and a non-indigenous desire to understand, learn and create new ways of knowing and being. As Chambers and Buzinde (2015, 11) and Holmes et al. (2016) have argued, it is significantly different when indigenous groups themselves draw on local capacities such as indigenous knowledge to inform knowledge production, development and planning.

My sincere hope is that in the future there will be more Nicaraguan and Central American tourism researchers, among others, who will participate in challenging and enriching the ways in which we know about tourism today. To complicate things, it is worth noticing that researchers from the so-called Global South can also strengthen the Western-centric ideas of tourism, development and participation. In fact, as my case study in San Ramón showed, the teachers and students from the local University of Matagalpa were visiting rural tourism communities with attitudes at least partly similar to those exhibited by their international colleagues. In fact, they expected every bit as much that the members of the local communities would be delighted to participate in their studies and considered that they should help the families to organize their lives for tourism development in the process.

6.4 Relationality of participation

While this research originated in my interest in rural communities' roles in tourism, my intention has not been to advocate community-based tourism development as a 'model' for poverty reduction or community development. I must also leave it to others with more insights into value chains and economic trickle-down effects to argue for and explain the economic implications of including local communities in tourism networks. I also find that any efforts intending to replace 'the grand narrative' of tourism growth with another universal solution could be seen as anathema. In other words, I do not find it meaningful to offer worldwide answers to questions of development or progress. It is in this same vein that Shalini Singh (2012, 117) argues that a 'progressive alternative to current models of participatory development could be seen as a repetition of the same mistake that the scholars are attempting to remedy'. In fact, I hope that current debates in tourism research would move beyond the dichotomy of promoting or condemning particular forms of tourism as models for sustainable development. I find it more important, for instance, to spread the word about the lost hospitality in development encounters and to call for more inclusive negotiations of hospitality in the encounters that take place in the name of tourism development.

My research on tourism encounters in San Ramón contributes to the academic discussions that find it *ill-devised* to dispose of the idea of participation as such (e.g. Singh 2012; Dredge et al. 2013). Instead of claiming that there is only one way that the reality of participation becomes constructed, there are many different ontologies, many different ways of being with self and with others (e.g. Veijola et al. 2014; Jóhannesson et al. 2015; Grimwood 2015; Munar and Jamal). Most importantly, curiosity and consciousness of different forms of participation belong here and can make the discussions of tourism ethics more meaningful and enjoyable (see Levinas 1969 112; Fennell 2008).[5] For this reason, I argue that we might need more time and space to articulate the visions and values of good life which support our ideas of community and participation. In the context of community-based tourism this would mean visualizing and explaining what is meant by the notion of participation and expressing why participation might be considered desirable, ethical, responsible or sustainable in the first place. Tourism ethics scholar David O. Fennell (2008, 4) has argued, drawing on Derrida's and Levinas's thoughts, that when it comes to 'responsible tourism', which has generated significant interest among theorists and practitioners, a failure to have a solid grounding on what responsibility means 'is in itself a lack of responsibility'.

I will now add few more arguments why we should continue to revitalize the transformative potential of participation and participatory approaches. Categorizing the participatory paradigm as a passé approach to development includes a palpable risk of throwing out the baby with the bathwater (Hickey and Mohan 2004). When considering the possible disposal or replacement of participation – or its cousin concepts – it is good to notice that the idea of participation might not be as new or modern as the tourism or development literature would like us to believe (Henkel and Stirrat 2001, 170–1; Cornwall and Brock 2005; Cohen and Uphoff 2011, 34; Singh 2012, 117). Where participation took place thousands of years ago, for instance, by collecting food, playing and eating together, today there exists a noticeably wider range of forms: physical, virtual, one-on-one, family, team, community, municipal elections, corporations and so on (Tökkäri 2010, 32). Hence, at least the most basic unit and case of participation – two people encountering and engaging with each other – is not something that scholars or practitioners could get rid of (ibid., 30). As I have argued throughout the book, I find it ambiguous to treat participation as a tap that could be turned on or off. Consequently, it is important that we keep tracing the more ancient and radical roots of participation where participation is seen as a starting point instead of a method or a goal (Leal 2010, 71; see Telfer 2009, 154–5; McRoberts 2012).

As this book has shown repeatedly, contemporary discussions on participatory tourism development have not been divided only based on questions of culture and market, but also along the dimension of individualism and communality. Thinking with Levinasian philosophy has guided my understanding about the differences between ontologies of *totality* – which is based on conditions and clear-cut subject positions – and the metaphysics of *infinity*, which calls for openness and receptivity. I have suggested that the frustration with and critique of participatory approaches in tourism studies and practices might spring from the ontologies that favour totalizing and dualistic ways of being and knowing. Thus, Levinas's (1969) idea of ethics calls for a readiness to interrupt the self as an individually responsible subject and to envision alternatives to essentializing ideas of participation. My ambition has been to argue that while participation and hospitality based on regulated techniques or knowledge can be seen as a form of domination, the possibilities and ethics of participation lie in the *impossibility* of controlling, deciding, or determining the conditions for participation. This means approaching hospitable encounters as something that cannot be planned; rather, the responsibilities between self and other become constantly negotiated in these encounters as such. In the context of this study, I have found the notion of readiness to be interrupted to be highly applicable to hosts and guests searching for more inclusive designs of participation. More generally, the idea of interruption provides a conceptual tool to facilitate reflection on welcoming encounters.

This research journey has been, most of all, an ontological movement from the individual self to the spaces between ourselves. Travelling with the notion of hospitality, I have sought to imagine hospitable, relational ways of being that can be seen as an alternative to solipsism and encounters between individual entities. Yet, the step that took me away from the self is still mobility within the anthropocentric ontology, where being is based on being among humans, and ethics is based on responsibilities between people (e.g. Braidotti 2013; Pyyhtinen 2015; Huijbens and Gren 2016). This ontology is like an enclave with closed gates against the more-than-human world. Frankly, I am currently suffering from a quite a bad hangover after partying all night at this Hotel Anthropocene. But that is already another story. While reaching out for my bottle of Coke with shaky hands, I believe that some of the ideas from this research journey could be used to envision and compose more inclusive, welcoming and caring gatherings among humans *and* nonhuman others (see also Grimwood 2015, 17–20; Kinnunen and Valtonen 2017; van der Duim et al. 2017; Puig de la Bellacasa 2017; Zylinska 2014).

Most of all, despite the context, the notion of hospitality encourages one to keep the door open to the unpredictable and the unexpected. In the end, perhaps one of the most salient 'results' of my research process that I want to carry with me in the future is the importance of readiness to be interrupted. Participation, responsibility and hospitality all build on the idea that we humans are capable of interrupting ourselves and of welcoming new ways of being, knowing and doing. In this spirit, I will let Gabriella, one of the local guides from San Ramón, close the story told in this book:

> I want hospitality to be a concept of humanity – to be a human.

Notes

1 For explanation of prepositions between welcome and the other, please see Derrida (1999, 23–4, 35). I have also discussed these prepositions briefly in Veijola et al. (2014, 146).
2 Wearing and Wearing (2014) suggest that the encounters between local communities and tourism intermediaries require codes of conduct for ethical action. See Raffoul's (2010, 1) work on responsibility, where he suggests that ethics today in general are approached less as a normative body of moral rules and more in terms of philosophical reflection on the meaning of ethics as such.
3 As Vrasti (2013, 71) points out, this false dichotomy can strengthen the elitist cliché 'they are poor but happy' and cause neglect of the material needs of the others and denying the other something that the self has (see also McEwan 2009, 301; Caton 2014b, 133).
4 See Caton's (2014a) research on 'Making messes with constructivism and critical theory'.
5 Levinas writes in *Totality and Infinity* (1969, 112) that '[W]e live in the consciousness of consciousness, but this consciousness is not reflection. It is not knowing but enjoyment, and, as we shall say, the very egoism of life'.

Bibliography

Abram, S., and Norum, R. (2016) 'An archaeology of Arctic travel journalism', *Studies in Travel Writing*, 20(3): 272–84.

Adler, J. (1989) 'Origins of sightseeing', *Annals of Tourism Research*, 16(1): 7–29.

Agamben, G. (1990/2007) *The Coming Community*, translated by M. Hardt, Minneapolis, MN: University of Minnesota Press.

Agar, M. (1980) *The Professional Stranger: An Informal Introduction to Ethnography*, New York: Academic Press.

Ahmed, S. (2000) *Strange Encounters: Embodied Others in Post-Coloniality*, London: Routledge.

Ahmed, S. (2012) *On Being Included: Racism and Diversity in Institutional Life*, Durham, NC: Duke University Press.

Aitchison, C. (2001) 'Theorizing other discourses of tourism, gender and culture: can the subaltern speak in (tourism)?', *Tourism Studies*, 1(2): 133–47.

Alt, S. (2016) *Beyond the Biopolitics of Development: Being, Politics and World*, Rovaniemi: Lapland University Press.

Alvesson, M., Gabriel, Y., and Paulsen, R. (2017) *Return to Meaning. A Social Science with Something to Say*, Oxford: Oxford University Press.

Andringa, S., Poulston, J., and Pernecky, T. (2016) 'Hospitality entrepreneurship: a link in the career chain', *International Journal of Contemporary Hospitality Management*, 28(5): 717–36.

Ankor, J. (2009) *Pleasure and Dread: The Paradox of Travel*, Sydney: University of Technology.

Ankor, J., and Wearing, S. (2012) 'Gaze, encounter and philosophies of Otherness', in O. Moufakkir and Y. Reisinger (eds), *The Host Gaze in Global Tourism*, Cambridge: CAB International.

Aref, F. (2011) 'Barriers to community capacity building for tourism development in communities in Shiraz, Iran', *Journal of Sustainable Tourism*, 19(3): 347–59.

Arendt, H. (1982) *Lectures on Kant's Political Philosophy*, Chicago: Chicago University Press.

Ashley, C., and Roe, D. (2002) 'Making tourism work for the poor: Strategies and challenges in southern Africa', *Development Southern Africa*, 19(1): 61–82.

Ateljevic, I., Harris, C., Wilson, E., and Collins, F. (2005) 'Getting "entangled": reflexivity and the "critical turn" in tourism studies', *Tourism Recreation Research: Theme – Tourism and Research*, 30(2): 9–21.

Atterton, P., and Calarcos, M. (2010) 'The third wave of Levinas' scholarship', in P. Atterton and M. Calarcos (eds), *Radicalizing Levinas*, Albany, NY: State University of New York Press.

Atterton, P. (2011) 'Levinas and our moral responsibility toward other animals', *Inquiry*, 54(6): 633–9.

Ayikoru, M., Tribe, J., and Airey D. (2009) 'Reading tourism education: neoliberalism unveiled', *Annals of Tourism Research*, 36(2): 191–221.

Babb, F. (2010) *The Tourism Encounter: Fashioning Latin American Nations and Histories*, Stanford, CA: Stanford University Press.

Baker, G. (2010) 'The "double law" of hospitality: rethinking cosmopolitan ethics in humanitarian intervention', *International Relations*, 24(1): 87–103.

Baker, G. (2011) *Politicising Ethics in International Relations: Cosmopolitanism as Hospitality*, London: Routledge.

Baker, G. (2013) 'Introduction', in G. Baker (ed.), *Hospitality and World Politics*, New York: Palgrave Macmillan.

Balslev, H., and Gyimóthy, S. (2016) 'Seizing community participation in sustainable development: Pueblos Magicos of Mexico', *Journal of Cleaner Production*, 111: 318–26.

Barnett, T. (2008) 'Tourism a tool for more humanized world?', in C. D'Mello (ed.), *Transforming Re-forming Tourism, Perspectives on Justice and Humanity in Tourism*, Thailand: Ecumenical Coalition on Tourism.

Barrera, O.D. (1997) *El sector turístico en Nicaragua: Actualidad y posibilidades de desarrollo. Un enfoque estratégico*, Managua: UCA.

Barrera, O.D. (1998) 'Turismo y globalización: un reto para Nicaragua', *Encuentro*, 48: 46–53.

Bauman, Z. (1998) *Globalization: The Human Consequences*, New York: Columbia University Press.

Belhassen, Y., and Caton, K. (2011) 'On the need for critical pedagogy in tourism education', *Tourism Management*, 32(6): 1389–96.

Bell, D. (2009) 'Tourism and hospitality', in T. Jamal and M. Robinson (eds), *The SAGE Handbook of Tourism Studies*, Los Angeles: SAGE.

Bell, D. (2017) 'Geographies of hospitality', in C. Lashley (eds), *The Routledge Handbook of Hospitality Studies*, London: Routledge.

Belli, G. (2002) *The Country Under My Skin: A Memoir of Love and War*, Managua: Knopf Borzot Books.

Belsky, J.M. (1999) 'Misrepresenting communities: the politics of community–based rural tourism in Gales Point Manatee, Belize', *Rural Sociology*, 64(4): 641–66.

Belsky, J.M. (2004) 'Contributions of qualitative research to understanding the politics of community ecotourism', in J. Phillimore and L. Goodson (eds), *Qualitative Methods in Tourism Research*, London: Routledge.

Bennett, T., and Joyce, P. (2010) *Material Powers: Cultural Studies, History and the Material Turn*, London: Routledge.

Benveniste, É. (1973) *Indo–European Language and Society*, translated by E. Palmer, London: Faber and Faber Limited.

Berkhöfer, U., and Berkhöfer, A. (2007) ' "Participation" in development thinking – coming to grips with a truism and its critiques', in S. Stoll-Kleemann and M. Welp (eds), *Stakeholder Dialogues in Natural Resource Management: Theory and Practice*, London: Springer.

Berking, H. (1999) *Sociology of Giving*, translated by P. Camiller, London: Sage.

Berno, T. (1999) 'When is a guest a guest? Cook Islanders conceptualize tourism', *Annals of Tourism Research*, 26(3): 565–675.

Bhabha, H. (1994) *The Location of Culture*, London: Routledge.

Bianchi, R.V. (2015) 'Towards a new political economy of global tourism revisited', in R. Sharpley and D. Telfer (eds), *Tourism and Development: Concepts and Issues*, 2nd edition, London: Channel View.

Blanchot, M. (1993) *The Infinite Conversation*, translated by Susan Hanson, London: University of Minnesota Press.

Blazer, M. (2010) *Storytelling Globalization from the Chaco and Beyond*, London: Duke University Press.

Blàzquez, M., and Cañada, E. (2011) *Turismo Placebo. Nueva colonización turística: del Mediterráneo a Mesoamérica y El Caribe. Lógicas espaciales del capital turístico*, Managua: Editorial Enlace.

Boluk, K. (2011) 'In consideration of a new approach to tourism: a critical review of fair trade tourism', *The Journal of Tourism and Peace Research*, 1(3): 27–37.

Bonilla, A., and Mordt, M. (2008) 'Turismo y conflictos territoriales en el pacifico de Nicaragua: El caso de Tola, más allá de los Titulares', *Prisma*: San Salvador.

Bonilla, A., and Mordt, M. (2011) 'Turismo en el Municipio de Tola (Nicaragua): Exclusión y Resistencia Local', *AlbaSud, Opiniones en Desarrollo, Programa Turismo Responsable*, 11.

Braidotti, R. (2013) *The Posthuman*, Cambridge: Polity Press.

Bramwell, B. (2014) 'Local participation in community tourism', in A.A. Lew, C.M. Hall and A.M. Williams (eds), *The Wiley Blackwell Companion to Tourism*, Oxford: John Wiley.

Brandth, B., and Haugen M.S. (2014) 'Embodying the rural idyll in farm tourist hosting', *Scandinavian Journal of Hospitality and Tourism*, 14(2): 101–15.

Branner, M. (2016) 'Nu ska du tänka negativt, interview of Ida Hallgren 4. Dec 2016'. GP, in Swedish. www.gp.se/livsstil/nu-ska-du-t%C3%A4nka-negativt-1.3998103, accessed 10 September 2017.

Briedenhann, J., and Ramchander, P. (2006) 'Township tourism – blessing or blight? The case of Soweto in South Africa', in M.K. Smith and M. Robinson (eds), *Cultural Tourism in a Changing World, Politics, Participation and (re)presentation*, Clevedon: Channel View.

Briggs, J., and Sharp, J. (2004) 'Indigenous knowledges and development: a postcolonial caution', *Third World Quarterly*, 2(4): 661–76.

Bruner, E.M. (2005) *Culture on Tour, Ethnographies of Travel*, London: University of Chicago Press.

Buades, J. (2009) *Do not disturb Barceló. Viaje a las entrañas de un imperio turístico*, Barcelona: Icaria.

Burns, P. (2004) 'Tourism planning: a third way?', *Annals of Tourism Research*, 31(1): 24–43.

Büscher, M., Urry, J., and Witchger, K. (2011) *Mobile Methods*, London: Routledge.

Butcher, J. (2007) *Ecotourism, NGOs and Development*, London: Routledge.

Butcher, J. (2012) 'The mantra of "community participation" in context', in T.V. Singh (ed.), *Critical Debates in Tourism*, Bristol: Channel View.

Butcher, J. (2014) 'Moralizing tourism: personal qualities, political issues', in M. Mostafanezhad and K. Hannam (eds), *Moral Encounters in Tourism*, Farnham: Ashgate.

Campbell, L.M. (1999) 'Ecotourism in rural developing communities', *Annals of Tourism Research*, 26(3): 534–53.

Cañada, E. (2010) *Perspectivas del Turismo Comunitario: Cómo Mantener Vivas las Comunidades Rurales*, Managua: Alba Sud.

Cañada, E. (2012) 'El turismo en la Soberanía Alimentaria', www.albasud.org/blog/es/284/el-turismo-en-la-soberania-alimentaria, accessed 20 September 2014.

Cañada, E. (2013) *Turismos en Centroamérica. Un diagnóstico para el debate*, Managua: Enlace.

Cañada, E. (2014) *Turismo Comunitario en Centroamérica. Experiencias y aprendizajes.* Editorial Enlace. Colección Mejores Prácticas, Managua: Alba Sud.

Cañada, E. (2015) *Las que limpian los hoteles: Historias ocultas de precariedad laboral*, Barcelona: Icaria Editorial.

Cañada, E., Delgado, L., and Gil, H. (2006) *Guía Turismo Rural Comunitario – Nicaragua*, Managua: Edisa.

Cañada, E., and Fandiño, M. (2009) *Experiencias de Turismo Comunitario en Nicaragua. Aportes a la economía campesina*, Managua: Editorial Enlace.

Cañada, E., and Gascón, J. (2007a) *El turismo y sus mitos*, Managua: Fundación Luciernaga.

Cañada, E., and Gascón, J. (2007b) *Turismo y Desarrollo, Herramientas para una mirada crítica*, Managua: Fundación Luciernaga.

Cañada, E., and Merodio, I. (2004) *Turismo rural comunitario en Nicaragua: La experiencia de la Unión de Cooperativas Agropecuarias "Tierra y Agua"*, Barcelona: Bilbao.

Carlisle, S. (2010) 'Access and marginalization in Beach Enclave Resort', in S. Cole and N. Morgan (eds), *Tourism and Inequality – Problems and Prospects*, London: CABI Publishing.

Carroll, R. (2007) Ortega banks on tourism to beat poverty, *The Guardian*. Available at: www.theguardian.com/world/2007/jan/07/rorycarroll.theobserver, accessed 14 August 2017.

Castañeda, Q. (2006) 'The invisible theatre of ethnography: performative principles of fieldwork', *Anthropological Quarterly*, 79(1): 75–104.

Caton, K. (2008) *Encountering the Other Through Study Abroad*, University of Illinois at Urbana-Champaign.

Caton, K. (2012) 'Taking the moral turn in tourism studies', *Annals of Tourism Research*, 39(4): 1906–28.

Caton, K. (2013) 'The risky business of understanding: philosophical hermeneutics and the knowing subject in worldmaking', *Tourism Analysis*, 18(3): 341–51.

Caton, K. (2014a) 'Humanism and tourism: a moral encounter', in M. Mostafanezhad and K. Hannam (eds), *Moral Encounters in Tourism*, Farnham: Ashgate.

Caton, K. (2014b) 'Between you and me: making messes with constructivism and critical theory', *Tourism, Culture and Communication*, 13(2): 127–37.

Caton, K., and Santos, C.A. (2008) 'Closing the hermeneutic circle? Photographic encounters with the other', *Annals of Tourism Research*, 35(1): 7–26.

Caton, K., and Santos, C.A. (2009) 'Images of the other: selling study abroad in a postcolonial world', *Journal of Travel Research*, 48(2): 191–204.

Cederström, C., and Spicer, A. (2015) *The Wellness Syndrome*, Cambridge: Polity Press.

Cernea, M.M. (1992) *Putting People First: Sociological Variables in Rural Development*, Oxford: Oxford University Press.

Cerwonka, A., and Malkki, L.H. (2007) *Improvising Theory: Process and Temporality in Ethnographic Fieldwork*, Chicago: University of Chicago Press.

Chalip, L., and Costa, C.A. (2012) 'Clashing worldviews: sources of disappointment in rural hospitality and tourism development', *Hospitality and Society*, 2(1): 25–47.

Chambers, D., and Buzinde, C. (2015) 'Tourism and decolonisation: locating research and self', *Annals of Tourism Research*, 51: 1–16.

Chambers, R. (1983) *Rural Development, Putting the Last First*, London: Pearson Education.

Chandler, D. (2013) 'Where is the human in human-centered approaches to development? A critique of Amartya Sen's "development as freedom"', in S. Mezzadra, J. Reid and R. Samaddar (eds), *The Biopolitics of Development: Reading Michel Foucault in the Postcolonial Present*, London: Springer.

Chen, L., Scott, N., and Benckendorff, P. (2017) 'Mindful tourist experiences: a Buddhist perspective', *Annals of Tourism Research*, 64: 1–12.

Cheong, S., and Miller, M. (2000) 'Power and tourism: a Foucauldian observation', *Annals of Tourism Research*, 27(2): 371–90.

Clifford, J., and Marcus, E.G. (1986) *Writing Culture: The Poetics and Politics of Ethnography*, Berkeley: University of California Press.

Cohen, E. (1979a) 'A phenomenology of tourist experiences', *Sociology*, 13(2): 179–201.

Cohen, E. (1979b) 'The impact of tourism on the hill tribes of Northern Thailand', *International Asian Forum*, 10(1/2): 5–38.

Cohen, J.M., and Uphoff, N.T. (2011) 'Participation's place in rural development: seeking clarity through specificity', in A. Cornwall (ed.), *The Participation Reader*, New York: Zed Books Reader.

Cohen, R.A. (1987) 'Foreword', in E. Levinas, *Time and the Other and Additional Essays*, Pittsburgh: Duquesne University Press.

Cohen, R.A. (1998) 'Foreword', in E. Levinas, *Otherwise than Being, or Beyond Essence*, Pittsburgh: Duquesne University Press.

Cole, S. (2006) 'Cultural tourism, community participation and empowerment', in M.K. Smith and M. Robinson (eds), *Cultural Tourism in a Changing World, Politics, Participation and (Re)presentation*, London: Channel View.

Cole, S. (2008) *Tourism, Culture and Development: Hopes, Dreams and Realities in East Indonesia*, Clevedon: Channel View.

Cole, S., and Eriksson, J. (2010) 'Tourism and human rights', in S. Cole and N. Morgan (eds), *Tourism and Inequality – Problems and Prospects*, London: CABI Publishing.

Cole, S., and Morgan, N. (2010) 'Introduction', in S. Cole and N. Morgan (eds), *Tourism and Inequality – Problems and Prospects*, London: CABI Publishing.

Cooke, B., and Kothari, U. (2001) 'The case for participation as tyranny', in B. Cooke and U. Kothari (eds), *Participation: The New Tyranny?*, London: Zed Books.

Córdoba Azcárate, M. (2014) 'Tourism development, architectures of escape and the passive beloved in contemporary Yucatán (Mexico)', in M. Mostafanezhad and K. Hannam (eds), *Moral Encounters in Tourism*. Farnham: Ashgate.

Cornwall, A. (2006) 'Historical perspectives on participation in development', *Commonwealth and Comparative Politics*, 44(1): 27–43.

Cornwall, A., and Brock, K. (2005) *Beyond Buzzwords "Poverty Reduction", "Participation" and "Empowerment" in Development Policy*, Geneva: United Nations Research Institute for Social Development UNRISD.

Correa Oquel, C. (2006) *The Nicaraguans, Los Nicaragüenses*, Colombia: Imprelibros SA.

Critchley, S. (1999) *The Ethics of Deconstruction: Derrida and Levinas*, Edinburgh: Edinburgh University Press.

Critchley, S. (2015) *The Problem with Levinas*, Oxford: Oxford University Press.

Crossley, N. (1996) *Intersubjectivity: The Fabric of Social Becoming*, London: Sage.

Csikszentmihalyi, M. (1975) *Flow: The Psychology of Optimal Experience*, New York: Harper Perennial.

Dahles, H., and Keune, L. (2002) 'Introduction', in H. Dahles and L. Keune (eds), *Tourism Development and Local Participation in Latin America*, New York: Cognizant Communication Corporation.

Davidson, T.L. (2005) 'What are travel and tourism: are they really an industry?', in W.F. Theobald (ed.), *Global Tourism*, 3rd edition, Burlington, MA: Elsevier.

de Bernardi, C., Kugapi, O., and Lüthje, M. (2017) 'Sámi indigenous tourism empowerment in the Nordic countries through labelling systems: strengthening ethnic enterprises and activities', in I.B. de Lima and V.T. King (eds), *Tourism and Ethnodevelopment: Inclusion, Empowerment and Self-determination*, Abingdon: Routledge.

de Kadt, E. (1979) *Tourism, Passport to Development?*, Oxford: Oxford University Press.

de Sardan, O. (2005) *Anthropology and Development: Understanding Contemporary Social Change*, London; Zed Books.

Derrida, J. (1967/1978) *Writing and Difference*, translated by A. Bass, Chicago: University of Chicago Press.

Derrida, J. (1976) *Of Grammatology*, translated by G.C. Spivak, Baltimore, MD: Johns Hopkins University Press.

Derrida, J. (1995) *The Gift of Death*, Chicago: University of Chicago Press.

Derrida, J. (1999) *Adieu to Emmanuel Levinas*, translated by P.A. Brault and M. Naas, Stanford, CA: Stanford University Press.

Derrida, J. (2000) *Of Hospitality: Anne Dufourmantelle Invites Jacques Derrida to Respond*, translated by R. Bowlby, Stanford, CA: Stanford University Press.

Derrida, J. (2001) *On Cosmopolitanism and Forgiveness*, translated by M. Dooley and M. Hughes, London: Routledge.

Derrida, J. (2003) *Sur Parole: Instantanés Philosophiques*, Paris: Editions de l'aube.

Derrida, J. (2005) 'The principle of hospitality', *Parallax*, 11(1): 6–9.

Derrida, J., and Rottenberg, E. (2002) *Negotiations: Interventions and Interviews, 19712001*, Stanford, CA: Stanford University Press.

Despret, V. (2005) 'Sheep do have opinions', in B. Latour and P. Weibel (eds), *Making Things Public*, Cambridge, MA: MIT Press.

Dicks, B. (2003) *Culture on Display: The Production of Contemporary Visitability*, Maidenhead: McGraw-Hill.

Dielemans, J. (2008) *Välkommen till Paradiset. Reportage om Turismindustrin* [Welcome to Paradise], Atlas: GGB Media.

Dixey, L. (2008) 'The unsustainability of community tourism donor projects: lessons from Zambia', in A. Spenceley (ed.), *Responsible Tourism: Critical Issues for Conservation and Development*, London: Earthscan.

Dowling, R.K. (2003) 'Community attitudes: tourism development in natural environments', in T. Singh, J.T. Dallen and R.K. Dowling (eds), *Tourism in Destination Communities*, Wallingford: CABI Publishing.

Drabinski, J.E. (2011) *Levinas and the Postcolonial: Race, Nation, Other*, Edinburgh: Edinburgh University Press.

Drabinski, J.E., and Nelson, E.S. (eds) (2014) *Between Levinas and Heidegger*, Albany, NY: State University of New York Press.

Dredge, D. (2010) 'Place Change and tourism development conflict: evaluating public interest', *Tourism Management*, 31(1): 104–12.

Dredge, D. (2011) 'Phronetic tourism planning research: reflections on critically engaged tourism planning research and practice', *IV Critical Tourism Studies Conference: Tourism Futures: Creative and Critical Action*, Cardiff: Welsh Centre for Tourism Research.

Dredge, D., and Hales, R. (2012) 'Community case study research', in L. Dwyer, A. Gill and N. Seetaram (eds), *Research Methods in Tourism: Quantitative and Qualitative Approaches*, Cheltenham: Edward Elgar.

Dredge, D., Hales, R., and Jamal, T. (2013) 'Community case study research: researcher operacy, embeddedness and making research matter', *Tourism Analysis*, 18(1): 29–43.

Duncan, T., Scott, D.G., and Baum, T. (2015) 'The mobilities of hospitality work: an exploration of issues and debates', *Annals of Tourism Research*, 41: 1–19.

Dussel, E. (2008) *Twenty Theses on Politics*, translated by G. Ciccariello-Maher, Durham, NC: Duke University Press.

Dussel, E. (2013) *Ethics of Liberation: In the Age of Globalization and Exclusion*, Durham, NC: Duke University Press.

Eadington, W.R., and Smith, V.L. (1993) 'Introduction: the emergence of alternative forms of tourism', in V.L. Smith and W.R. Eadington (eds), *Tourism Alternatives: Potentials and Problems in the Development of Tourism*, Philadelphia, PA: University of Pennsylvania Press.

Easterly, W. (2006) *The White Man's Burden: Why the West's Efforts to Aid the Rest Have Done So Much Ill and so Little Good?*, Oxford: Oxford University Press.

Edelheim, J. (2013) 'Vieraanvaraisuus – mitä se todellisuudessa on?' Multidimensional Tourism Institute, *Newsletter June 19 2013*.

Edelheim, J. (2015) *Tourist Attractions: From Objective to Narrative*, Clevedon: Channel View.

Edensor, T. (1998) *Tourists at the Taj: Performance and Meaning at a Symbolic Site*, London: Routledge.

Edensor, T. (2009) 'Tourism and performance', in T. Jamal and M. Robinson (eds), *The SAGE Handbook of Tourism Studies*, Los Angeles: SAGE.

EduTourism (2009) 'Welcome to Nicaragua', tourist brochure, Managua: Grafi Print.

Ek, R. (2015) 'The tourist-vampire and the citizen as ontological figures: human and nonhuman encounters in the postpolitical', in G. Jóhannesson, C. Ren and R. van der Duim (eds) *Tourism Encounters and Controversies: Ontological Politics of Tourist Development*, Farnham: Ashgate.

Eksell, J. (2013) 'Värdeskapande Gästfrihet. Hur gästfrihet som värde ramas in, etableras och förhandlas i hotellbranchen', Lund: Media-Tryck.

Equipo Nitlapan – Envió (2008a) 'Hasta cuándo?', *Envio, Revista Mensual de la Universidad Centroamericana (UCA)*, 318: 3–12.

Equipo Nitlapan – Envió (2008b) 'Las Reglas del Juego', *Envio, Revista Mensual de la Universidad Centroamericana (UCA)*, 319: 3–13.

Eriksson Baaz, M. (2005) *The Paternalism of Partnership: A Postcolonial Reading of Identity in Development Aid*, London: Zed Books.

Escobar, A. (2010) 'Latin America at a crossroads', *Cultural Studies*, 24(1): 1–65.

Escobar, A. (2012) *Encountering Development: The Making and Unmaking of the Third World*, Princeton, NJ: Princeton University Press.

Fagan, M. (2009) 'The inseparability of ethics and politics: rethinking the third in Emmanuel Levinas', *Contemporary Political Theory*, 8(1): 5–22.

Fennell, D.A. (2006) *Tourism Ethics*, Clevedon: Channel View.

Fennell, D.A. (2008) 'Responsible tourism: a Kierkegaardian interpretation', *Tourism Recreation Research*, 33(1): 3–12.

Fennell, D.A. (2009) 'Ethics and tourism', in J. Tribe (ed.), *Philosophical Issues in Tourism*, Bristol: Channel View.

Fennell, D.A., and Malloy, D.C. (2007) *Codes of Ethics in Tourism: Practice, Theory, Synthesis*, Bristol: Channel View.

Fennell, D.A., and Przeclawski, K. (2003) 'Generating goodwill in tourism', in T. Singh, J.T. Dallen and R.K. Dowling (eds), *Tourism in Destination Communities*, Wallingford: CABI Publishing.

Fleischer, A., and Felsentein, D. (2000) 'Support for rural tourism: does it make a difference?', *Annals of Tourism Research*, 27(4): 1007–27.

Francesch Díaz, A. (2016) 'Antropólogos, turistas, confusiones y reflexiones', *Pasos* 14(1): 11–21.

Freire, P. (1970/2000) *Pedagogy of the Oppressed*, New York: Continuum.

Gadamer, H.G. (1975) *Truth and Method*, translation revised by J. Weinsheimer and G.M. Donald, New York: Seabury Press.

Ganem-Cuenca, A. (2011) *Gender Equity and Health within Fair Trade Certified Coffee Cooperatives in Nicaragua: Tensions and Challenges*, Saskatoon: University of Saskatchewan.

García-Rosell, J.-C. (2013) *A Multi–Stakeholder Perspective on Sustainable Marketing: Promoting Sustainability through Action and Research*, Rovaniemi: Lapland University Press.

Geleta, E.B. (2015) *The Microfinance Mirage: The Politics of Poverty, Social Capital and Women's Empowerment in Ethiopia*, Farnham: Ashgate.

George, E.W., Mair, H., and Reid, D.G. (2009) *Rural Tourism Development Localism and Cultural Change*, Bristol: Channel View.

Germann Molz, J. (2007) 'Cosmopolitans on the couch: mobile hospitality and the internet', in J. Germann Molz and S. Gibson (eds), *Mobilizing Hospitality, The Ethics of Social Relations in a Mobile World*, Aldershot: Ashgate.

Germann Molz, J. (2009) 'Representing pace in tourism mobilities: staycations, slow travel and the amazing race', *Journal of Tourism and Cultural Change*, 7(4): 270–86.

Germann Molz, J. (2011) 'Connectivity, collaboration, search', in M. Büscher, J. Urry and K. Witchger (eds), *Mobile Methods*, London: Routledge.

Germann Molz, J. (2012) *Travel Connections: Tourism, Technology and Togetherness in a Mobile World*, London: Routledge.

Germann Molz, J. (2014) 'Camping in clearing', in S. Veijola, J. Germann Molz, O. Pyyhtinen, E. Höckert and A. Grit, *Disruptive Tourism and Its Untidy Guests: Alternative Ontologies for Future Hospitalities*, New York: Palgrave MacMillan.

Germann Molz, J. (2017) 'Giving back, doing good, feeling global: the affective flows of family voluntourism', *Journal of Contemporary Ethnography*, 46(3): 334–60.

Germann Molz, J., and Gibson, S. (2007) 'Introduction: Mobilizing and Mooring Hospitality', in J. Germann Molz and S. Gibson (eds), *Mobilizing Hospitality, The Ethics of Social Relations in a Mobile World*, Aldershot: Ashgate.

Gibson, S. (2003) 'Accommodating strangers: British hospitality and the asylum hotel debate', *Journal for Cultural Research*, 7(4): 367–86.

Gindling, T.H. (2008) 'South–south migration: the impact of Nicaraguan immigrants on earnings, inequality, and poverty in Costa Rica', *World Development*, 37(1): 116–26.

Gmelch, G. (2012) *Behind the Smile: The Working Lives on Caribbean Tourism*, Indianapolis: Indiana University Press.

Goodwin, H. (2011) *Taking Responsibility for Tourism: Responsible Tourism Management*, Oxford: Goodfellow Publishers.

Goodwin, H., and Boekhold, H. (2010) 'Beyond Fair Trade: enhancing the livelihoods of coffee farmers in Tanzania', in L. Jolliffe (ed.), *Coffee Culture, Destinations and Tourism*, Bristol: Channel View.

Goodwin, H., Santilli, R., and Armstrong, R. (2014) 'Community-based tourism in the developing world: delivering the goods?', *Progress in Responsible Tourism*, 3(1): 31–56.

Gössling, S. (2003) *Tourism and Development in Tropical Islands: Political Ecology Perspectives*, Cheltenham: Edward Elgar.

Gotman, A. (2001) *Le sens de l'hospitalité: Essai sur les fondements sociaux de l'accueil classique*, Paris: Seuil.

Gould, J., and Secher Marcussen, H. (eds) (2004) *Ethnographies of Aid: Exploring Development Texts and Encounters*, Roskilde: Roskilde University.

Gramsci, A. (1971) *Selections from the Prison Notebooks*, New York: International Publisher.

Greig, A., Hulme, D., and Turner, M. (2007) *Challenging Global Inequality*, New York: Palgrave Macmillan.

Gren, M., and Huijbens, E.H. (2012) 'Tourism theory and the earth', *Annals of Tourism Research*, 39: 155–70.

Grimwood, B.S.R. (2015) 'Advancing tourism's moral morphology: relational metaphors for just and sustainable Arctic tourism', *Tourist Studies*, 15(1): 3–26.

Grimwood, B.S.R., and Doubleday, N.C. (2013) 'Illuminating traces: enactments of responsibility in practices of Arctic river tourists and inhabitants', *Journal of Ecotourism*, 12(2): 53–74.

Grimwood, B.S.R., Yudina, O., Muldoon, M., and Qiu, J. (2015) 'Responsibility in tourism: a discursive analysis', *Annals of Tourism Research*, 50: 22–38.

Grimwood, B.S.R., Doubleday, N.C., Laidler, G.J., Donaldson, S.G., and Blangy, S. (2012) 'Engaged acclimatization: towards responsible community-based participatory research in Nunavut', *The Canadian Geographer*, 56(2): 211–30.

Grimwood, B.S.R., and Caton, K. (2017) 'Pausing at the intersections of tourism moralities and mobilities: some neighbourhood history and a traffic report', *Tourist Studies*, 17(1): 3–16.

Grit, A. (2010) *The Opening Up of Hospitality Spaces to Difference: Exploring the Nature of Home Exchange Experiences*, unpublished PhD thesis, University of Strathclyde.

Grit, A. (2014) 'Messing around with serendipities', in S. Veijola, J. Germann Molz, O. Pyyhtinen, E. Höckert and A. Grit, *Disruptive Tourism and Its Untidy Guests. Alternative Ontologies for Future Hospitalities*, New York: Palgrave MacMillan.

Grit, A., and Lynch, P. (2012) 'An analysis of the development of home exchange organisations', *Research in Hospitality Management*, 1(1): 1–7.

Grosfoguel, R. (2008) 'Developmentalism, modernity, and dependency theory in Latin America', in M. Moraña, E. Dussel and C.A. Jáuregui (eds), *Coloniality at Large: Latin America and the Postcolonial Debate*, Durham, NC: Duke University Press.

Grosz, E. (1995) 'Women, chora, dwelling', in S. Watson and K. Gibson (eds), *Postmodern Cities and Spaces*, Cambridge, MA: Blackwell.

Gyimóthy, S. (2017) 'Dinnersharing: casual hospitality in the collaborative economy', in C. Lashley (eds), *The Routledge Handbook of Hospitality Studies*, London: Routledge.

Haanpää, M. (2017) *Event Co-Creation as Choreography: Autoethnographic Study on Event Volunteer Knowing*, Rovaniemi: Lapland University Press.

Hakkarainen, M. (2009) 'Matkailu maaseudun uutena työnä' [Tourism as new work in rural areas], in S. Tuulentie (ed.), *Turisti tulee kylään. Matkailukeskukset ja lappilainen arki* [Tourist comes to visit], Helsinki: Minerva Kustannys Oy.

Hakkarainen, M. (2017) *Matkailutyön ehdot syrjäisessä kylässä* [The Conditions of Tourism Work in a Remote Village], Acta Universitatis Lapponiensis 357, Rovaniemi: Lapland University Press.

Hakkarainen, M., and García-Rosell, J.C. (2018) 'An ethnographic action research approach to tourism development in peripheral areas: insights from projects in Finnish Lapland', *International Journal of Tourism Policy*.

Hales, R., and Caton, K. (2017) 'Proximity ethics, climate change and the flyer's dilemma: ethical negotiations of the hypermobile traveler', *Tourist Studies*, 17(1): 9–113.

Hall, C.M. (1994) *Tourism and Politics: Policy, Power and Place*, Chichester: John Wiley and Sons.

Hall, C.M. (2003) 'Politics and place: an analysis of power in tourism communities', in T. Singh, J.T. Dallen and R.K. Dowling (eds), *Tourism in Destination Communities*, Wallingford: CABI Publishing.

Hall, C.M. (2007) 'Pro–poor tourism: do tourism exchanges benefit mainly people from the south?', In C.M. Hall (ed.), *Pro–Poor Tourism: Who Benefits?: Perspectives on Tourism and Poverty Reduction*, Clevedon: Channel View Publishing.

Hall, C.M. (2007) 'North–South perspectives on tourism, regional development and peripheral areas', in D.K. Müller and B. Jansson (eds), *The Difficult Business of Making Pleasure Peripheries Prosperous: Perspectives on Space, Place and Environment*, Wallingford: CABI.

Hall, C.M. (2010a) 'Changing paradigms and global change: from sustainable to steady–state tourism', *Tourism Recreation Research*, 35(2): 131–14.

Hall, C.M. (2010b) 'Fieldwork in tourism/touring fields: where does tourism end and fieldwork begin?', in C.M. Hall (ed.), *Fieldwork in Tourism: Methods, Issues and Reflections*, London: Routledge.

Hall, C.M. (2013) 'Tourism, visas and the geopolitics of mobility: "We are all terror suspects now"', in B. Lovelock and K.M. Lovelock (eds), *The Ethics of Tourism: Ciritical and Applied Perspectives*, London: Routledge.

Hall, C.M., Amelung, B., Cohen, S., Eijgelaar, E., Gössling, S., et al. (2015) 'No time for smokescreen scepticism: a rejoinder to Shani and Arad', *Tourism Management*, 47: 341–7.

Hall, C.M., and Tucker, H. (2004) *Tourism and Postcolonialism: Contested Discourses, Identities and Representations*, London: Routledge.

Hand, S. (2009) *Emmanuel Levinas, Routledge Critical Thinkers*, London: Routledge.

Hannerz, U. (1996) *Transnational Connections: Culture, People, Places*, London: Routledge.

Haraway, D. (2016) *Staying with the Trouble: Making Kin in the Chthulucene*, Durham, NC: Duke University Press.

Harvey, B., and Kelsay, D. (2010) 'La Ruta del Café and Los Santos coffee tourism: a Central America Project to develop coffee-related tourism to augment coffee families' Incomes', in L. Jollife (ed.), *Coffee, Culture, Destinations and Tourism*, Bristol: Channel View.

Hashimoto, A. (2014) 'Tourism and socio-cultural development issues', in R. Sharpley and D.J. Telfer (eds), *Tourism and Development, Concepts and Issues*, 2nd edition, Bristol: Channel View.

Hatton, M.J. (1999) *Community-based Tourism in the Asia–Pacific*, Toronto: School of Media Studies.

Heidegger, M. (1927/1972) *Being and Time*, translated by J. Stambaugh, Albany: State University of New York Press.

Heinämaa, S. (1996) *Ele, tyyli ja sukupuoli. Maurice Merleau-Pontyn ruumiinfenomenologia ja sen merkitys sukupuolikysymykselle* [Gesture, Style and Sex: Beauvoir's and Merleau-Ponty's Phenomenology of the Body and its Relevance to the Problem of Sexual Difference], Helsinki: Gaudeamus.

Heinämaa, S. (2002) Loogisista tutkimuksista ruumiinfenomenologiaan, in I. Niiniluoto and E. Saarinen (eds), *Nykyajan filosofia*, Helsinki: WSOY.

Heinämaa, S., and Oksala, J. (2011) *Rakkaudesta toiseen: kirjoituksia vuosituhannen vaihteen etiikasta*, Helsinki: Gaudeamus Kirja.

Heldt Cassel, S., and Pettersson, K. (2015) 'Performing gender and rurality in Swedish farm tourism', *Scandinavian Journal of Hospitality and Tourism*, 15(1–2): 138–151.

Henkel, H., and Roderick, S. (2001) 'Participation as spiritual duty; empowerment as secular subjection', in B. Cooke and U. Kothari (eds), *Participation: The New Tyranny?*, London: Zed Books.

Hennig, C. (2002) 'Tourism: enacting modern myths', in G.M.S. Dann (ed.), *The Tourist as a Metaphor of the Social World*, Wallington: CABI.

Hergenrather, K.D., Rhodes, S.G., and Bardhoshi, G. (2010) 'Photovoice as community-based participatory research: a qualitative review', *American Journal of Health Behavior*, 33(6): 686–98.

Hickey, S., and Mohan, G. (eds) (2004) *Participation: From Tyranny to Transformation?*, New York: Zed Books.

Hiddleston, J. (2009) *Understanding Postcolonialism*, Stocksfield: Acumen Publishing.

Hietalahti, J., and Nygren A. (2014) 'Microcredit as a socio-political institution in South Africa: the complexity of rules, logic and power relations', in F. Hossain, C. Rees and T. Knight–Millar (eds), *Microcredit and International Development Contexts, Achievements and Challenges*, London: Routledge.

Higgins–Desbiolles, F. (2006) 'More than an "industry": the forgotten power of tourism as a social force', *Tourism Management*, 27: 1192–208.

Higgins–Desbiolles, F., and Powys Whyte, K. (2013) 'No high hopes for hopeful tourism: a critical comment', *Annals of Tourism Research*, 40(1): 428–33.

Hill, L. (2010) *Radical Indecision: Barthes, Blanchot, Derrida, and the Future of Criticism*, Notre Dame, IN: University of Notre Dame Press.

Hirschman, A.O. (1982/2002) *Shifting Involvements: Private Interest and Public Action*, London: Princeton University Press.

Höckert, E. (2009) *Sociocultural Sustainability of Rural Community-based Tourism: Case Study of Local Participation in Fair Trade Coffee Trail, Nicaragua*. Master's thesis, University of Lapland.

Höckert, E. (2011) 'Community-based tourism in Nicaragua: a socio–cultural perspective', *The Finnish Journal of Tourism Research*, 7(2): 7–25.

Höckert, E. (2014) 'Unlearning through hospitality', in S. Veijola, J. Germann Molz, O. Pyyhtinen, E. Höckert and A. Grit, *Disruptive Tourism and Its Untidy Guests: Alternative Ontologies for Future Hospitalities*, New York: Palgrave MacMillan.

Höckert, E. (2017) 'Review: the Routledge handbook of hospitality studies', *Scandinavian Journal of Hospitality and Tourism*, 1–3.

Höckert, E., Hakkarainen, M., and Jänis, J. (2013) 'Matkailun paikallinen kehittäminen maaseudulla', in S. Veijola (ed.), *Matkailututkimuksen lukukirja*, Rovaniemi: Lapin Yliopistokustannus.

Hollander, P. (1986) *Political Hospitality and Tourism: Cuba and Nicaragua*, Washington DC: Cuban American National Foundation.

Hollinshead, K. (1998) 'Tourism, hybridity, and ambiguity: the relevance of Bhabha's "third space" cultures', *Journal of Leisure Research*, 30(1): 121–56.

Hollinshead, K. (2004) 'Tourism and new sense: worldmaking and the enunciative value of tourism', in C.M. Hall and H. Tucker (eds), *Tourism and Postcolonialism: Contested Discourses, Identities and Representations*, London: Routledge.

Hollinshead, K. (2007) 'Worldmaking and the transformation of place and culture: the enlargement of Meethan's analysis of tourism and global change', in I. Ateljevic, N. Morgan, and A. Pritchard (eds), *The Critical Turn in Tourism Studies: Innovative Research Methodologies*, Oxford: Elsevier.

Hollinshead, K., and Jamal, T. (2007) 'Tourism and "the third ear": further prospects for qualitative inquiry', *Tourism Analysis*, 12: 85–129.

Hollinshead, K., Ateljevic, I., and Ali, N. (2009) 'Worldmaking agency: worldmaking authority. The sovereign constitutive role of tourism', *Tourism Geographies*, 11(4): 427–43.

Hossain, F., Rees, C., and Knight–Millar, T. (2014) *Microcredit and International Development Contexts, Achievements and Challenges*, London: Routledge.

Holmes, A.P., Grimwood B.S.R., King, L.J., and the Lutsel K'e Dene First Nation (2016) 'Creating an Indigenized visitor code of conduct: the development of Denesoline self-determination for sustainable tourism', *Journal of Sustainable Tourism*, 24(8–9): 1177–93.

Huijbens, E., and Benediktsson, K. (2013) 'Inspiring the visitor? Landscapes and horizons of hospitality', *Tourist Studies*, 13(2): 189–208.

Huijbens, E.H., and Gren, M. (2016) 'Tourism and the Anthropocene: an urgent and emerging encounter', in M. Gren and E.H. Huijbens (eds), *Tourism and the Anthropocene*, London: Routledge.

Hultman, J., and Andresson Cederholm, E. (2012) 'Bed, breakfast and friendship: intimacy and distance in small-scale hospitality businesses', *Culture Unbound*, 2(3): 365–80.

Humberstone, B. (2004) 'Standpoint research: multiple versions of reality in tourism theorising and research', in J. Phillimore and L. Goodson (eds), *Qualitative Research in Tourism*, London: Routledge.

Hunt, C. (2011) 'Passport to development? Local perceptions of the outcomes of post-socialist tourism policy and growth in Nicaragua', *Tourism Planning and Development*, 8(3): 265–79.

Hunt, C. (2016) 'A political ecology of tourism in the shadow of an inter-oceanic canal in Nicaragua: displacing poverty or displacing social and environmental welfare?', in S. Nepal and J. Saarinen (eds), *Political Ecology and Tourism*, London: Routledge.

Hunt, C., Durham, W., Driscoll, L., and Honey, M. (2014) 'Can ecotourism deliver real economic, social, and environmental benefits? A study of the Osa Peninsula, Costa Rica', *Journal of Sustainable Tourism*, 23(3): 1–19.

Hunt, C., and Stronza, A. (2011) 'Missing the forest for the trees?: Incongruous local perspectives on ecotourism in Nicaragua converge on ethical issues', *Human Organization*, 70(4): 376–86.

Hunt, C., and Stronza, A. (2014) 'Stage-based tourism models and resident attitudes towards tourism in an emerging destination in the developing world', *Journal of Sustainable Tourism*, 22(2): 279–98.

Hytten, K., and Madison, S.D. (2012) *Critical Ethnography: Method, Ethics, and Performance*, 2nd edition, London: SAGE.

Inayatullah, S. (1995) 'Rethinking tourism: unfamiliar histories and alternative futures', *Tourism Management*, 16(6): 411–15.

Innerarity, D. (2017) *The Ethics of Hospitality*, translated from the Spanish by S. Williams and S. Champeau, London: Routledge.

INTUR (2006) *Instituto Nicaraguense de Turismo Nicaragua: Boletin de Estadísticas de Turismo 2006*, Managua: Instituto Nicaragüense de Turismo.

INTUR (2009) *Definición de la Política y Estrategias para el Turismo Rural Sostenible de Nicaragua*, Managua: Instituto Nicaragüense de Turismo.

INTUR (2010a) *Instituto Nicaraguense de Turismo, Informe de Logros*, Managua: Instituto Nicaragüense de Turismo.

INTUR (2010b) *Politica y Estrategia de Turismo Rural Sostenible. Fincas Agroturisticas de Nicaragua*, Managua: Instituto Nicaragüense de Turismo.

INTUR (2011a) *Plan Nacional de Desarrollo Turistico Sostenible de Nicaragua. Estrategia de Desarrollo 2011–2020*, Managua: Instituto Nicaragüense de Turismo.

INTUR (2011b) *Plan Nacional De Desarrollo Turistico Sostenible de Nicaragua. Estrategia de Marketing 2011–2020*, Managua: Instituto Nicaragüense de Turismo.

INTUR (2012a) *Plan de Negocios. Fincas Agroturisticas, Nicaragua*, Managua: Instituto Nicaragüense de Turismo.

INTUR (2012b) *Politica y Estrategia de Turismo Rural Sostenible. Turismo Rural Sostenible y sus beneficiarios*, Managua: Instituto Nicaragüense de Turismo.

INTUR (2016) *Comportamiento de las Estadísticas de Turismo. No.3 Año 2016*, Managua: Instituto Nicaragüense de Turismo.

INTUR (2017) *Programa de bonos para Pequeños y Medianos Negocios Turísticos*, Managua: Instituto Nicaragüense de Turismo.

Irigaray, L. (1994/2000) *Democracy Begins between Two*, London: The Athlone Press.

Jafari, J. (2001) 'The scientification of tourism', in V.L. Smith and M. Brent (eds), *Hosts and Guests Revisited: Tourism Issues of the 21st Century*, New York, Cognizant Communication.

Jamal, T. (2004) 'Virtue ethics and sustainable tourism pedagogy: phronesis, principles and practice', *Journal of Sustainable Tourism*, 12(6): 530–45.

Jamal, T., Budke, C.M., and Barradas-Bribiesca, I. (2014) 'Health and sustainable development: new directions forward', in H. Balslev Clausen, S. Gyimóthy and V. Andersson (eds), *Global Mobilities and Tourism Development: A Community Perspective*, Aalborg: Aalborg University Press.

Jamal, T., and Camargo, B. (2013) 'Sustainable tourism, justice and an ethic of care: towards the just destination', *Journal of Sustainable Tourism*, 22(1): 11–30.

Jamal, T., and Dredge, D. (2014) 'Tourism and community development issues', in R. Sharpley and D. Telfer (eds), *Tourism and Development: Concepts and Issues*, 2nd edition, Bristol: Channel View.

Jamal, T., Everett, J., and Dann, G. (2003) 'Ecological rationalization and performative resistance in natural area destinations', *Tourist Studies*, 3(2): 143–69.

Jamal, T., and Everett, J. (2007) 'Rationalization in the natural and academic Lifeworld: critical research or hermeneutic charity?', in I. Ateljevic, N. Morgan and A. Pritchard (eds), *The Critical Turn in Tourism Studies: Innovative Research Methodologies*, Oxford: Elsevier.

Jamal, T., and Getz, D. (1995) 'Collaboration theory and community tourism planning', *Annals of Tourism Research*, 22(1): 186–204.

Jamal, T., and Hill, S. (2002) 'The home and the world: (post)touristic spaces if (in) authenticity?', in D. Graham (ed.), *The Tourist as a Metaphor of the Social World*, London: CABI.

Jamal, T., and Hollinshead, K. (2001) 'Tourism and the forbidden zone: the underserved power of qualitative inquiry', *Tourism Management*, 22(1): 63–82.

Jamal, T., and Menzel C. (2009) 'Good actions in tourism', in J. Tribe (ed.), *Philosophical Issues in Tourism*, Bristol: Channel View.

Jamal, T., and Stronza, A. (2009) ' "Dwelling" with ecotourism in the Peruvian Amazon: cultural relationships in local–global spaces', *Tourist Studies*, 8(3): 313–36.

Jänis, J. (2011) *The Tourism–Development Nexus in Namibia – A Study of National Tourism Policy and Local Tourism Enterprises' Policy Knowledge*, Helsinki: Interkont Books.

Järvinen-Tassopoulos, J. (2010) 'Vieraanvarainen koti' [Hospitable Home], in A. Vilkko, A. Suikkanen and J. Järvinen-Tassopoulos (eds), *Kotia Paikantamassa*, Rovaniemi: Lapland University Press.

Jenkins, C.L. (1982) 'The effects of scale in tourism projects in developing countries', *Annals of Tourism Research*, 9(2), 229–49.

Jennings, G.R. (2009) 'Methodologies and methods', in T. Jamal and M. Robinson (eds), *The SAGE Handbook of Tourism Studies*, Los Angeles: SAGE.

Jóhannesson, G.T (2015) 'A fish called tourism: emergent realities of tourism policy in Iceland', in G. T. Jóhannesson, C. Ren and R. van der Duim (eds), *Tourism Encounters and Controversies: Ontological Politics of Tourism Development*, Farnham: Ashgate.

Jóhannesson, G.T., and Lund, K.A. (2017) 'Creative connections? Tourists, entrepreneurs and destination development', *Scandinavian Journal of Hospitality and Tourism*, 1–15.

Jóhannesson, G.T., Ren, C., and van der Duim, R. (2015) 'Postscript: making headways, expanding the field and slowing down', in G.T. Jóhannesson, C. Ren and R. van der Duim (eds), *Tourism Encounters and Controversies: Ontological Politics of Tourism Development*, Farnham: Ashgate.

Johnston, A.M. (2006) *Is the Sacred for Sale? Tourism and Indigenous Peoples*, London: Earthscan.

Jokinen, E., and Veijola, S. (1997) 'The disoriented tourist: the figuration of the tourist in contemporary cultural critique', in C. Rojek and J. Urry (eds), *Touring Cultures: Transformations of Travel and Theory*, London: Routledge.

Jokinen, E., and Veijola, S. (2012) 'Time to hostess: reflections on borderless care', in C. Minca and T. Oakes (eds), *Real Tourism: Practice, Care and Politics in Contemporary Travel Culture*, London: Routledge.

Jollife, L. (ed.) (2010) *Coffee, Culture, Destinations and Tourism*, Bristol: Channel View.

Joppe, M. (2016) 'International tourism policy', in H. Siller and A. Zehrer (eds), *Entrepreneurship und Tourismus*, Vienna: Linde Verlag.

Jordan, S., and Yeomans, D. (1995) 'Critical ethnography: problems in contemporary theory and practice', *British Journal of Sociology of Education*, 16(3); 389–408.

Junka-Aikio, L. (2014) 'Can the Sámi speak now? Deconstructive research ethos and the debate on who is a Sámi in Finland', *Cultural Studies*, 30, 205–33.

Kalisch A. (2010) 'Fair Trade in tourism: a marketing tool for transformation?', in S. Cole and N. Morgan (eds), *Tourism and Inequality*, Wallingford: CABI.

Kallio-Tavin, M. (2013) *Encountering Self, Other and the Third: Researching the Crossroads of Art Pedagogy, Levinasian Ethics and Disability Studies*, Helsinki: Aalto University.

Kant, I. (1996 [1795]) 'Toward perpetual peace: a philosophical project', in *Practical Philosophy: The Cambridge Edition of the Works of Immanuel Kant*, translated by M.J. Gregor, Cambridge: Cambridge University Press.

Kapoor, I. (2004) 'Hyper self-reflexive development? Spivak on representing the Third World "Other"', *Third World Quarterly*, 25(4): 627–47.

Karst, H. (2017) ' "This is a holy place of Ama Jomo": buen vivir, indigenous voices and ecotourism development in a protected area of Bhutan', *Journal of Sustainable Tourism*, 25(6): 746–62.

Kearney, R., and Dooley, M. (1999) *Questioning Ethics*, London: Routledge.

Keen, D., and Tucker, H. (2012) 'Future spaces of postcolonialism in tourism', in J. Wilson, (ed.) *The Routledge Handbook of Tourism Geographies*, London: Routledge.

Keogh, B. (1990) 'Public participation in community tourism planning', *Annals of Tourism Research*, 17: 449–65.

Kincaid, J. (1988) *A Small Place*, New York: Farrar, Strauss and Giroux.

King, B., and Pearlman, M. (2009) 'Planning for tourism at local and regional levels: principles, practices and possibilities', in T. Jamal and M. Robinson (eds), *The SAGE Handbook of Tourism Studies*, Los Angeles: SAGE.

Kinloch Tijerino, F. (2008) *Historia de Nicaragua, 3era edición*, Managua: IHNCA–UCA.

Kinnunen, V. (2017) Tavarat Tiellä, Sosiologinen tutkimus esinesuhteista muutossa, Rovaniemi: Lapland University Press.

Kippendorf, J. (1989) *The Holiday Makers: Understanding the Impact of Leisure and Travel*, London: Routledge.

Kinnunen, V. and Valtonen A. eds (2017) *Living Ethics in a More-than-human World*, Rovaniemi: Lapland University Press.

Knapman, C. (2011) *When is a right not a right? Assessing the translation of the international legal guarantees for the right to food to rural Nicaragua through the state programme, Hambre Cero*, School of Oriental and African Studies, University of London.

Knudsen, D.C., Rickly J.M., and Vidon, E.S. (2016) 'The fantasy of authenticity: touring with Lacan', *Annals of Tourism Research*, 58: 33–45.

Knut, W. (1993) *The Regime of Anastasio Somoza, 1936–1956*, The University of North Carolina Press.

Kontogeorgopoulos, N., Churyen, A., and Duangsaeng, V. (2014) 'Success factors in community-based tourism in Thailand: the role of luck, external support, and local leadership', *Tourism Planning and Development*, 11(1): 106–24.

Kuokkanen, R. (2007) *Reshaping the University: Responsibilities, Indigenous Epistemes, and the Logic of the Gift*, Vancouver: UBC Press.

Kvale, S. (1996) *InterViews: An Introduction to Qualitative Research Interviewing*, London: SAGE.

Laachir, K. (2007) 'Hospitality and the limitations of the national', in J. Germann Molz and S. Gibson (eds), *Mobilizing Hospitality, The Ethics of Social Relations in a Mobile World*, Aldershot: Ashgate.

Ladyga, Z. (2012) 'Tracing Levinas in Gayatri Spivak's ethical representations of subalternity', in E.B. Luczak, J. Wierzchowska and J. Ziarkowska (eds), *In Other Words: Dialogizing Postcoloniality, Race, and Ethnicity*, Warszawa: Encounters.

Lane, B. (2009) 'Rural tourism, an overview', in T. Jamal and M. Robinson (eds), *The SAGE Handbook of Tourism Studies*, Los Angeles, CA: SAGE.

Larsen, J. (2014) 'The tourist gaze 1.0, 2.0, and 3.0', in A.A. Lew, C.M. Hall and A.M. Williams (eds), *The Wiley Blackwell Companion to Tourism*, Oxford: John Wiley and Sons.

Lashley, C. (2000) 'Towards a theoretical understanding', in C. Lashley and A. Morrison (eds), *In Search of Hospitality: Theoretical Perspectives and Debates*, Oxford: Butterworth–Heinemann.

Lashley, C. (2017) 'Introduction. Research on hospitality: the story so far/ways on knowing hospitality', in C. Lashley (ed.), *The Routledge Handbook of Hospitality Studies*, London: Routledge.

LaVanchy, G. (2017) 'When wells run dry: water and tourism in Nicaragua', *Annals of Tourism Research*, 64: 37–50.

Leal, P.A. (2010) 'Participation: the ascendancy of a buzzword in the neo-liberal era', in A. Cornwall and D. Eade (eds), *Deconstructing Development Discourse: Buzzwords and Fuzzwords*, Oxford: Oxfam GB.

Levinas, E. (1969) *Totality and Infinity: An Essay of Exteriority*, Pittsburgh: Duquesne University Press.

Levinas, E. (1985) *Ethics and Infinity: Conversations with Philippe Nemo*, translated by R.A. Cohen, Pittsburgh: Duquesne University Press.

Levinas, E. (1987) *Time and the Other and Additional Essays*, translated by R.A. Cohen, Pittsburgh: Duquesne University Press.

Levinas, E. (1990) *Nine Talmudic Readings*, translated by A. Aronowicz, Indianapolis: Indiana University Press.

Levinas, E. (1998) *Otherwise than Being, or Beyond Essence*, translated by A. Lingis, Pittsburgh: Duquesne University Press.

Li, T. (2007) *The Will to Improve: Governmentality, Development, and the Practice of Politics*, London: Duke University Press.

Li, W. (2006) 'Community decision-making: participation in development', *Annals of Tourism Research*, 33(1), 132–43.

Lincoln, Y.S., Lynham, S.A., and Guba, E.G. (2011) 'Paradigmatic controversies, contradictions, and emerging confluences revisited', in N.K. Denzin and Y.S. Lincoln (eds), *The Sage Handbook of Qualitative Research*, 4th edition, Los Angeles: Sage.

Lovelock, B., and Lovelock, K. (2013) *The Ethics of Tourism, Critical and Applied Perspectives*, London: Routledge.

Lugosi, P. (2008) 'Hospitality spaces, hospitable moments: consumer encounters and affective experiences in commercial settings', *Journal of Foodservice*, 19(2): 139–49.

Lugosi, P. (2017a) 'Consuming hospitality', in C. Lashley (ed.), *Routledge Handbook of Hospitality Studies*, London: Routledge.

Lugosi, P. (2017b) 'Cultivating academic imagination in (and through) hospitality', *Hospitality and Society*, 6(3): 217–21.

Lund, C. (2014) 'Of what is this a case?: analytical movements in qualitative social science research', *Human Organization*, 73(3): 224–34.

Lüthje, M. (2005) Se mukava maaseutu siellä jossain. Maaseutumatkailu kokemusten, mielikuvien ja markkinoinnin kohteena [That pleasant countryside somewhere out there: rural tourism as an object of experiences, mental images and marketing], Rovaniemi: Lapin Yliopistopaino.

Lynch, P. (2017) 'Mundane welcome: hospitality as life politics', *Annals of Tourism Research*, 64: 174–84.

Lynch, P., Di Domenico, M.L., and Sweeney, L. (2007) 'Resident hosts and mobile strangers: temporary exchanges within the topography of the commercial home', in J. Germann Molz and S. Gibson (eds), *Mobilizing Hospitality, The Ethics of Social Relations in a Mobile World*, Aldershot: Ashgate.

Lynch, P.A., McIntosh, A.J., and Tucker, H. (2009) *Commercial Homes in Tourism: An International Perspective*, London: Routledge.

Lynch, P., Germann Molz, J., McIntosh, A., Lugosi, P., and Lashley, C. (2011) 'Theorizing hospitality', editorial in *Hospitality and Society*, 1(1): 3–24.

Länsman, A.S. (2004) *Väärtisuhteet Lapin Matkailussa. Kulttuurianalyysi suomalaisten ja saamelaisten kohtaamisesta*, Kustannus–Puntsi.

MacCannell, D. (1976) *The Tourist: A New Theory of the Leisure Class*, New York: Schocken Books.

Mair, H. (2014) 'Trust and participatory tourism planning', in R. Nunkoo and S.L.J. Smith (eds), *Trust, Tourism Development and Planning*, London: Routledge.

Maldonado, C. (2005) *Pautas Metodológicas para el análisis de experiencias de turismo comunitario* [Methodologies for analysing experiences of community-based tourism], Geneva: ILO.

Maldonado-Torres, N. (2010) 'On the coloniality of being: contribution to the development of a concept', in W.D. Mignolo and A. Escobar (eds), *Globalization and the Decolonial Option*, London: Routledge.

Matarrita-Cascante, D. (2010) 'Beyond growth: reaching tourism-led development', *Annals of Tourism Research*, 37(4): 1141–63.

Matarrita-Cascante, D., Brennan, M.A., and Luloff, A.E. (2010) 'Community agency and sustainable tourism development: the case of La Fortuna, Costa Rica', *Journal of Sustainable Tourism*, 18(6): 735–56.

Mathieson, A., and Wall, G. (1982) *Tourism: Economic, Physical and Social Impacts*, London: Longman.

Matteucci, X., Lund-Durlacher, D., and Beyer, M. (2008) 'The socio-economic and environmental impacts of second home tourism: the South Pacific coast of Nicaragua example', in P. Keller and T. Bieger (eds), *Real Estate and Destination Development in Tourism*, Berlin: Erich Schmidt Verlag.

Mauss, M. (2008/1924) *The Form and Reason for Exchange in Archaic Societies*, London: Routledge.

McEwan, C. (2009) *Postcolonialism and Development*, London: Routledge.

McIntyre, A. (2008) *Participatory Action Research*, Thousand Oaks, CA: Sage.

McLeod, J. (2010) *Beginning Postcolonialism*, Manchester: Manchester University Press.

McNaughton, D. (2006) 'The host as uninvited guest: hospitality, violence and tourism', *Annals of Tourism Research*, 33(3): 645–65.

McRoberts, D. (2012) *Building a Movement – Solidarity, Activism and Travel from North America to Nicaragua*, Master's thesis, University of Waterloo, Ontario.

Medina Chavarria, M.E. (2017) 'Propuesta de desarrollo del turismo accesible en la reserva de biósfera Isla de Ometepe (Nicaragua)' *Pasos*, 15(4): 913–24.

Meijrt-van Wijk, K. (2017) 'Levinas, hospitality and the feminine Other', in C. Lashley (ed), *The Routledge Handbook of Tourism Studies*, London: Routledge.

Mendieta, E. (2008) 'Remapping Latin American studies: postcolonialism, subaltern studies, post-occidentalism, and globalization theory', in M. Moraña, E. Dussel and C.A. Jáuregui (eds), *Coloniality at Large: Latin America and the Postcolonial Debate*, Durham, NC: Duke University Press.

Mettiäinen, I., Uusitalo, M., and Rantala, O. (2009) 'Osallisuus matkailukeskusten suunnittelussa' [Participation in tourism planning], in S. Tuulentie (ed.), *Turisti tulee kylään. Matkailukeskukset ja lappilainen arki* [Tourist comes to visit], Helsinki: Minerva Kustannus Oy.

Meyer, A., and Huete-Perez, J.A. (2014) 'Nicaragua canal would wreak environmental ruin', *Nature*, 506(7488): 287–9.

Midgley, J. (2011) 'Community participation: history, concepts and controversies', in A. Cornwall (ed.), *The Participation Reader*, New York: Zed Books Reader.

Miettinen, S. (2007) *Designing the Creative Tourism Experience: A Service Design Process with Namibian Crafts People*, Publication series of University of Art and Design Helsinki A 81, Jyväskylä: Gummerus kirjapaino Oy.

Mignolo, W.D. (2005) *The Idea of Latin America*, Malden: Blackwell.

Mignolo, W.D. (2008) 'The geopolitics of knowledge and the colonial difference', in M. Moraña, E. Dussel and C.A. Jáuregui (eds), *Coloniality at Large: Latin America and the Postcolonial Debate*, Durham, NC: Duke University Press.

Mignolo, W.D., and Escobar, A. (2010) *Globalization and the Decolonial Option*, London: Routledge.

Mitchell, J., and Muckosy, P. (2008) *A Misguided Quest: Community-based tourism in Latin America*, London: Overseas Development Institute.

Mohanty, C.T. (1999) 'Med västerländska ögon. Feministisk forskning och kolonial diskurs', in C. Eriksson et al. (eds), *Globaliseringens kulturer: Den postkoloniala paradoxen, rasismen och det mångkulturella samhället*, Nora: Nya Doxa.

Moraña, M., Dussel, E., and Jáuregui, C.A. (2008) *Coloniality at Large: Latin America and the Postcolonial Debate*, Durham, NC: Duke University Press.

Morgan, N., and Cole, S. (2010) 'Introduction: tourism and inequalities', in N. Morgan and S. Cole (eds), *Tourism and Inequality – Problems and Prospects*, London: CABI Publishing.

Morton, S. (2007) *Gayatri Spivak. Ethics, Subalternity and the Critique of the Postcolonial Reason*, Cambridge: Polity Press.

Moscardo, G. (2008) 'Community capacity building: an emerging challenge for tourism development', in G. Moscardo (ed.), *Building Community Capacity for Tourism Development*, Wallingford: CABI.

Moscardo, G., Blackman, A., and Murphy, L. (2014) 'Tourism development as Greek tragedy: implications for tourism development policy and education', paper presented in BEST EN Think Tank XIV entitled, 'Politics, policy and governance in sustainable tourism', at the Faculty of Economics, University of Ljubljana, Slovenia, 24 June 2014.

Mostafanezhad, M. (2014) *Volunteer Tourism: Popular Humanitarianism in Neoliberal Times*, Farnham: Ashgate.

Mostafanezhad, M., and Hannam, K. (2014) 'Introducing moral encounters in tourism', in M. Mostafanezhad and K. Hannam (eds), *Moral Encounters in Tourism*, Farnham: Ashgate.

Mostafanezhad, M., Norum, R., Shelton, E., and Thompson-Carr, A. (eds) (2015) *Political Ecology of Tourism Community, Power and the Environment*, London: Routledge.

Mowforth, M., and Munt, I. (1998) *Tourism and Sustainability: New Tourism in the Third World*, London: Routledge.

Mowforth, M., and Munt, I. (2003) *Tourism and Sustainability. Development and New Tourism in the Third World*, 2nd edition, London: Routledge.

Mowforth, M., Charlton, C., and Munt, I. (2008) *Tourism and Responsibility. Perspectives from Latin America and the Caribbean*, London: Routledge.

Müller, D.K., and Jansson, B. (2007) 'The difficult business of making pleasure peripheries prosperous: perspectives on space, place and environment', in D.K. Müller and B. Jansson (eds), *Tourism in Peripheries: Perspectives from the Far North and South*, Wallingford: CABI.

Munar, A.M., and Jamal, J. (2016) 'What are paradigms for?' in A.M. Munar and T. Jamal (eds), *Tourism Research Paradigms: Critical and Emergent Knowledges*, Bingley: Emerald.

Murchison, J.M. (2010) *Ethnography Essentials: Designing, Conducting, and Presenting Your Research*, San Francisco, CA: Jossey–Bass.

Murphy, P.E. (1985) *Tourism: A Community Approach*, London: Routledge.

Murphy, P.E., and Murphy, A.E. (2004) *Strategic Management for Tourism Communities: Bridging the Gaps*, Clevedon: Channel View.

Murphy, P., and Pauleen, D. (2007) 'Managing paradox in a world of knowledge', *Management Decision*, 45(6): 1008–22.

Naas, M. (2008) *Derrida From Now On*, New York: Fordham University Press.

Navas-Camargo, F., and Zwerg-Villegas, A. (2014) Community-based tourism: is this progress?/Turismo Comunitario: ¿Es Progreso?/Turismo Comunitário: É Progresso?, *Revista Ciencias Estrategicas*, 22(32): 249–59.

Närman, A. (2006) 'Paolo Freire', in D. Simon (ed.), *Fifty Key Thinkers of Development*, London: Routledge.

Nederveen Pieterse, J. (2001) *Development Theory: Deconstructions/Reconstructions*, London: Sage.

Nepal, S., Saarinen, J., and McLean-Purdon, E. (2016) 'Tourism and political ecology: introduction', in S. Nepal and J. Saarinen (eds) *Political Ecology and Tourism*, London: Routledge.

New York Times (2013) 'The 46 places to go in 2013. Whether you travel to eat or shop, surf or ski, new adventures await', article published 11 January 2013.

Nisbett, G.S., and Strzelecka, M. (2017) 'Appealing to Goodwill or YOLO – promoting conservation volunteering to Millennials', *VOLUNTAS: Journal of the International Society for Third-Sector Research*, 288–306.

Nkyi, E., and Hashimoto, A. (2014) 'Human rights issues in tourism development', in R. Sharpley and D.J. Telfer (eds), *Tourism and Development, Concepts and Issues*, 2nd edition, Bristol: Channel View.

Noblit, G.W., Flores, S.Y., and Murillo, E.G. (2004) *Postcritical Ethnography: An Introduction*, Cress, NJ: Hampton Press.

Noddings, N. (2002) *Starting at Home: Caring and Social Policy*, Berkeley, CA: University of California Press.

Nunkoo, R., and Gursoy, D. (2016) 'Rethinking the role of power and trust in tourism planning', *Journal of Hospitality Marketing and Management*, 25(4): 512–22.

Nygren, A. (1999) 'Local knowledge in the environment– development discourse. From dichotomies to situated knowledges', *Critique of Anthropology*, 19(3): 267–88.

O'Gorman, K.D. (2007) 'Discovering commercial hospitality in ancient Rome', *Hospitality Review*, 9(2): 44–52.

O'Gorman, K.D. (2010) *The Origins of Hospitality and Tourism*, Oxford: Goodfellow Publishers.

Oksala, J. (2001) 'Järjen ja tahdon tuolla puolen. Etiikan mahdoton subjekti' [Beyond understanding and will. The impossibility of a subject in ethics], in S. Heinämaa and J. Oksala (eds), *Rakkaudesta toiseen: kirjoituksia vuosituhannen vaihteen etiikasta*, Helsinki: Gaudeamus Kirja.

Olam (2013) Coffee Report, Briefing note 1 – January 2013, La Roya. www.olamspecialtycoffee.com/index.php/downloads/dl/file/id/36/la_roya_briefing_ note_ olam_coffee_jan_2013.pdf, accessed 10 September 2014.

Olsen, B. (1997) 'Environmentally sustainable development and tourism: lessons from Negril, Jamaica', *Human Organization*, 56(3): 285–93.

Page, S., and Dowling, R.K. (2002) *Ecotourism*, Harlow: Prentice Hall.

Pakkasvirta, J. (2005) *¿Un continente, una nación? Intelectuales latinoamericanos, comunidad política y las revistas culturales en Costa Rica y en el Perú (1919–1930)*, San José: Editorial de la Universidad de Costa Rica.

Pakkasvirta, J. (2010) *Policies and Practices of Tourism Industry: A Comparative and Interdisciplinary Study on Central America*. Research proposal for the Academy of Finland.

Palmer, S. (1988) 'Carlos Fonseca and the construction of Sandinismo in Nicaragua', *Latin American Research Review*, XXIII(1): 100–21.

Palomo Pérez, S. (2003) *El Turismo y la cooperación internacional al desarrollo*, Malaga: Fuengirola.

Panosso Netto, A. (2009) 'What is tourism? Definitions, theoretical phases and principles', in J. Tribe (ed.), *Philosophical Issues in Tourism*, Bristol: Channel View.

Parry, B. (2004) *Postcolonial Studies: A Materialist Critique*, London: Routledge.

Parsons, J.B., and Harding, K.J. (2011) 'Post-colonial theory and action research', *Turkish Online Journal of Qualitative Inquiry*, 2(2): 1–6.

PEMCE (2008) *Estudio de cadena de valor, Turismo rural en Nicaragua*, DFID and UNOPS, Managua, Nicaragua.

Peperzak, A.T. (ed.) (1995) *Ethics as First Philosophy: The Significance of Emmanuel Levinas for Philosophy, Literature and Religion*, New York: Routledge.

Pérez, F.P., Barrera, O.P., Peláez, A.V., and Lorío, G. (2010) *Turismo Rural Comunitario como Alternativa de reducción de la pobreza rural en Centroamérica*, Managua: EDITASA.

Pernecky, T., and Jamal, T. (2010) '(Hermeneutic) phenomenology in tourism studies', *Annals of Tourism Research*, 37: 1055–75.

Phillimore, J., and Goodson, L. (2004) 'Progress in qualitative research in tourism: epistemology, ontology, methodology', in J. Phillimore and L. Goodson (eds), *Qualitative Methods in Tourism Research*, London: Routledge.

Piffa, P.K., Stancatoa, D.M., Côtéb, S., Mendoza-Dentona, R., and Keltnera, D. (2011) 'Higher social class predicts increased unethical behaviour', *Proceedings of the National Academy of Sciences of the United States of America*, 109(11): 4086–91.

Pleumarom, A. (2012) 'The politics of tourism and poverty reduction', in D. Leslie (ed.), *Responsible Tourism: Concepts, Theory and Practice*, Wallingford: CABI.

Plog, S.C. (1991) *Leisure Travel: Making it a Growth Market…Again*, New York: John Wiley and Sons.

Plunkett, H. (2007) *Nicaragua in Focus: A Guide to the People, Politics and Culture*, New York: Interlink.

PNDH (2008) *Plan Nacional de Desarrollo Humano 2008–2012*, Managua, Nicaragua.

PNDH (2012) *Plan Nacional de Desarrollo Humano 2012–2016*, Managua, Nicaragua.

Potts, T.D., and Harrill, R. (1998) 'Enhancing communities for sustainability: a travel ecology approach', *Tourism Analysis*, 3: 133–142.

Poulston, J. (2015) 'Expressive labour and the gift of hospitality', *Hospitality and Society*, 5(2): 145–65.

Pratt, M.L. (1986) 'Fieldwork in common places', in J. Clifford and E.G. Marcus (eds), *Writing Culture: The Poetics and Politics of Ethnography*, Berkeley: University of California Press.

Pratt, M.L. (1992) *Imperial Eyes Travel Writing and Transculturation*, London: Routledge.

Pritchard, A., Morgan, N., and Ateljevic, I. (2011) 'Hopeful tourism, a new transformative perspective', *Annals of Tourism Research*, 38(3): 941–63.

Prince, S., and Ioannides, D. (2017) 'Contextualizing the complexities of managing alternative tourism at the community level: a case study of a Nordic eco-village', *Tourism Management*, 60: 348–59.

PRONicaragua (2014) *Doing Business in Nicaragua, Guía del Inversionista*, PRONicaragua in cooperation with AMCHAM and MIFIC.

PRONicaragua (2015) *Country Presentation: Nicaragua, let's grow together*, http://pronicaragua.org/images/resource_library/Presentacin%20Pas%202015.pdf.

PRONicaragua (2017) *High Levels of Citizen Security*, http://pronicaragua.gob.ni/en/why-invest-in-nicaragua/1769-high-levels-of-citizen-security, accessed 20 August 2017.

Puig de la Bellacasa, M. (2017) *Matters of Care: Speculative Ethics in More Than Human Worlds*, London: University of Minnesota Press.

Pyyhtinen, O. (2009) 'Being-with: Georg Simmel's sociology of association', *Theory, Culture and Society*, 26: 108–28.

Pyyhtinen, O. (2014) *The Gift and its Paradoxes: Beyond Mauss*, Farnham: Ashgate.

Pyyhtinen, O. (2015) *More-than-Human Sociology: A New Sociological Imagination*, New York: Palgrave Macmillan.

Quesada, F. (2014) 'Sustainable tourism planning, and the demolition conflict in the South Caribbean coastal area of Costa Rica', in H. Balslev Clausen, S. Gyimóthy and V. Andersson (eds), *Global Mobilities and Tourism Development: A Community Perspective*, Aalborg: Aalborg University Press.

Raffoul, F. (1998) 'The subject of the welcome. On Jacques Derrida's Adíeu á Emmanuel Levinas', *Symposium*, 2(2): 211–22.

Raffoul, F. (2010) *The Origins of Responsibility*, Bloomington: Indiana University Press.

Raffoul, F. (2014) 'The question of responsibility between Levinas and Heidegger', in J.E. Drabinski and E.S. Eric (eds), *Between Levinas and Heidegger*, Albany, NY: State University of New York Press.

Rakic, T., and Chambers, D. (2012) 'Rethinking the consumption of places', *Annals of Tourism Research*, 39(3): 1612–33.

Ramirez, S. (1985) *Estás En Nicaragua*, Barcelona: Muchnik.

Ramirez, S. (2011) *Adios muchachos: A Memoir of the Sandinista Revolution*, Durham, NC: Duke University Press.

Ranta, E.M. (2014) *In the Name of Vivir Bien. Indigeneity, state formation, and politics in Evo Morales' Bolivia*, Helsinki: Unigrafia.

Rantala, O. (2011a) *Metsä Matkailukäytössä. Etnografinen tutkimus luonnossa opastamisesta*, Rovaniemi: Lapland University Press.

Rantala O. (2011b) 'An ethnographic approach to nature-based tourism', *Scandinavian Journal of Hospitality and Tourism*, 11(2): 150–65.

Rantala, O., and Valtonen, A. (2014) 'A rhythmanalysis of touristic sleep in nature', *Annals of Tourism Research*, 47: 18–30.

Reid, D., Mair, H., and George, W. (2004) 'Community tourism planning: a self-assessment instrument', *Annals of Tourism Research*, 31(3): 623–39.

Ren, C. (2010) 'Beyond hosts and guests: translating the concept of cultural misconception', *International Journal of Culture, Tourism and Hospitality Research*, 4(4): 287–98.

Ren, C., Pritchard, A., and Morgan, N. (2010) 'Constructing tourism research: a critical inquiry', *Annals of Tourism Research*, 37(4): 885–904.

Replogle, J. (2014) 'Why Nicaraguan kids aren't fleeing to U.S.', www.kpbs. org/news/2014/jul/29/why-nicaraguan-kids-arent-fleeing-to-the-us/, accessed 10 February 2015.

Richards, G., and Hall, D. (2000) 'Conclusions', in D. Hall and G. Richards (eds) *Tourism and Sustainable Community Development*, London: Routledge.

Rivas Choza, E. (2008) *San Ramon Indigena y Fertil*, Matagalpa: Publitec.

Rocha, J.L. (2008) 'Esplendor y Miserias del Ecoturismo Nacional', *Envio, Revista Mensual de la Universidad Centroamericana (UCA) Managua*, 318: 3–13.

Ronkainen, S. (1999) *Ajan ja paikan merkitsemät. Subjektiviteetti, tieto ja toimijuus*, Helsinki: Gaudeamus.

Rosello, M. (2001) *Postcolonial Hospitality: The Immigrant as Guest*, Palo Alto, CA: Stanford University Press.

Ross, S., and Wall, G. (1999) 'Ecotourism: towards congruence between theory and practice', *Tourism Management*, 20: 122–32.

Saarinen, J. (2006) 'Traditions of sustainability in tourism studies', *Annals of Tourism Research*, 33(4): 1121–40.

Saarinen, J. (2010) 'Local tourism awareness: community views in Katutura and King Nehale Conservancy, Namibia', *Development Southern Africa*, 27(5): 713–24.

Saarinen, J., Rogerson, C.M., and Hall, C.M. (2017) 'Geographies of tourism development and planning', *Tourism Geographies*, 19(3): 307–17.

Sachs, W. (1992) *The Development Dictionary*, London: Zed Books.

Said, E. (1993) *Culture and Imperialism*, New York: Vintage Books.

Said, E. (1994) *Orientalism*, revised edition, New York: Vintage Books.

Salazar, N.B. (2010) *Envisioning Eden: Mobilizing Imaginaries in Tourism and Beyond*, Oxford: Berghahn.

Salazar, N.B. (2012a) 'Community-based cultural tourism: issues, threats and opportunities', *Journal of Sustainable Tourism*, 20(1): 9–22.

Salazar, N.B. (2012b) 'Tourism imaginaries: a conceptual approach', *Annals of Tourism Research*, 39: 863–882.

Salazar, N.B. (2013) 'Imagineering otherness: anthropological legacies in contemporary tourism', *Anthropological Quarterly*, 86(3): 669–96.

Salazar, N.B. (2014) 'Seduction: learning the trade of tourist enticement', in D. Picard and M.A. Giovine (eds), *Tourism and the Power of Otherness: Seductions of Difference*, Bristol: Channel View.

Sammels, C.A. (2014) 'Bargaining under thatch roofs: tourism and the allure of poverty in highland Bolivia', in D. Picard and M.A. Giovine (eds), *Tourism and the Power of Otherness. Seductions of Difference*, Bristol: Channel View.

Scheyvens, R. (1999) 'Case study: ecotourism and the empowerment of local communities', *Tourism Management*, 20: 245–49.

Scheyvens, R. (2002) *Tourism for Development: Empowering Communities*, Harlow: Pearson Education.

Scheyvens, R. (2003) 'Local involvement in managing tourism', in T. Singh, J.T. Dallen and R.K. Dowling (eds), *Tourism in Destination Communities*, Wallingford: CABI Publishing.

Scheyvens, R. (2007) 'Poor cousins no more valuing the development potential of domestic and diaspora tourism', *Progress in Development Studies*, 7(4): 307–25.

Scheyvens, R. (2011) *Tourism and Poverty*, London: Routledge.

Schilcher, D. (2007) 'Growth versus equity: the continuum of pro-poor tourism and neoliberal governance', in M. Hall (ed.), *Pro-Poor Tourism: Who Benefits? Perspectives on Tourism and Poverty Reduction*, Clevedon: Channel View.

Schyst Resande (2015) Travel life's broken promises to hotel workers. A study of labour rights at hotels in Turkey contracted by Apollo (Kuoni), Fritidsresor (TUI) and Ving (Thomas Cook).

SECTUR / Moderniza (2015) Programa de calidad, para la micro, pequeña y mediana empresa turística. www.sectur.gob.mx/sub/revistas/CertificacionTuristica/Moderniza/#libro/, accessed 14 August 2015.

Sen, A. (1999) *Development as Freedom*, Oxford: Oxford University Press.

Seppälä, T. (2013) 'Hallintaa, vastarintaa ja uusliberaalia kehityspolitiikkaa Etelä-Aasiassa' [Governance, Resistance and Neoliberal Development in South-Asia], *AGON, Northern Philosopher's Association*, 39: 11–13.

Serres, M. (2007) *The Parasite*, translated by L.R. Schehr, Minneapolis: University of Minnesota Press.

Serres, M., with Latour, B. (1995) *Conversations on Science, Culture, and Time*, translated by R. Lapidus, Ann Arbor, MI: University of Michigan Press.

Sharpe, J., and Spivak, G.C. (2002) 'A conversation with Gayatri Chakravorty Spivak: politics and the imagination', *Signs*, 28(2): 609–24.

Shen, F., Hughey, K., and Simmons, D. (2008) 'Connecting the sustainable livelihoods approach and tourism: a review of the literature towards integrative thinking', research paper presented in Gauthe 2008 Conference: 'Where the Bloody Hell Are We?', Lincoln University, New Zealand.

Simmons, B.A. (2004) 'Saying the same old things: a contemporary travel discourse and the popular magazine text', in C.M. Hall and H. Tucker (eds), *Tourism and Postcolonialism: Contested Discourses, Identities and Representations*, London: Routledge.

Simpson, M. (2008) 'Community benefit tourism initiatives: a conceptual oxymoron?', *Tourism Management*, 29(1): 1–18.

Singh, S. (2012) 'Community participation – in need of a fresh perspective', in T.V Singh (ed.), *Critical Debates in Tourism*, Bristol: Channel View.

Singh, S., Timothy, D.J., and Dowling, R.K. (2003) 'Tourism and destination communities', in S. Singh, D.J. Timothy and R.K. Dowling (eds), *Tourism in Destination Communities*, Wallingford: CABI Publishing.

Sklar, H. (1988) *Washington's War on Nicaragua*, Cambridge, MA: South End Press.

Smith, M. (2009a) 'Development and its discontents: ego-tripping without ethics or Idea(l)s?', in J. Tribe (ed.), *Philosophical issues in Tourism*, Bristol: Channel View.

Smith, M. (2009b) 'Ethical perspectives: exploring the ethical landscape of tourism', in T. Jamal and M. Robinson (eds), *The SAGE Handbook of Tourism Studies*, Los Angeles: SAGE.

Smith, M.K. (2009c) *Issues in Cultural Tourism Studies*, 2nd edition, Abingdon: Routledge.

Smith, M., and Duffy, R. (2003) *The Ethics of Tourism Development*, Abingdon: Routledge.

Smith, P. (2014) 'International volunteer tourism as (de)commodified moral consumption', in M. Mostafanezhad and K. Hannam (eds), *Moral Encounters in Tourism*, Farnham: Ashgate.

Smith, V.L. (ed.) (1978) *Hosts and Guests: The Anthropology of Tourism*, Philadelphia: University of Pennsylvania Press.

SNV (2007) *Linea base de Renitural.com. Servicio Holandes de Cooperación al Desarrollo* (SNV), Managua, Nicaragua.

Spivak, G.C. (1987) *In Other Worlds: Essays in Cultural Politics*, London: Routledge.

Spivak, G.C. (1988) 'Can the subaltern speak?', in C. Nelson and L. Grossberg (eds), Marxism and Interpretation of Culture, Chicago: University of Illinois Press.

Spivak, G.C. (1990) *The Postcolonial Critic: Interviews Strategies, Dialogue*, London: Routledge.

Spivak, G.C. (1993) *Outside in the Teaching Machine*, London: Routledge.

Spivak, G.C. (1994) 'Responsibility', *Boundary 1*, 21(3): 19–64.

Spivak, G.C. (1995) 'Translator's preface and afterword', in *Imaginary Maps: Three Stories*, London: Routledge.

Spivak, G.C. (1999) *A Critique of Postcolonial Reason: Toward a History of the Vanishing Present*, Cambridge, MA: Harvard University Press.

Spivak, G.C. (2001) 'A note on the new international', *Parallax*, 7(3): 12–16.

Stiefel, M., and Wolfe, M. (1994) 'The many faces of participation', in A. Cornwall (ed.), *The Participation Reader*, London: Zed Books.

Still, J. (2006) 'France and the paradigm of hospitality', *Third Text*, 20(6): 703–10.

Still, J. (2010) *Derrida and Hospitality: Theory and Practice*, Edinburgh: Edinburgh University Press.

Strasdas, W., Corcoran, B., and Petermann, T. (2007) 'Capacity–building for ecotourism: training programmes for managers of protected areas', in R. Bushell and P. Eagles (eds), *Tourism and Protected Areas: Benefits Beyond Boundaries: the Vth IUCN World Parks Congress*, Wallingford: CABI.

Strhan, A. (2012) *Levinas, Subjectivity, Education: Towards an Ethics of Radical Responsibility*, Chichester: Wiley Blackwell.

Stronza, A. (2001) 'Anthropology of tourism: forging new ground for ecotourism and other alternatives', *Annual Review of Anthropology*, 30: 261–83.

Stronza, A. (2005) 'Hosts and hosts: the anthropology of community-based ecotourism in the Peruvian Amazon', *NAPA Bulletin*, 23: 170–90.

Stronza, A. (2008) 'Through a new mirror: reflections on tourism and identity in the Amazon', *Human Organization*, 67(3): 244–57.

Strzelecka, M. (2015) 'The prospects for empowerment through local governance for tourism – the LEADER approach', *Journal of Rural and Community Development*, 10(3): 78–97.

Strzelecka, M., and Wicks, B. (2015) 'Community participation and empowerment in rural post-communists societies: lessons from the leader approach in Pomerania, Poland', *Tourism Planning and Development*, 12(4): 381–97.

Strzelecka, M., Nisbett, G.S., and Woosnam, K.M. (2017) 'The hedonic nature of conservation volunteer travel', *Tourism Management*, 63: 417–25.

Svanberg, J. (2014) *Varför kom du hit?*, Månpocket: Stockholm.

Swarbrooke, J. (2002) *Sustainable Tourism Management*, Wallingford: CABI Publishing.

Szczesiul, A. (2017) *The Southern Hospitality Myth: Ethics, Politics, Race, and American Memory*, Athens, GA: University of Georgia Press.

Taylor, G. (1995) 'The community approach: does it really work?', *Tourism Management*, 16(7): 487–9.

Teivainen, T. (2004) *Pedagogía del poder mundial*, Helsinki: INTO eBooks.

Teivainen, T. (2014) 'Vasemmistohallitukset 2000–luvun Latinalaisessa Amerikassa' [Leftist Governments in Latin America in the 21st century], in H. Kettunen and E. Vuola (eds), *Latinalainen Amerikka: Ihmiset kulttuuri ja yhteiskunta* [Latin America: people, culture and society], Tampere: Vastapaino.

Telfer, D.J. (2003) 'Development issues in destination communities', in S. Singh, J.T. Dallen and R.K. Dowling (eds), *Tourism in Destination Communities*, Wallingford: CABI Publishing.

Telfer, D.J. (2009) 'Development studies and tourism', in T. Jamal and M. Robinson (eds), *The SAGE Handbook of Tourism Studies*, Los Angeles: SAGE.

Telfer, D.J. (2014) 'The evolution of development theory in tourism', in R. Sharpley and D. Telfer (eds), *Tourism and Development: Concepts and Issues*, 2nd edition, Bristol: Channel View.

Telfer, D.J., and Sharpley, R. (eds) (2008) *Tourism and Development in the Developing World*, Abingdon: Routledge.

Telfer, E. (2000) 'The philosophy of hospitableness', in C. Lashley and A. Morrison (eds), *In Search of Hospitality: Theoretical Perspectives and Debates*, Oxford: Butterworth Heinemann.

Terazono, E. (2013) 'Coffee fungus threatens disaster for Central America's farmers', in *Financial Times*, 14 July 2013.

Timothy, D.J. (2002) 'Tourism and community development issues', in R. Sharpley and D.J. Telfer (eds), *Tourism and Development, Concepts and Issues*, Clevedon: Channel View.

Tlostanova, M., and Mignolo, W.D. (2012) *Learning to Unlearn. Decolonial Reflections from Eurasia and the Americas*, Ohio: Ohio University Press.

Todaro, M.P., and Smith, S.C. (2006) *Economic Development*, Harlow: Pearson.

Todorov, T. (1984) *The Conquest of America: The Question of the Other*, translated by R. Howard, Oklahoma: University of Oklahoma Press.

Tökkäri, V. (2010) 'Ihmiseksi osallistumalla' [Becoming a human though participation], in J. Perttula, A. Pietiläinen, T. Salonen, E. Sorjonen and V. Tökkäri, *Ihmistyminen: suhteisuusteoreettisia punoksia*, Rovaniemi: Lapin Yliopistokustannus, 30–41.

Tosun, C. (2000) 'Limits to community participation in the tourism development process in developing countries', *Tourism Management*, 21(6): 613–33.

Tosun, C. (2005) 'Stages in the emergence of a participatory tourism development approach in the developing world', *Geoforum*, 36(3): 333–52.

Tribe, J. (2004) 'Knowing about tourism: epistemological issues', in J. Phillimore and L. Goodson (eds), *Qualitative Research in Tourism: Ontologies, Epistemologies and Methodologies*, London: Routledge.

Tribe, J. (ed.) (2009) *Philosophical Issues in Tourism*, Bristol: Channel View.

Trousdale, W.J. (2001) 'Appropriate tourism impact assessment: a case study of Kaniki Point Resort, Palawan, Philippines', in V.L. Smith and M. Brent (eds), *Hosts and Guests Revisited: Tourism Issues of the 21st Century*, New York: Cognizant Communication Corporation.

Truman, H. (1949) 'Inauguration of the President: address by Harry S. Truman', www.inaugural.senate.gov/swearing-in/address/address-by-harry-s-truman-1949, accessed 10 September 2017.

Tucker, H. (2003) *Living with Tourism: Negotiating Identities in a Turkish Village*, London: Routledge.

Tucker, H. (2007) 'Undoing shame: tourism and women's work in Turkey', *Journal of Tourism and Cultural Change*, 5(2): 87–105.

Tucker, H. (2009) 'Recognizing emotion and its postcolonial potentialities: discomfort and shame in a tourism encounter in Turkey', *Tourism Geographies*, 11(4): 444–61.

Tucker, H. (2010) 'Peasant entrepreneurs: a longitudinal ethnography', *Annals of Tourism Research*, 37(4): 927–46.

Tucker, H. (2014) 'Mind the gap: opening up spaces of multiple moralities in tourism encounters', in M. Mostafanezhad and K. Hannam (eds), *Moral Encounters in Tourism*, Farnham: Ashgate.

Tucker, H. (2016) 'Empathy and tourism: limits and possibilities', *Annals of Tourism Research*, 57: 31–43.

Tucker, H. (2017) 'CTS 7 Keynote Address: Contaminated Tourism. On Pissed Off-Ness, Passion, and Hope', Critical Tourism Studies Proceedings, Article 147.

Tucker, H., and Akama, J. (2009) 'Tourism as postcolonialism', in T. Jamal and M. Robinson (eds), *The SAGE Handbook of Tourism Studies*, Los Angeles: SAGE.

Tuhiwai Smith, L. (2012) *Decolonizing Methodologies: Research and Indigenous Peoples*, 2nd edition, London: Zed Books.

Turner, L., and Ash, J. (1976) *The Golden Horses*, New York: St. Martin's Press.

Tuulentie, S. (2006) 'The dialectic of identities in the field of tourism. The discourses of the indigenous Sámi in defining their own and the tourists' identities', *Scandinavian Journal of Hospitality and Tourism*, 6(1): 25–36.

Tuulentie, S., and Mettiäinen, I. (2007) 'Local participation in the evolution of ski resorts: the case of Ylläs and Levi in Finnish Lapland', *Forest, Snow and Landscape Research*, 81(1/2): 207–22.

UCA San Ramón (2008) Project Document 13th of May 2008 'Convocatoria Especial 2008: Agencia Luxemburguesa de cooperación, Programa de las Naciones Unidas para el Desarrollo – Programa de Pequeñas Donaciones (PPD)', UCA San Ramón.

UNDP (2016) Human Development Report 2016, Human Development for Everyone, http://hdr.undp.org/sites/default/files/2016_human_development_report.pdf accessed 20 August 2017.

UNWTO (2004) *Making Tourism More Sustainable: A Guide for Policy Makers*, Madrid: United Nations World Tourism Organization UNWTO.

Urry, J. (1990) *The Tourist Gaze*, London: Sage.

Urry, J., and Larsen, J. (2011) *The Tourist Gaze 3.0*, London: Sage.

Vainikka, V. (2013) 'Rethinking mass tourism', *Tourist Studies*, 13(3): 268–86.

Vakis, R., Kruger, D., and Mason, A. (2004) *Shocks and Coffee: Lessons from Nicaragua*, Social Protection Discussion Paper Series No. 0415, Washington DC: The World Bank.

Valkila, J., and Nygren, A. (2009) 'Impacts of Fair Trade certification on coffee farmers, cooperatives and laborers in Nicaragua', *Agriculture and Human Value*, doi:10.1007/s10460-009-9208-7.

Valkonen, J., Lehtonen, T.-K., and Pyyhtinen, O. (2013) 'Sosiologista materiaalioppia' [Sociological Materiology], *Sosiologia*, 50(3): 217–21.

Valtonen, A. (2009) 'Small tourism firms as agents of critical knowledge', *Tourist Studies*, 9(2): 127–43.

van der Duim, R., Peters, K., and Akama, J. (2006) 'Cultural tourism in African communities: a comparison between cultural Manyattas in Kenya and cultural tourism project in Tanzania', in M.K. Smith and M. Robinson (eds), *Cultural Tourism in a Changing World, Politics, Participation and (Re)presentation*, Clevedon: Channel View.

van der Duim, R., Ren, C., and Jóhannesson, G.T. (2017) 'ANT: a decade of interfering with tourism', *Annals of Tourism Research*, 64: 139–49.

van Manen, M. (1990) *Researching Lived Experience: Human Science for an Action Sensitive Pedagogy*, Albany, NY: State University of New York Press.

Veijola, S. (1994) 'Metaphors of mixed team play', *International Review for the Sociology of Sport*, 29(1): 32–49.

Veijola, S. (1999) 'Tourism as a violent narrative? Epistemological and methodological inquiries', an invited paper at the Second Annual Colloquium of the Centre for the Study of Spaces in Modernity, Mobilities. 26–28 November 1999, in Gregynog, Newtown, Powys, Wales.

Veijola, S. (2005) 'Turistien yhteisöt' [Tourist Communities], in A. Hautamäki, T. Lehtonen, J. Sihvola, I. Tuomi, H. Vaaranen and S. Veijola (eds), *Yhteisöllisyyden paluu* [The Return of Communality], Helsinki: Gaudeamus.

Veijola, S. (2006) 'Heimat tourism in the countryside. Paradoxical sojourns in self and place', in T. Oakes and C. Minca (eds), *Travels in Paradox: Remapping Tourism*, New York: Rowman and Littlefield.

Veijola, S. (2009) 'Gender as work in the tourism industry', *Tourist Studies*, 9(2): 109–26.

Veijola, S. (2014) 'Towards silent communities', in S. Veijola, J. Germann Molz, O. Pyyhtinen, E. Höckert and A. Grit, *Disruptive Tourism and Its Untidy Guests. Alternative Ontologies for Future Hospitalities*, New York: Palgrave MacMillan.

Veijola, S., and Falin, P. (2014) 'Mobile neighbouring', *Mobilities*, 11(3): 382–99.

Veijola, S., and Jokinen, E. (1994) 'The body in tourism', *Theory, Culture and Society*, 11(3), 125–51.

Veijola, S., and Jokinen, E. (1998) 'The death of the tourist', *European Journal of Cultural Studies*, 1(3): 327–51.

Veijola, S., and Jokinen, E. (2008) 'Towards a hostessing society? Mobile arrangements of gender and labour', *NORA: Nordic Journal of Feminist and Gender Research*, 16(3): 166–81.

Veijola, S., Germann Molz, J., Pyyhtinen, O., Höckert, E., and Grit, A. (2014) *Disruptive Tourism and Its Untidy Guests. Alternative Ontologies for Future Hospitalities*, New York: Palgrave MacMillan.

Veijola, S., Ilola, H., and Edelheim, J. (2013) 'Johdanto matkailun tukimukseen' [Introduction to tourism research], in S. Veijola (ed.), *Matkailututkimuksen lukukirja*, Rovaniemi: Lapin Yliopistokustannus.

Veijola, S., and Säynäjäkangas, J. (eds) (2018) *Hitaiden matkojen sanakirja* [A Dictionary of Slow Travels], co-authors: David Carlin, Janne Honkasilta, Emily Höckert, Ann Light, Janne Säynäjäkangas, Soile Veijola and Noora Vikman, Helsinki: Ntamo.

Vennesson, P. (2008) 'Case studies and process tracing: theories and practices', in D.D. Porta and M. Keating (eds), *Approaches and Methodologies in the Social Sciences: A Pluralist Perspective*, Cambridge: Cambridge University Press.

Vianica (n.d.) 'Rural tourism at the la Pita community', www.vianica. com/activity/118/rural-tourism-at-the-la-pita-community, accessed April 2014.

Viswanath, R. (2008) 'Can we transform tourism?', in C. D'Mello (ed.), *Transforming Re-forming Tourism, Perspectives on Justice and Humanity in Tourism*, Ecumenical Coalition on Tourism, Thailand.

Vogler, C. (2002) 'Social imaginary, ethics and methodological individualism', *Public Culture*, 14: 625–7.

Vrasti, W. (2010) 'Dr Strangelove or how I learned to stop worrying about methodology and love writing', *Millennium: Journal of International Studies*, 39(1): 79–88.

Vrasti, W. (2013) *Volunteer Tourism in the Global South: Giving Back in Neoliberal Times*, London: Routledge.

Wall, G., and Mathieson, A. (2006) *Tourism: Change, Impacts, and Opportunities*, 2nd edition, Harlow: Pearson Prentice Hall.

Watts, J. (2015) 'Land of opportunity – and fear – along the route of Nicaragua's giant new canal', *The Guardian*, 20 January 2015.

Wearing, B. (1998) *Leisure and Feminist Theory*, London: Sage.

Wearing, S. (2001) *Volunteer Tourism: Experiences That Make a Difference*, New Wallingford: CABI.

Wearing, S., Deville, A.M., and Lyons, K. (2008) 'The volunteer's journey through leisure into the self', in K.D. Lyons and S.L. Wearing (eds), *Journeys of Discovery in Volunteer Tourism*, Wallingford: CABI.

Wearing, S., and McDonald, M. (2002) 'The development of community-based tourism: re-thinking the relationships between tour operators and development agents as intermediaries in rural and isolated area communities', *Journal of Sustainable Tourism*, 10(2): 31–45.

Wearing, S.L., Stevenson, D., and Young, T. (2010) *Tourist Cultures: Identity, Place and the Traveller*, London: SAGE.

Wearing, S., and Wearing, M. (1999) 'Decommodifying ecotourism: rethinking global–local interactions with host communities', *Leisure and Society*, 22(1): 39–70.

Wearing, S., and Wearing, M. (2014) 'On decommodifying ecotourism's social value: neoliberal reformism or the new environmental morality?', in M. Mostafanezhad and K. Hannam (eds), *Moral Encounters in Tourism*, Farnham: Ashgate.

Weaver, D. (2012) 'Community-based tourism as strategic dead-end', in T.V. Singh (ed.), *Critical Debates in Tourism*, Bristol: Channel View.

Welten, R. (2017) 'On the hospitality of cannibals', in C. Lashley (ed.), *The Routledge Handbook of Hospitality Studies*, London: Routledge.

Westwood, S., Morgan, N., and Pritchard, A. (2005) 'Situation, participation and reflexivity in tourism research: furthering interpretative approaches to tourism enquiry', *Tourism Recreation Research*, 31(2): 33–41.

WFP (2008) *Executive Brief: Central America. Prices, Markets and Food and Nutritional Security*, May 2008, United Nations World Food Programme.

Wild, J. (1969) 'Introduction', in E. Levinas, *Totality and Infinity*, Pittsburgh: Duquesne University Press.

Wilson, E., and Hollinshead, K. (2015) 'Qualitative tourism research: opportunities in the emergent soft sciences', *Annals of Tourism Research*, 54: 30–47.

Wilson, S. (2014) 'To boldly go where no van has gone before: auto–ethnographic experimentation and mobile fieldwork', in M. Mostafanezhad and K. Hannam (eds), *Moral Encounters in Tourism*, Farnham: Ashgate.

Wood, R. (2000) 'Caribbean cruise tourism: globalisation at sea', *Annals of Tourism Research*, 27(2): 345–70.

Woods, T. (1997) 'The ethical subject: the philosophy of Emmanuel Levinas', in K. Simms (ed.), *Ethics and the Subject*, Amsterdam: Rodopi.

Woosnam, K.M., Aleshinloye, K.D., Strzelecka, M., and Erul, E. (2016) 'The role of place attachment in developing emotional solidarity with residents', *Journal of Hospitality and Tourism Research*, 1–9.

Young, G. (1973) *Tourism: Blessing or Blight?*, Harmondsworth: Penguin.

Zapata Campos, M.J. (2014) 'Partnerships, tourism, and community impacts', in A.A. Lew, C.M. Hall and A.M. Williams (eds), *The Wiley Blackwell Companion to Tourism*, Oxford: John Wiley and Sons.

Zapata, M.J., Hall, C., Lindo, P., and Vanderschaeghe, M. (2011) 'Can community-based tourism contribute to development and poverty alleviation? Lessons from Nicaragua', *Current Issues in Tourism*, 14(8): 725–49.

Zoomers, A. (2008) 'Global travelling along the Inca Route: is international tourism beneficial for local development?', *European Planning Studies*, 16(7): 971–83.

Zorn, E., and Farthing, L. (2007) 'Communitarian tourism hosts and mediators in Peru', *Annals of Tourism Research*, 34(3): 673–89.

Zylinska, J. (2014) *Minimal Ethics for the Anthropocene*, Ann Arbor, MI: Open Humanities Press.

Index

Adieu to Emmanuel Levinas 14–5, 31, 40,
46; *see also* Derrida, J.
Ahmed, S. 21, 56
all-inclusive resorts 2, 76–8, 161–2, 169
alterity *see* otherness
authenticity 17, 36, 38, 110, 130,
154–5, 164

backpacking 152–4
Baker, G. 61–3, 124
becoming 13, 138–9, 149–50
becoming-with 149
being 6–7, 14–5, 19–20, 28, 41–4, 60,
145–6, 159–60, 168–70; *Being and
Time* 43; dualistic ways of 169; ethics
as basis of 17, 44, 60, 159–60; freedom
of 157; human 13, 169; relational
41–4, 159–60, 168–9; self–subsistent
20, 145; in the fieldwork 24, 166;
totalizing concepts of 42, 143–4, 150;
unprepared 150–1; welcoming ways of
58, 156, 159–60; *see also* ontologies;
otherwise than being; well-being
'being-for-the-other' 14–5, 17, 95, 139;
see also responsibility-for-the-other
being taught 139, 148–51; *see also*
learning; teaching; unlearning
being-with 41–2, 138
being-with-others 6, 60, 62
Bhabha, H. 141
bilateral aid 1–5, 23–4; *see also* conditions
of aid; development cooperation
binaries 6, 53, 140; subject positions 6,
14, 139, 169
Bruner, E. 6, 20–1, 123
bottom-up *see* participatory
development
borders 16, 40, 50–1, 59, 126; *see also*
categories; totality; *said* and *saying*
Butcher, J. 30, 85, 90

camping ix, 20
'can the subaltern speak?' 52, 56, 86, 14;
see also Spivak, G.
Cañada, E. 9–10, 39, 77–9, 97
care 6, 15, 17, 140–2, 158, 165;
hospitality 15, 113, 128; mutual 141–2;
privilege 34; self-centred 145
categories 15, 20, 50–1, 57, 121–2,
144–5, 146, 152; *see also* borders;
totality; *said* and *saying*
Caton, K. 18, 30–1, 135
Chambers, D. and Buzinde, C. 10, 21, 167
Chambers, R.: 'rapid rural appraisal' 144
codes of conduct 45, 62, 125–6, 135, 170
coffee 3, 23, 88; cooperatives 3, 88–9,
114, 128; crisis 3, 24, 89, 127, 150, 152;
encounters 146; fair trade certificate
89, 104, 144; farmers 140; history 88–9;
tourism 4, 88–9, 100, 105, 110–12, 127,
140, 143; *see also* Ruta del Café
colonial: conditions 140; difference 50,
70; encounters 66–7, 83; history and
tourism 1, 20–1, 51, 53, 66–9, 73,
82–3, 96, 161; history and community
development 8, 30; hospitality 69;
legacy 34, 49–50, 53; subject positions
21; travel writing 20–1; *see also Ruta
Colonial*
colonialism 5–6, 8, 70, 141; internal 52,
75; in Latin America 69–70; tourism
as 67, 77, 108, 161–2
colonialized imaginings 52, 67, 82–3, 149,
155–6; disruption of 94, 156, 162,
149–50; *see also* homework; unlearning
commodification of hospitality
102–31, 163
communities: academic viii; Agamben 13;
coffee 2–4, 88–9, 115, 127–8, 140–2;
definition 9, 30, 91; displacement
161; guests in development projects

13, 23, 91–2, 118–20, 167; home 12, 59, 68–9, 106–7, 117, 125, 137, 140–2, 154–5; host 6–10, 13, 23, 81–2, 86, 93, 118–19, 125–30, 141, 152; indigenous 19, 21, 67, 70, 78, 80, 87–8, 131, 167; individuals 12–13, 16–18, 27, 87, 110, 164, 166; sense of 18, 130; rural viii, 69, 76, 81–6, 101, 154–5

community-based tourism viii, 2–6, 117; attractions in 3, 82, 108–12, 148–55; as responsible form of tourism viii, 2–3, 7, 79, 80, 98, 108–9, 139, 161–2, 167–8; care 10, 140–3; conflicts 92–3; critique 2, 4–5, 10–13; dependency 5; distribution of benefits 2–4, 93; empowerment 3–4, 9, 79, 114–15, 122; experts 5, 82, 84–7, 138–40; financing 4, 92–5, 103–6, 129; guides 9, 91, 112–3, 125, 137; history of 9–10, 72–3, 89–90; inequality 4–5, 154–6; intermediaries 4–5, 9–10, 23, 93, 108–9, 118–19, 147–8; material development 102–41, 148; motivation 93; NGOs 2–5, 69, 77–9, 108–13, 118, 162; networks 79, 91, 109, 137–8, 150–1; poverty reduction 98; power relations 4–5, 11–12; resistance towards 4, 90, 112–13, 121–6, 162–3; risks of 4, 90, 96, 103–6; San Ramón 2–5, 28, 89; skills and capacity 9, 11, 106, 109, 120, 162–3; sustainability 3–4, 57, 9–10

community-case study research 2–4, 10–13, 21–27, 30, 91, 101, 135, 167; Dredge, D., Hales, R. and Jamal, T. 10; worldmaking 11–12, 30

community development 7–9, 162; colonialism 8, 12, 30; good life 7, 168; modernization 8, 30, 118–19; projects 7–8, 127–9; radical roots of 8, 10; resistance 4–5, 90, 112–13, 121–6

community participation *see* participation

conditions: aid 83, 127–31; colonial 140; hospitality 15–6, 33–4, 40–1, 57–62, 74, 95, 102–33, 169; juridical and political 40, 74, 83, 95; material 28–9, 101–3, 111–24, 132, 148–9, 163; participation 16, 22–3, 83, 118, 121, 169; rural 100–24, 156–7

conflictive ontological encounters 6, 41–2, 167–9

consciousness: conscience 123; hospitality 46, 60; individualism

145–6; Levinas, E. 95, 145, 151, 170; moral 42, 61; relationality 145–6, 168; *see also* hospitality; Kant, I.; mindfulness; totality; negotiations

continuum: in hosting and guesting 28, 46–7, 51, 115, 120–1, 148; in teaching and learning 146–52; *see also* ethical subjectivity; *hôte*; Levinas, E.; Rosello, M.

Critical Turn in Tourism Studies, The 10–11

curiosity 55, 168; *see also* Irigaray, L.

decolonization: of minds 52–8, 159, 164; *see also* homework; unlearning

decolonizing: imaginings 159–60, 164; research methodologies 21, 27, 166; participation 12; research methodologies 21, 27; *see also* hermeneutic phenomenology; Tuhiwai Smith, L.

democratization: knowledge production 21; participation 7–8, 148; responsibility towards the other 95, 146; tourism development 68, 78, 148

Derrida, J. 13–20, 33–4, 39–47; deconstruction 31, 40, 50, 59, 62, 65; *see also Adieu to Emmanuel Levinas*; double law of hospitality

dependency: aid 7, 72; community participation 5, 12–3, 90–3, 103, 105, 108–9, 162; tourism development 97; *see also* interdependency

dependistas 8

development: aid 1–2, 4, 7, 72; alternative development theory 9, 162, 167–8; cooperation 1–2, 23; cooperation 2–3, 69–70, 123–4; as economic growth 19, 149; as freedom 48–9, 64; studies 2, 5–8, 23–4, 83–4, 167; Eurocentrism 6, 36, 69, 144, 167; Global North as model of 51, 69–70, 97; hosts and guests 7–13, 28, 39, 54, 67, 85–6, 105, 109–9, 120–3, 133, 139; human 7–13, 48; mainstream 9; neoliberal idea of economic 19, 5, 80; parodies of 119; participatory theory 7–8, 12–13; post-development 70; postcolonial critique of 7–8, 51–8, 119, 164; poverty reduction 12; practitioners 2, 6, 23, 28, 52, 55, 115–24; projects 106, 151; Rostow's stages of growth 149, 158n13; theories 7–9; thinking 8, 19, 69–70; top-down 5, 117–19; *see also* developmentalism; Eriksson Baaz, M.; Sen, A.; tourism development

developmentalism 4, 12, 19, 97, 149; critique towards 8, 119, 160

displacement 2, 158, 161

disruption 50–1, 151; clear-cut subjects and categories 20; roles between hosts and guests 23, 60; paternalism 151; social imaginings 13; *see also* decolonization; interruption

Disruptive Tourism and Its Untidy Guests 20

domestic epistemic violence 121–2, 160, 163–5; *see also* epistemic violence

domestic tourism 5, 111–12

double law of hospitality 15–17, 34, 39–45, 68, 122–3; *see also* Derrira, J.; ethics of hospitality; laws of hospitality

double session of representation 27, 55; *see also* Spivak, G.

Drabinski, J. E. 15, 44, 49–50, 59

Dualist subject positions 16, 21, 120, 169

Dussel, E. 50, 70

Edelheim, Johan 25, 108

Edensor, T. 78

El Güeguense 66–7

emancipation 13, 26–8, 34, 51–5, 123, 132, 149

empowerment 2–4, 9–10, 12, 24, 48, 78, 93, 113–14, 122, 125

enclaves *see* all-inclusive resorts

encounters 22–3; colonial 51–8, 68; hospitable 148; moral 141; participatory 13–14; responsible 131, 159; slow 146; tourism development 5–6, 23–9, 45, 77, 84, 92, 160, 163

Enlightment 56–7; hospitality 35; participation 12; post-enlightment 50

entrepreneurship *see* rural tourism entrepreneurship

epistemic ignorance *see* epistemic violence

epistemic violence 6, 53–5, 121–2, 155, 163; development projects 163–4; domestic 121–2; maintenance of European theatres of responsibility 53; material exploitation 141;

unconditional hospitality 154–5; unlearn privilege 34; *see also* Spivak, G.

Eriksson Baaz, M. 34, 54, 63, 123; *see also* paternalism of partnership

Escobar, A. 7, 135, 140; *see also* decolonization

ethical encounters 7, 21, 29, 45, 61; at home 58–61; decolonization 159; hospitality 46, 61; in tourism 28–9, 45, 147; mutual welcoming 45–6, 50–1, 61, 147–8; *see also* continuum; interruption, negotiations; Levinas, E.

ethical epistemologies: Veijola, S. 27

ethical saying: Levinas, E. 27, 55; *see also said* and *saying*; Spivak, G.; double session of representation

ethical subjectivity 7, 14–19, 28, 33, 45–58, 151; Levinas, E. 14–15, 40, 43, 55, 58–61, 144, 151; other-orientedness 15, 29, 42–3, 60–1, 95; phenomenological philosophy 14–15, 53, 144; postcolonial philosophy 7, 13–14, 28, 33, 55; receptivity 29, 34; responsibility 29, 45–9; that begins from the other 15, 19, 46, 60, 195; welcoming 14, 49, 60, 68; *see also Adieu to Emmanuel Levinas*; continuum; hospitality; intersubjectivity; subjectivity

ethics of hospitality 15–16, 33–4, 39–45, 145–6; *see also* laws of hospitality

ethics 10–18, 33–63; in academic research 25–6, 166; codes of 45, 62, 125–6, 135, 170; of deconstruction 31n11; Fennell, D. A. 18, 168; as first philosophy 19; in tourism 17–18, 39; Kant, I. 34, 40; Levinasian 15–19, 40–50; of participation 169; post-enlightment 50; Smith, M. 17–18

ethnocentrism 6, 11, 21, 30n7, 50, 53, 60, 167

ethnography 13, 20–5; reflective turn in 21

experience 22–3; historicity and materiality 58; *see also* hermeneutic phenomenology

face, Levinasian 143–8; face-to-face 143–8; holiness 42; infinite alterity 15, 42; of the other 15

failure 24; failure as success 24, 151–2

fair trade 3, 104

Fennell, D. A. 18, 168

freedom 48–9, 64; *see also* Sen, A.
Freire, P. 8, 151

Gadamer, H. G. 25; *see also* hermeneutic phenomenology
gaze: expert 165; humanitarian, Mostafanezhad, M. 6, 134; tourist (Urry, J. and Larsen, J.) 6, 165
Germann Molz, J. 15–16, 20, 35–6, 61, 151
gift 103, 130–1, 159; tourists' (Länsmann, A. S.) 131; Mauss, M. 131; *see also* Kuokkanen, R.; Pyyhtinen, O.
good life 7, 10–11, 19, 168; *see also* vivir bien; well-being

happiness 7, 145–6
Heidegger, M. 14–15, 19, 31n16, 41–4; homesickness 60; phenomenology 19, 41, 60
helping 51, 115–22, 141; *see also* paternalism
hermeneutic phenomenology 22–3; analysis 25–6; decolonizing research methodologies 27; *see also* hospitable methodologies; van Manen, Max; phenomenology
Hollinshead, K. 140–1; *see also* worldmaking
home 58–62; community 4, 12, 59, 88–9, 117; ethical encounters 58–61; being at home with oneself 60; being at home with others 60; hospitality 4, 35, 39, 60–2, 126, 142; metaphysical 59–60; nation 59; political 68; sharing 60–2; *see also* domestic epistemic violence
homestay tourism 37, 101, 107; backstage 37–8, 124, 153; commercial friendship 37; intimacy 101, 107, 124; *see also* hospitality
homesickness 60
homework 59, 123, 156; *see also* decolonizing imaginings; Kuokkanen R.; unlearning
hope 4, 41–2
hopefulness 10
hospitality: act of sharing 16; altruistic 38, 82; as being, doing and knowing with others 159; asymmetry of hospitality 23, 47; bargaining 152–3, 156; being-for-the-other 139; between strangers 35; care 37, 39, 141, 146; commercial 37, 102–7, 116, 124, 163; condition of humanity 35, 170; conditions of 15–16, 33–4, 40–1, 57–62, 74, 95, 102–33, 169; cosmopolitan 36; definitions of 34, 143, 147, 149; domains of 38, 107; domestic 102, 35, 39, 60–2; double law of 15–16, 31, 39–45, 68, 122–3; ethics of 15–6, 19, 15–16, 33–65, 145–6; etymology 35–6, 107–8; as interruption 17, 28–9, 49, 51, 58, 115, 128, 131, 142, 166; history of 13–14, 35; home 35, 39, 60–2, 126, 142; humanity 13–14, 147, 170; lack of 5, 29, 113, 138, 147; making space for the other 58, 101, 107, 138–9, 142, 159–62; management 4, 14, 16, 19, 33–4, 37–9, 73, 103, 116–19, 123, 149; material fabric of 4, 112–13, 116, 123, 130, 147–9, 163; mobilizing 16, 39; mutual virtue 35, 45–6, 81, 146; negotiating 39–40, 59, 83, 94–6, 100–9, 160–1; Nicaraguan 22, 28, 71, 81–7; openness of 18, 29, 34, 147, 169–70; other-orientedness 15, 29, 42–3, 60–1, 95; participation 14–15, 33, 45, 62, 121, 145, 160, 168–9; paying for 86, 124–9, 152–3; political 72, 83; postcolonial philosophy of 14, 59–60, 70, 135; reciprocity 45; relationality 14, 20, 94, 146–7, 168–9; renaissance 13–14; risks of 94, 106, 162; rural 13, 7, 82–8, 94, 102–7, 163; sacred obligation 35; and society 31, 35; subject of welcome 45–50, 68, 152–60; thinking with 165–7; time 139, 145; unconditional 28, 33–9, 54–5, 61, 73, 87, 94, 124; in universities 52, 165–9; volunteering 127–9; as a way of being 58, 139; work 37–8, 102–15; *see also* Derrida, J.; Kant, I.; Levinas E.; O'Gorman, K.; *Totality and Infinity*; welcome
hospitable methodologies 20–7, 165–7; *see also* ethical saying; hermeneutic phenomenology; knowing with hospitality
hospitable spaces 16, 27, 29, 35, 50–1, 58, 101, 107, 138–9, 156
hospity (Grit, A.) 138–9
hostage 47, 121; *see also* Levinas, E.
hostessing (Veijola, S. and Jokinen, E.) 107
hostility 35–6, 123; *see also* Kant, I.

hosting and guesting: continuum in 28, 46–7, 51, 115, 120–1, 148
hostis 35–6
hosts and guests 5–6, 23, 39, 45, 94, 102; care 141; inseparability 17, 35–6, 46; in participatory tourism development 9–13, 106–7, 120, 138; Levinas, E. 60, 120–1, 138; relation 4, 106–7; roles of 23, 51–4, 67, 83, 113, 120–1; roles in development 7–13, 28, 39, 54, 58, 67, 85–6, 105, 109–9, 120, 123, 133, 139; *see also* continuum; ethical encounters; hosting and guesting; *hôte*
hôte 17, 35–6, 46, 120–1
humanitarian gaze *see* gaze
humanity: hospitality 36, 40, 170; more-than-human-world 169; participation 13
Hunt, C. 68–74, 161–2
Husserl, Edmund 19, 41
hybrid subject positions 13, 141; *see also* Tucker, H.

imaginings 13, 18, 27, 57–9, 63; being and becoming 138–40; disrupting colonized 155, 159–50, 164–5; *see also* phenomenology
impoverishment *see* poverty
indigenous knowledge 5, 10, 31, 167; *see also* local knowledge
indigenous: cosmologies 11, 19; epistemes 52–3; cultures as tourist attraction 2, 73, 101, 108; *see also* communities; decolonizing methodologies
individualism 11–12, 18, 30, 41–2, 45, 48, 52, 144–5, 160, 170; alternatives to 18–20, 45–1, 145–6, 150–1, 169; autonomous subject 17–18; community 12–3, 169; ethics 18; limitations of 18, 160; mindfulness 145; ontology 18–20, 46; participation 12, 28–9, 33, 45, 115–16, 169; tourism 12, 19; self-centredness 18, 113; self-gratification 48, 116, 145; *see also* intersubjectivity; relationality; subjectivity; totality
infinity 14–7, 40–7, 54–5, 151, 169–70; *see also* totality; Levinas, E.; saying; relationality
interdependency *see* relationality
intermediaries 5, 118–19, 126–7, 147–8
international development aid *see* bilateral aid

international solidarity movement *see* Nicaragua
interoceanic canal route; *see* Nicaragua
interruption 19; colonial imaginings 155, 159–50, 164–5; hospitality as 28–9, 49, 51, 58, 115, 128, 131, 142, 166, 170; self 29, 34, 46–9, 131, 139, 141–6, 157; *see also* disruption
intersubjectivity 14–16, 23, 43–4, 47, 53, 109, 158, 160; ethics 50; *see also* ethical subjectivity; individualism; relationality; subjectivity
INTUR *see* Nicaragua
Irigaray, L.: wonder 20, 55

Jamal, T. 10, 22, 99n31, 158n7; *see also* community-case study research; hermeneutic phenomenology
Jokinen, E. 16–17

Kant, I. 17, 34, 36–7, 58–61
Kincaid, J. 51–2, 141
knowing with hospitality 20–7, 165–7; *see also* epistemic violence; hospitable methodologies
Kuokkanen, R. 46–6, 52, 59, 69, 121–3, 166; *see also* homework; continuum of teaching and learning

Lashley, C.: domains of hospitality 38–9, 107, 125
Latin American theorists 6, 69–70; *see also* Dussel, E.; Escobar, A.; Mignolo, W.
laws of hospitality 15–16, 33–4, 39–45; *see also* Derrida, J.; double law of hospitality; ethics of hospitality; hospitality
learning, being taught: Levinas, E. 139–40; learning anew 58; learning anew the welcome of the other 152–6; *see also* unlearning
Levinas, E. 14–17, 40–7, 54–5, 151, 169; critique towards Levinas's philosophy 44; ethical subjectivity 14–15, 40, 43, 55, 58–61, 144, 151; phenomenology 14–15, 22, 41, 59–61, 101; postcolonial philosophy 6, 15, 17, 49–50; posthumanism 44; responsibility 16, 19, 21n16, 41–9, 59; Spivak, G. 44, 49–50, 54–5, 58, 121–2, 151; third 17, 43, 95; *Totality and Infinity* 14, 40–3, 47, 54, 143–4; *see also* Derrida, J.; ethical saying; welcome of/to the other; West

Liberation pedagogy 8; *see also* Freire, P.
listening 54–5, 86, 132–3, 143–4, 148
local knowledge 5, 10, 81, 167; critique
    51–8, 167; *see also* indigenous
    knowledge
local tourism coordinators 23–5, 93, 105,
    119, 125–30
Lynch, P. 31n11, 35–8; *see also*
    hospitality

mass tourism 37, 48, 98n18
messiness 12, 19–20, 164; *see also*
    disruption; untidy guests
method 21–2; absence of 62;
    hermeneutic phenomenology 22,
    32n26; violence of 22, 144; *see also*
    Gadamer, H.
microcredits 4, 99n34, 103–6, 129
Mignolo, W. 6, 70, 140; *see also*
    decolonization
migration 39–40, 50, 59
mindfulness 145; *see also* consciousness
modernization: Moderniza 4;
    understanding of subjectivity 18,
    42, 48, 52, 112; *see also* community
    development
more-than-human others 21, 44, 169
Mostafanezhad, M. 6, 13, 134n20, 141;
    see also humanitarian gaze; volunteer
    tourism
multiculturalism 10, 51–2, 69, 140, 164
Murphy, P. 9

naivety; 4, 15, 140, 146, 160; *see also*
    unicorns
negotiations 22–3, 40, 58–9, 95–60
Nicaragua: Belli, G. 71; bilateral aid
    1–4, 23, 67–8, 79–91, 83–7, 116;
    colonial guests 69–70, 88; community-
    based tourism 2–5, 79–80; contra war
    71; cooperatives 89–93; emigration
    72–3; Güeguense, El 66–7; helping
    Finland 67–8; international solidarity
    movement 3, 71–2, 80–1, 89–90, 103,
    146–7; inter-oceanic canal project
    67, 71, 94–6, 161; INTUR 1, 2, 23,
    78–87; National plan for Human
    Development in Nicaragua 79; Ortega
    D. 1, 83, 161; PRONicaragua 74–5;
    political hospitality 72–7, 84, 94–5;
    Ruta del Café 2, 89; *Ruta Colonial* 66,
    80; rural tourism; development 4–5,
    78–95; safety and low levels of violence

72; Sandinista revolution 1979 3, 72;
    Sandino, A. 70–1; San Ramón 2–5,
    84–152; social justice 71–7; Somoza,
    A. 71, 88; tourism development 1–3,
    72–95; tourism laws 73–9; tourism and
    poverty 74–84; tranquillity of life
    72–3, 82–31, 140–6; Western
    imaginaries of 72; *see also* coffee;
    Cañada, E.; Hunt, C.

objectivity 30
O'Gorman, K. 35–6
openness 16, 18–20, 27, 36; between
    ourselves 33; *see also* ethics of
    hospitality, infinity; Levinas, E.;
    phenomenology
other/Other 5–6, 11–12, 16–7, 33–60;
    being-for-the 17; Levinasian 15–17,
    18–19, 34, 40–51, 54–9; lowercasing
    'other' 17; mastering the other 16,
    37, 51–9; multiple others 6, 16–17,
    33; othering 53, 64n14; other Others
    44, 49–50; responsibility-for-the
    17–18; subaltern 27, 52, 55; as an
    object of knowledge 20–1, 26–7, 144;
    orientedness 15, 29, 42–3, 60–1, 95;
    more-than-human 21, 44, 169; *see also*
    alterity
otherness 5–6, 12–17, 21, 27–9, 37, 42,
    44, 51; alterity 15–17, 28, 43–4
ownership 2, 5, 9, 85

paternalism 33, 53–4, 57, 107, 119, 132,
    151; of partnership 86, 133; *see also*
    Eriksson Baaz, M.
participation viii, 1–2, 7–13; in academic
    research 22; basis of ethical relations
    13; conditions of 16, 169; critique
    5, 7, 10–12, 165, 168; ethics of
    participation 169; history of 7–8,
    168–9; and hospitality 45, 120–1,
    145, 160, 169; and humanity 13,
    168–9; invitation to 6, 12, 33, 85;
    limitations of 5, 11–12, 45, 57, 86,
    105–6, 120–1; openness of 160, 169;
    other-orientedness 15; orthodoxy
    of participation 12; radical roots
    of participation 8–9, 30n6, 169;
    relationality of participation 45,
    167–70; resistance as 63–5, 90, 122;
    subject formation 12, 33, 115–24,
    146–52; third sector 78–9; tyranny of
    participation 12; *see also* community

participatory: action research 25;
development 1, 8, 12, 14, 22, 45, 85,
167–8; observation 3; paradigm 9,
151, 168; projects 120–2; planning 11,
98n21; theory 7–14, 167–9; research
methodologies 21, 25, 139n28,
166–7; Grimwood, B. S. R. et al, 53;
see also development; emancipation;
empowerment
Perpetual Peace (Kant, I.) 36, 40
phenomenology: hermeneutic 25–6,
63; Gadamer, H. 32; Heidegger, M.
19, 41, 60; Husserl, Edmund 19, 41;
Levinas, E. 14–15, 22, 41, 59–61, 101;
of tourist experience 22; of the other
15; representation 26; van Manen, M.
25; *see also* ethical saying
phenomenological: analysis 22–6, 169–70;
ethical subjectivity 14–15, 53, 144;
hermeneutic circle 26; methodology
20–7, 32; nod 25; philosophy 19, 32,
41, 59–61, 101
pluralism 7, 8, 10, 30n6, 42, 145–6
postcolonial: critique 6, 8, 21, 63, 101;
encounters 140–1; ethics 50, 64;
limitations of postcolonial approach
140–1; Marxism 50; post-structuralism
50; xenophobia 14; *see also* Ahmed,
S.; colonial; decolonization;
Derrida, J.; Spivak, G.; Rosello, M.;
worldmaking
postcolonialism 7, 49, 51–3
postcolonial philosophy 6, 14, 16,
47; Drabinski, J. E. 15, 49, 59–61;
Hiddleston, J. 49–50; Latin America
6, 69–70; Levinas, E. 6, 15, 17, 49–50;
ethical subjectivity 7, 13–14, 28, 33,
55; of hospitality 14, 59–60, 70, 135,
145, 156–7
post-host-guest-society 16–17
poverty: hosts and guests 4, 155;
impoverishment 4, 71, 101, 141, 155;
reduction and tourism development 4,
12, 74–5, 101, 167; romanticising 111,
132, 140–1, 149, 155, 163–4; tourism
12, 73–4, 76–7, 101; tourist attraction
155, 163–4; vulnerability 127–8;
see also Scheyvens, R.
Pratt, M. L. 20, 140
prejudices 6, 44, 56
prepositions between welcome and the
other 46–7
pre-tour narratives 6, 56

privilege 56–7, 111; Spivak, G. 34, 53–7,
140–1; *see also* unlearning privilege
as loss
Pyyhtinen, O. 20

Rantala, O. 24
readiness to welcome 107–15,
150–1, 169
refugees 48, 59, 135n21
relationality 6–7, 11, 167–70; gaze
6; interdependency 12–13, 108–9;
in academic research 25–6, 57; of
hospitality 16, 24, 58; participation
11, 45, 167–70; subjectivities 19, 23,
40–9, 53–4, 58, 109, 152; in tourism
7, 13, 20; Jóhannesson, G. T., Ren, C.
and van der Duim, R. 6–7, 94, 109
relational ontologies 6–7, 11–16, 19–20,
86–7; indigenous cosmologies 19;
see also Levinas, E.
representation 22, 26–7, 52, 55;
consequences of 164–5; democratic 7;
double session of 27, 55; ethical 55;
imaginaries 116; research 10, 27, 53–4,
58, 161–6; Spivak, G. 53–4; subject
formation 27, 53–4, 68; of the other
20, 27, 52–4, 107, 119, 163–6; tourism
marketing 52, 72; *see also* speaking
for/about the other; ethical saying;
worldmaking
resistance 4, 128; of categorization 144;
of tourism 154; participation 63–5, 90,
122, 165
responsibility: care 18, 146; corporate
social responsibility 39, 108, 130;
encounters 131, 159, 140–6; ethical
subjectivity as 29, 45–9; for-the-other
14–15, 17–18, 43, 47, 49, 95, 146;
Grimwood, B. S. R. et al. 6–7, 15,
53, 169; and hospitality 15, 19, 29,
45–7, 61, 160–170; Levinas, E. 16, 19,
21n16, 16, 41–9, 59; negotiating 62,
90, 95, 126, 157, 160; relationality 45,
167–70; research 63, 82, 123, 166–7;
theatres of 53; to welcome 4, 26, 47,
51, 47, 147
responsible: individual 47–9, 53,
86–7, 139
responsible tourism 109, 122, 140,
166–8; Goodwin, H. 122
risks of welcoming 40, 94–6, 96,
115–24, 163–5
Rivas Choza, E. 87–88

romanticisation: of poverty 132, 140–1, 149, 155, 163–4; of the subaltern other 51–2, 112, 140–1

Rosello, M. 17, 28, 31, 46, 121, 135; *see also* continuum in hosting

rural tourism 4–5, 80–2, 102–15; policy-making 79–82; poverty 100–1; sustainability 2, 5, 79–80

rural tourism entrepreneurship 79, 82, 86; calculating risks 28, 94–6; lack of vision 82, 96, 106, 108, 122, 124; peasant entrepreneurship Tucker, H. 149; recognition 114–15, 124, 126, 128–31, 149–50; risks e.g. 96, 122–3, 163–5

Ruta Colonial 67, 80; *see also* colonialism

Ruta del Café 2, 30, 80, 89, 134; *see also* coffee

Salazar, N. 115–16, 153–4, 164; *see also* tourism imaginaries

Sandinistas *see* Nicaragua

Sandino, A. *see* Nicaragua

said and *saying* 27, 43, 55; *see also* double session of representation; ethical saying

self: centeredness 18, 113; gratification 48, 116, 145; identity 23, 46, 113, 131–3; interrupting 29, 34, 46–9, 131, 139, 141–6, 157; responsible 47–9, 53, 86–7, 139; *see also* individualism; other

Scheyvens, R. 98n18, 101, 113–14

Sen, A. 48–9

serendipity 20, 81, 139

silence 20, 39, 157; culture of (Freire, P.) 8; disruption of the social (Veijola, S.) 20, 157; *see also* silencing

silencing 57–9, 94; guests silencing the hosts 29, 86, 102, 121–2, 160; in participatory projects 6, 86, 122, 163; the other 17, 29, 52–3, 57, 132; other ways of knowing 28, 53, 102, 121; *see also* domestic epistemic violence; epistemic violence; paternalism; Spivak, G.

sharing 29, 60, 148, 156–7

social justice 10–11

solidarity viii, 1, 10, 12, 18, 162; Levinas, E. 95; *see also* Nicaragua international solidarity movement

Somoza, A. *see* Nicaragua

spaces: between self and other 16, 23, 34, 61, 95, 156, 169; discursive 56–9, 78, 82, 132; enclavic, Edensor, T. 78; epistemic 59; ethical 50–1, 156; hospitable 16, 27, 29, 35, 50–1, 58, 101, 107, 138–9, 156; making space for the other 58, 101, 107, 138–9, 142, 159–62; marginalized 56; purifying one's space (Serres, M.) 100–1; sharing 29, 60; metaphysical 58–9; politicized 50, 95

speaking for/about the other 22, 26–7, 55; double session of representation 27, 55; *see also said* and *saying*; ethical saying

Spivak, G. 6, 22, 25–8, 34, 52–8, 165; 'can the subaltern speak?' 52, 56, 86, 149; Derrida, J. 54; double session of representation 27, 55; failure as success 151–2; homework 123; Kuokkanen, R.; Levinas, E. 44, 49–50, 54–5, 58, 121–2, 151; Marxism 50; pessimism 59, 140–1; poststructuralism 50; privilege 34, 53–7, 140–1; representation of the subaltern 27; worlding, worldmaking 11, 164–5; *see also* epistemic violence; silencing; unlearning privilege

stranger 20, 35, 39–40, 47, 68–9, 81, 101, 106, 115, 125–6

subjectivity: being-for-the-other 14, 19, 42–3, 60–1; binary oppositions 6, 14, 139, 169; cosmopolitan 57; flexible 112; Heidegger, M. 43–4; hybrid subject positions 13, 141; individual 11–12, 17–18, 30, 41–2, 45–9, 144–5, 160, 170; modern understanding of 18, 42, 48, 52, 112; openness 46; privilege 56–7; relational 19, 23, 40–9, 53–4, 58, 109, 152; renewing 18; subaltern 5, 54, 156; subject of welcome 45–50, 68, 101, 152; totalizing definitions of 14–15, 20–1, 23, 58, 169; *see also* ethical subjectivity; individualism; intersubjectivity; subjectivity; Tucker H.

subject formation: clear cut 23; ontinuum 167; contradictions 12, 47–8; dualist 16; entangled 152; free 43; in research 22, 24–5, 27, 56, 161; interrupting individual subject 29, 34, 46–9, 131, 139, 141, 146, 157; Levinas, E. 14, 46; mobile 16–17, 23, 28, 51–2, 56–7, 131, 139–40, 156; participation 12, 33, 115–24, 146–52; representation 27, 53–4, 68; Spivak, G. 52–3; stranger

20; subaltern 50–2, 56, 86, 149; subaltern hosts 155–6; tourism 18, 45, 48, 56–7, 129
subject of welcome 18, 45–50, 68, 101, 152; *see also* intersubjectivity; relationality
sustainability 2, 5, 7, 9–10, 7, 74, 77, 122, 142, 159

teaching 148–51; *see also* being taught
tidy guests 109, 110, 115–24; untidy guest teaching the hosts 117–18
Totality and Infinity see Levinas, E.
totality 14–17, 40–7, 54–5, 151, 169; *see also* infinity; Levinas, E.; *said* and *saying*
tourism development 116; alternative forms of 11; bilateral aid 2–5; decentralization 9; displacement 2, 161; emigration 89; enclaves 75–8, 161–2; encounters 5–6, 23–4, 26–9, 45, 56–7, 77, 102, 106, 148–50, 160, 164; experts 5–6, 115; growth 73, 116, 142; growth fetish 75; hosts and guests 115–24; imaginaries 115–16, 164; inclusion 78–87, 92; inequality 76–7; myths of 97; neo-colonialism 67, 77, 108, 161–2; non-governmental organisations 66, 78–9, 98, 114–24, 162; poverty 75–7, 120, 153, 161; rural 4–5, 80–2, 102–15, 142; subject positions 18, 45, 48, 56–7, 129; sustainability 5, 9–10, 57, 82–3, 86, 122; technical assistance 91–2, 102–24; welcoming 87–95, 131–2, *see also* community-based tourism; development; participatory development; Salazar, N.
tourism as work 81–2, 104–7, 109–15, 124–6
tourism research 5, 12–13, 45, 164; critical turn 10; curriculums 11; participatory paradigm 9–13; relational turn in tourism 6–7, 13, 20, 94; Western epistemological lenses 21
tourist guides 2–3, 124–5
tourists 16–18, 38; decline in number 4, 114, 126–8; domestic 111–12; experience 22; postpolitical (Ek, R.) 18; *see also* hosts and guests
tranquillity 139–45

travel literature 20, 24; *see also* Pratt, M. L.; Kincaid, J.
Tucker, H. 12, 13, 129, 141
Tuhiwai Smith, L. 20–2

unconditional hospitality 46, 61, 94, 153–4; Global South 94; in rural communities 94; Nicaragua 69–93; *see also* Derrida, J.; hospitality; infinity; utopia
undedicability 62; *see also* negotiations
unfinishedness 20, 149–51
unicorns *see* utopia; wonder
unlearning: unlearning privilege as loss (Spivak, G.) 34, 55–6; unlearning the privilege to enter 51–8
untidy guest 20, 30n10; *see also* tidy guest
utopia 8, 58, 128; Levinasian 19, 29

Van Manen, M. 25
Veijola, S. ix, 16–17, 19–20, 27, 37–8
visitability (Dicks, B.) 3, 116, 130, 164
vivir bien 19; *see also* good life, well-being
volunteer tourism 5, 48, 51–2, 11–12, 127, 134n20, 155; antecedents 71–2; San Ramón 127–20; *see also* Mostafanezhad, M.
Vrasti, W. 13, 51, 111, 130, 155

welcome of/to the other (Levinas, E.) 26, 46–7, 160
welcome; cancelling 119–20; dance 66–7; face 143; lack of 160; mutual 156–7; teaching 151, *see also* hospitality; subject of the welcome; welcome of/to the other
well-being 10, 82; living-well-between-ourselves 10; *see also* vivir bien
wellness syndrome 145
West, the 4, 6–7, 36, 50–2; epistemes 10, 21, 27, 64n19, 72; Levinas's philosophy as an alternative to Western essential ontology 15, 33–4, 42, 47, 55, 58; postcolonial critique 6, 10, 15, 50–2, 55
white man's burden 51–6, 130–1
wonder 9, 55; *see also* Irigaray, L.
worlding *see* worldmaking
worldmaking 11, 64; violence of 164–5; *see also* Spivak, G.